D0056008

A NEW PAIR OF GLASSES

by CHUCK "C"

NEW-LOOK PUBLISHING COMPANY
P.O. Box 17496
Irvine, CA 92623

For information, address the publisher:
NEW-LOOK PUBLISHING COMPANY
P.O. Box 17496
Irvine, CA 92623
                           ISBN: 0-916733-00-9

Library of Congress Catalog Card Number: 84-90798

Manufactured in The United States of America

A limited first edition of this book was printed May, 1984
———— • ————
Second Printing September, 1984
———— • ————
Third Printing March, 1985
———— • ————
Fourth Printing July, 1986
———— • ————
Fifth Printing March, 1988
———— • ————
Sixth Printing September, 1989
———— • ————
Seventh Printing May, 1993
———— • ————
Eighth Printing February, 1998

To Elsa—the lady in my life, without whose love, interest, encouragement and help, this never could have happened.

CONTENTS

CHUCK "C"

CHARLES A. CHAMBERLAIN
1902-1984

PREFACE

In a world of proliferating pop-psychology and self-help publications, a reasonable questioner might wonder if "A New Pair of Glasses" serves any purpose whatsoever. And, if so, what makes it different.

I think the two most significant factors contributing to the special value of the following pages are that they represent the backbone of applied principles from the single most dynamic and successful philosophy of this century ... discussed by a man who literally went from a "tongue-chewing, babbling idiot" to one of the most charismatic men in the world.

The philosophy, of course, is that of Alcoholics Anonymous, which has dramatically changed more alcoholic lives during the past half century than have likely been changed through all other therapeutics combined in the history of alcoholic treatment. Founded in the mid-1930's by an alcoholic stockbroker and an alcoholic doctor whose paths crossed in Akron, Ohio, the fellowship of AA has now taken root throughout the entire world, with a practicing membership of well over a million sober alcoholics.

What sets AA head and shoulders above other attempts to reverse the disease of alcoholism, however, is in its immensely successful efforts to literally alter the relationship of the alcoholic to his or her world—in effect, to provide a *different perception* of the same environment. The most baffling characteristic of alcoholism—both to the alcoholic and to those who must deal with him—is the paradox in which the conflict of sober reality eventually always become untenable, leading to the return to alcohol and/or drugs for relief. (Scientists who study alcoholics have stated that the patient may get to a point in sobriety where he actually must drink to preserve his sanity!)

Then the "relief" chemical begins to present an obvious problem. The outside pressures begin to mount regarding its use, and the pain and discomfort in the patient begins to increase. Neither sobriety nor its chemical counterpoint can provide a meaningful cessation of the conflict. This almost hopeless condition of mind and body is known as *alcoholism...* a truly strange disease in which withdrawal from alcohol has little if any salutary effect, and often makes the emotional agony intensify.

The so-called "miracle" of AA is in its ability—if its principles be rigorously applied—to gradually alter the perceptions of reality within these distraught personalities. The goal, often achieved, is to eventually experience life with a degree of comfort never before possible for people sharing this affliction of mind and body.

And, since the symptoms of the sober alcoholic seem to be almost identical to those of the acute or intense neurotic, these same AA principles can be applicable to a great many additional lives. (But, as is stated again and again in this book, the principles must be *used,* not just evaluated or analyzed or passively accepted.)

The man who explains his own interpretation and understanding of the AA program of recovery in the following pages is almost as remarkable as the program he describes. Chuck C. (initials only are used for surnames in Alcoholics Anonymous, as a spiritual tool which helps remind its members not to use its teachings for self-aggrandizement) has been a deeply involved activist in AA since shortly after he achieved sobriety in the 1940's.

In 1946 he was a husband (whose wife had filed for divorce), a father (whose two sons viewed him with fear and contempt), a businessman (whose employer had told him he would be "thrown through the window" if he ever reappeared at his desk.) In short, Chuck C. was a failure in every area of his life.

Today, this remarkable man has become as near a legend in his own time as is possible to achieve in a program of anonymity. Over the years he has become probably the best-known, most-loved, highly-successful living example of the AA principles. And, as he carefully explains, his success is due entirely to what he learned from the AA program, and its continued use in his life today. A contented marriage that has now passed its golden anniversary, the continuing love and respect of his two sons, his retirement as owner of the same company that summarily discharged him in 1946... all are merely surface indications of the far deeper change he has brought about in himself.

"Uncover, discover and discard!" This has been the root of his evolving philosophy. But, unlike most philosophies which get enmeshed in clever phrases and pseudo-psychological mumbo jumbo, he uses these pages to describe a *pragmatic* way to live, to love, and to bring a meaning to existence.

I have had the inestimable pleasure of knowing Chuck C. for many years, and have discovered his living *example* to be more encouraging to me than all the countless pages of "How to..." books in which I for many years immersed my discomfort and discouragement. (There are many who will *tell* you how

...there are few who can *demonstrate* it!)

Over the years I have been staggered by his almost inexhaustible store of energy and dedication. And, even more astonishing in this crass and materialistic world, it remains astonishing to remember there is absolutely no financial recompense to him for these efforts. As he says, "...we do it for *free* and for *fun.*" Most of us have heard many distinguished leaders in the field of spiritual thought preach their equivalent to this approach, but it seems rarely practiced that way.

"A New Pair of Glasses" may seem strange and unrelated to specific problems at first reading; most of us who have needed help the most desperately have taken refuge behind a dismal veneer of cynicism, which we use as a tattered cloak of self protection.

I have had the opportunity, however, to watch these principles gradually work in my own life for over a quarter of a century, and there is still much further to go. I most earnestly suggest you not allow yourself to fall into that trap described by Herbert Spencer which so often undoes our own best efforts:

> "There is a principle which is a bar against all information, which is proof against all arguments and which cannot fail to keep a man in everlasting ignorance—that principle is contempt prior to investigation."

In short, friend, give yourself a break. Take what you can now, and file the rest for future reference. It's amazing how well such an apparently simple approach can alter the perception of life. And, after all isn't that why we get a new pair of glasses....

Clancy I.
Los Angeles
1983

FOREWORD

The day that changed my life began like every other day during those last months. I was drunk. Through drinking I had managed to lose just about everything, including my family, my business and my self-respect. Everything, that is, except my ego. Incredibly, even while lying in bed suffering alcoholic withdrawal, shaking and sweating with empty bottles and trash strewn all over the house, I still somehow thought that I could do anything I set my mind to—including quit drinking. I had been attending Alcoholics Anonymous meetings off and on for years, and even managed to stay dry without a drink for almost a year. But although I knew first hand that many people had quit drinking and were recovering through the help of this fellowship, I could not identify with the people or their program, and consequently I was back in my same drunken condition.

I was trying to decide whether I really wanted to see the man I had telephoned the day before. He was known all over the world in the fellowship of Alcoholics Anonymous, and my ego told me that if anyone could help someone as important as I thought I was, he could. So I called him again and said that I would like to see him if he could come to my place. (He had asked me to go to his house, but in my condition there was no way I could make it to my car, let alone drive somewhere.) I had no idea how much I was asking, and it wasn't until weeks later that I learned he rarely drove anywhere by himself because of his failing health.

Later that morning, after becoming lost and calling en route for clearer instructions, he arrived. He sat in my grandmother's rocking chair and talked to me all afternoon and into the night...

After he had been with me for several hours I began to withdraw from the alcohol in my body and was shaking so much I could no longer hear what he was saying. By way of apology I asked if he minded if I had a drink to calm my nerves, and he said sure, to do whatever I had to do.

And then he talked some more.

But what changed my life occurred as he was leaving. I followed him out and found him in pain, doubled over and leaning on the kitchen counter in the midst of my trash and empty bottles. I asked what I could do and he said not to worry, that he would be alright in a few minutes and be on his way. After a while he recovered enough to walk out to his car and drive off. But during those minutes in the kitchen I understood the program of Alcoholics Anonymous. This man, who had once been a drunken alcoholic just like me, had disregarded his comfort and well being to come to my home and share his experience, strength and hope with me, and his sole motivation was to try to comfort a fellow alcoholic who was in trouble. This man, who had never heard of me, loved me so much that there was no pain or inconvenience that could keep him from trying to help me.

To this day, over a year later, the miracle that this

man brought me, the miracle of Alcoholics Anonymous, has allowed me not to take another drink since the last one I took in front of him that night. But more importantly, the spiritual philosophy of the program of Alcoholics Anonymous, as personified by this man, has completely changed my attitude and way of life. Embracing this philosophy to the best of my ability has given me the thing I was forever looking for in the bottle. I am comfortable. I am comfortable with myself and the world in which I live.

This man who came to see me, Chuck C., is the first human being I have ever met who truly has something I want. I want what he has. I once asked him which of the hundreds of tapes that have been recorded of his talks over the years best represented his thinking. He did not hesitate when he replied that the talks he gave at the Pala Mesa Retreat, a gathering of fellow alcoholic men in 1975, included just about all his thoughts on the program of Alcoholics Anonymous and the Program of Life.

With the help of Chuck C. and his wife, Elsa, we have put these tapes into writing so that the countless number of people that Chuck has touched and will touch in the future may have a volume to pick up and gain comfort from.

Here then, as told to sixty-four men at Pala Mesa, are the thoughts of Chuck C. Thoughts which will help you see the world through a new pair of glasses.

Lee T.
August 16, 1983

Chapter 1

THE PROBLEM

My name is Chuck C., and I'm a alcoholic. I don't know when I've felt any more grateful than I do tonight. This gang that has come down here to hear me bark for about six sessions is something else. It's a great tribute from those of you who came down here to listen. And for those of you who came down here to get away from your wives, I thank you for coming, too. It's a beautiful sight, standing here and looking at you—you're a great bunch. And I love you.

This has been an eventful week, so far. I had to give a funeral on Monday in Pasadena for a chap who was fifty-one. He was giving an AA pitch, and right in the middle of it he went down and didn't get up. Heart attack. That was Monday, and Tuesday I had another one. He was one of the original members of the Compton Group. He came in just after it was started. Old Tex M., and Tex had been sober for twenty-one years. He did it the hard way, because he was a compulsive gambler, too. He loved to gamble. And he won and he lost once in a while. The last time I knew him to be in Las Vegas, he won seventeen thousand dollars at the crap table. He took it up to his wife and said, "Now you send this home", but she didn't. She put it in the safe in the hotel, and he lost most of it before he got out of the place! It wasn't too bad for him, because he thought it was a great joke. He blamed his wife, entirely, because he had told her to send it home. Well, this time he went up to gamble again, and he had a heart attack and left us. So I had to put him away on Tuesday.

Wednesday, I got my twenty-ninth birthday cake, which is something for a tongue-chewing, babbling idiot drunk. Twenty-nine years without a drink or pill. That was pretty nice. And here, to finish the week out, I have you people to share with and to be shared with. And again, I'm very grateful to you for coming.

I thought tonight we might just think a little about the problem and get started. This retreat is supposed to be "in all of our affairs." The Twelfth Step* says "Having had a spiritual awakening as the result of these steps…"(meaning the first eleven) "…we tried to carry this message to alcoholics, and to practice these principles in all our affairs." *In all of our affairs.*

And thinking a little about the problem, I have to think a little about a Texan who was the first chap that sobered up in Houston. I guess he has close to, if not already, thirty-five years sobriety. He's half a Texan wide and a Texan-and-a-half tall.

And he tells this story. He says if you're going to solve a problem, it helps if you know what the problem is. For instance, says he, "I've always been afraid of dogs. Some little ol' girl comes walkin' down the sidewalk, with a great dane on the leash, and says she's not afraid of him at all. (A poodle runs out, and I take off!)" He's over six feet tall—I can just see him running from a poodle! He says this caused him a lot of embarrassment in his life, and it finally became necessary for him to look at the reason that he was afraid of dogs. And he looked and looked, and he

---

*Throughout this book chapters and quotations are referenced from the book, "Alcoholics Anonymous", published by Alcoholics Anonymous World Services, Incorporated, New York City. The Twelve Steps of Alcoholics Anonymous are contained in Chapter Five of that book.

started to turn the pages of his life back, and he got clear back to where he was seven years old. He remembered that when he was seven a little dog bit him, and that was the reason he was afraid of dogs. But he said that didn't completely satisfy him. So he looked at it again, and he saw that the reason the dog bit him was that he was chasing the little girl at the time. Now says he, "All my life I've been chasin' women and gettin' in trouble and runnin' from dogs, and dogs never were my problem in the first place!" So he says it helps to know the problem.

I think it helps to know the problem. I'm going to tell you what I think the problem is, and I'm going to tell you what I think the solution is. There will be some of you that will not agree with my thinking, and that's perfectly alright. But if I talk, I have to say it as I see it. Our immediate problem when we came here was booze. Alcohol. That's the thing that ran us in here. It ran me here in a hurry after twenty-five years, because I had used every resource I had, and I had lost the battle. So I got here at the ripe old age of forty-three, a failure in every department of life; failure as a husband, a father, a businessman, a man and a drunk. I had run out of everything, including people, places, things, money, whiskey and home and everything else. And there wasn't any place else for me to go but here. However, on my last trip out I had a very great, good fortune. The bottle killed me! The bottle beat me to death, beat me into total and absolute nothingness, and only then could I come to investigate Alcoholics Anonymous. Up until that time there was no way that anybody could have talked me into coming here. As long as I had the power of choice, my choice was never to come to Alcoholics Anonymous, and I never came until I had lost everything, including the power of choice.

So I would say to you right off the bat that the

greatest single event that has ever happened in my life, and I'm seventy-two years old, happened in January, 1946, when the bottle beat me to death. Had it been necessary for me to consciously surrender the first time, I would have died without coming to this program. There was no way that I could surrender. I had never admitted defeat one time in forty-three years of life. Not to God, man, woman or the Devil. The word "surrender" wasn't in my vocabulary. It had been bred out of me for generations. So, thank God, on my last trip out, the bottle did it for me. The road block was burned out, and I got to the program in a state of total abandonment of self. And everything in the fifth chapter of the book, "Alcoholics Anonymous" was something I wanted to do, the first time I ever heard it. The very first night, when I heard Chapter Five read, everything in it was something I wanted to do. And I'm certain it was because of the total state of abandonment of self in which I got here.

Now, there was one thing that I didn't think I could do, and that was Step Three, and it wasn't because I didn't want to. I had no objection to Step Three.* I would have turned my will and my life over to a jackass, if I could have gotten rid of me. But, where it says we made a decision to turn our will and our lives over to the care of God as we understood him, I didn't think that this was possible for anybody like me, because I didn't think it was cricket to believe that I could give the mess that was me to anybody, let alone to God. I wouldn't have taken me with a large dowry, and I didn't figure God liked me any better than I did, and I hated my guts. So I let it lay. I

---

*Step Three in the book "Alcoholics Anonymous": "...made a decision to turn our will and our lives over to the care of God as we understood Him."

just let it lay. I picked up the last third of Step Twelve, and "practiced these principles in all of my affairs."

After attending a meeting every night for six months, I discovered that I was sober and had been without a drink or a pill for six months. This was quite a discovery, because I'd attended everyone of those meetings with a great fear upon me that I couldn't have this thing, that I didn't have enough left physically or mentally to get it. But after six months of a meeting every night, I discovered that I was sober and had been all the time. Then I started giving a little attention to Step Three, because I was thinking, "Well, maybe there's some way that I could come to feel that God would take a package like mine." But I couldn't get any solution to the thing. I was messin' with it for quite a little while, and finally it occurred to me, "You're a father". Then I started conjuring up the most heinous crimes I could imagine, and laying them on these two boys of mine. I let my imagination go crazy, buildin' the worst possible kind of crimes that anybody could perpetrate, and when I'd done that I would say to myself, "Now, would this keep me from wanting to see my boys? Would these things make me want to cast them into Perdition, to burn for eternity?" And I had to say, "No, I couldn't do it." No way could I, regardless of what they did, no way could I assign them to Hell. So I came to believe that maybe the Heavenly Father, being a good guy, and me an evil one, maybe He would forgive me. And I got comfortable. But it had to come through that kind of procedure with me.

Now the funny part of it is that when I discovered that I'd been sober for six months, I had to get lost in trying to give this thing to alcoholics, because they had given it to me. Drunks had given it to me. I lost myself working with drunks, and after a while I had another discovery, that something had happened in our household. A year before, Mrs. C. was divorcing me, the kids wouldn't come home when I was around, the boss-man was going to throw me through the window if I ever stepped foot in the plant again, I had no health, no sanity, no home, no job, no nothing, and it appeared that the war was over. Now, the household was living like kittens. And that was a good discovery. It was about a year after I got here. Another six to eight months went by, and I made another discovery, and that was that I was still trying to clean up my desk at the office. (We will talk a little about this when we talk about AA in business–of practicing these principles in business.) But here I was, still trying to clean up my desk at the office, and business was good. It was plum good. That was a pretty good discovery! Maybe another year went by, and I discovered that my Being was better than anything that I had ever dreamed of in my life. My *liv-ing-ness*, being myself, was better than anything that I ever dreamed of. And that was a good discovery.

And now five, maybe six years have passed, and I made another discovery, which I believe to be the Great Discovery. When we make this discovery, the search is over and life begins—life isn't over, life just begins. Really! And this discovery was that I was never alone anymore. I, who had walked alone for forty-three years, totally alone, I was never alone anymore. I had a God of my very own. And where I am, He is. I'm often by myself, but never alone. And this has been the way it's been ever since the discovery, and it's the way it was before the discovery. Because I hadn't been alone since my first Alcoholics Anonymous meeting. I believe that this program of ours, the Alcoholics Anonymous program, is a program of uncovering, discovering, and discarding. That's the AA program to me. Uncovering, Discovering, and Discarding.

The first nine steps of the program are the uncovering steps, clearing away the wreckage of the past. Squeezing us out of ourselves, ego-wise; to get rid of the human ego, temporarily, because we never get rid of it totally, in my opinion. I am convinced that nobody can honestly take the first nine steps in this program without making the discovery that something has happened, and it's terrific! Because when we honestly apply the first nine steps of this program, ego is temporarily gone.

Now I am convinced in my own mind, totally and completely convinced from my toenails to the top of my longest hair, that there's only one problem in this life. One problem that includes all problems, and one answer that includes all answers. Now that's oversimplification, isn't it? One problem that includes all problems, and one answer that includes all answers. I am totally convinced that the only roadblock between me and you and me and my God is the human ego. The only roadblock there is. I further believe that the best definition you'll ever hear of the human ego is, "The feeling of conscious separation from." The feeling of conscious separation from. From what? From everything. From God. (I like to use three words: Life, Good, God, which to me are synonymous words.) Conscious separation from God, from each other, and eventually from ourselves. That is the thing that says to me, "Here are my big me, little me, smart me, dumb me, rich me, poor me against the whole world. I've got to out-think, out-perform and out-maneuver in order to eke out a miserable living out of an unfriendly universe." That's what they laid on me as a kid. The very cliches of life, "The early bird gets the worm", "The Devil takes the hindmost", "You've got to be there firstest with the mostest" and build on that premise. Here am I against the whole world. I've got to out-think, out-perform and out-maneuver. Consciously separated from each other and from God. I think that's the greatest roadblock there is, the only one, as a matter of fact, the only roadblock there is between me and you and me and my God. And that's the human ego. The seat of all the obsessions of the mind. That's where they come from.

It is also my total conviction that there is no possibility under Heaven to satisfy the human ego. It is a divine impossibility. I like to sit up there in my big chair (Many of you have seen it. Some of you have sat in it for a minute, but I won't let you sit in it much longer!), and I look down over that little town, Laguna Beach, to the beautiful shoreline and the channel (right straight in front of my chair is Avalon) to Catalina Island. It's about thirty-four or thirty-five miles from where I live. I look down at that water, that channel, and that thirty-five miles is just the top of it. It's deep, too. And I say to myself, "Suppose that entire channel was bourbon whiskey." Now, that's quite a few drinks! Would that satisfy my obsession for whiskey? And I have to say no. The whole damn thing could not satisfy my obsession to drink, because when I get started drinking, before long I'm flat on my back in bed, drinking the clock around, and every time I open my eyes I drink, and there's no way to satisfy that obsession. No way.

Now suppose my obsession had been for money instead of drinking. How about that? It's totally impossible to satisfy an obsession for dough. I had a client through many years who lived in Phoenix. He was a Syrian named Eddy who had gone from one head of lettuce to thirty-five million bucks, and he was one of the poorest men I ever saw. Because, unfortunately, he had a partner in one of his business enterprises, which happened to be oil, and this old boy was worth one-hundred and fifty million. They had a suite in the Jonathan Club, most beautiful

thing you ever looked at in your life, all paneled with
the finest wood in the world, gun racks and elephant
tusks all over it, and feet and gazelles and everything
else. And when I'd be sitting there with the two of
them, Eddy was trying to get under the davenport.
Poor thing, he had only thirty-five million, and here
was old Steele with one-hundred and fifty million.
Poor man! Eddy used to say to me, "Charley (I was
'Charley' in business.), how can I be like you?", and I'd
say, "Eddy, you can't.". He'd say, "Why?", and I'd say,
"Eddy, who needs God if you've got thirty-five million
bucks?! Don't be silly! You can buy anything you want,
including women, and you do. Who needs God when
you've got thirty-five million bucks? You go ahead and
make one hundred and fifty million, and you will, if you
live. (Because everything that old boy touched turned
to gold.) And when you've made one hundred and fifty
million, you will have then found that it won't do for
you what you have to have done inside you. And you
will come to me and say, 'Charley, how can I be like
you?' Then I'll tell you, and you can do it, but not until
then. He'd say, "Well, talk to me about it, anyway." And
we'd drive all over the state of Arizona, talking just like
we'll be talking here. But poor Eddy didn't make his
one hundred and fifty; he got so many things in his
head that it exploded. He was ten years younger that I,
and he's been gone five or six years. He died.
Impossible to satisfy an obsession for money.

Suppose my obsession had been for power. How
about that? No possibility. Witness Watergate; there's
a nice power struggle. It's absolutely impossible to
satisfy an obsession for power. If you were President of
the United States, no good, because every dictator in
the world has more power than our President. Old
Genghis Khan had more than all of them. So, no
way. What about women? I started to say sex, but that

brings up a bad connotation! (I've been getting invitations, lately, to gab and talk to the deviates and God bless me, I can't hardly make it. So far I've been able to sort of have some other thing to do, or get something else to do.) So, let's say women. Suppose my obsession had been for women. And suppose that I had been the greatest lothario of all times, and suppose I had captured every chick I set out to catch, but one. Now at my age that would be a pretty good size army, don't you think? Would they satisfy my obsession for women? Uh-uh. This one kills me! The one I can't get kills me dead. So, if you can't beat 'em, join 'em. We've got to get rid of the obsessions of the mind. And in order to get rid of the obsessions of the mind, we have to be rid of the ego, because that's where they come from. I want, I don't want, I like, I don't like, I - I - I - I - I. That's it.

Now that's the reason that the wording in the book, "Alcoholics Anonymous" is like it is. There are four hundred and fifty-two pitches in the first page and two paragraphs in our Chapter Five. Boy, there's a lot of things said in that deal! "Rarely have we seen a person fail who has thoroughly followed our path."* Even yet I hear people get up here and say they have heard Bill Wilson** say that there's one word in the book he would change if he was doing it again. And that would be to take out the "Rarely" and put in "Never have we seen a person fail who has thoroughly followed our path." Well, Bill didn't say that to anybody, because he knew why he put "Rarely" in there. If he had said, "Never have we seen a person fail who has thoroughly followed our path...", I see about four people here at the front table look-ing right at me that would have said, "Oh, they've never seen a failure. Well, by God, I'll show 'em one!". That's the reason it's "Rarely". And Bill did tell me that, himself. (I happened to know him pretty well.)

"Rarely have we seen a person fail who has thoroughly followed our path."* I heard that read one time in a way I think may be even better than it's written. Some guy got up here and he read it, "Rarely have we seen a person fail who has thoroughly enjoyed our path." I think that's terrific. "Those who do not recover are people who cannot or will not completely give themselves to this simple program, usually men and women who are constitutionally incapable of being honest with themselves."* Being honest with themselves. Honesty and following the path. There're two pitches, right there. To be honest, and to follow the path, thoroughly follow the path. "They are naturally incapable of grasping and developing a manner of living which demands rigorous honesty."* Now there's a pitch. Grasping and developing. You see, we're people who never were able to settle for status quo. Never in our lives, long before we had a drink, were we able to settle for status quo. Nothing that was normal ever merited our attention for more than a split second. If it wasn't better than normal, we didn't like it. And that's *before* we ever had a drink. So, we had better jolly well grasp and develop, because a happy sobriety will turn into a drunk unless we develop. We've got to walk. We've got to keep going. All we need to do is get fat and complacent and quit walking, and we're in trouble. So grasping and developing a manner of living which demands rigorous honesty is a full time job.

"There are such unfortunates. They are not at fault; they seem to have been born that way."* I don't like that line, because in twenty-nine years, I have had probably five hundred people tell me they're

11

sure that they're naturally incapable of being honest with themselves—actually incapable of it. Well, I'm sure that if you're still breathing and you don't have two or three of those wheels missing entirely, there's no way you can hide behind that, but it's the sort of thing that we use once in a while.

"Their chances are less than average. There are those, too, who suffer from grave emotional and mental disorder, but many of them do recover if they have the capacity to be honest."* I've got to tell you a little story. Many of you have heard it, I'm sure. In the early days in Los Angeles, we didn't have anybody out here that had ever been in an AA meeting, and then a Jewish gentleman came out here with a book. He didn't know he had it. He "came to" in Palm Springs, and started looking through his luggage for some whiskey, and he found this book. (Alcoholics Anonymous—the first edition, that red one.). And he didn't know how it had gotten in his suitcase. But he didn't have any whiskey, so he read it, and he just kept reading it, and he liked it; he liked what he read.

And he came into Los Angeles with this book, and he got hold of some people and they started a meeting, but they didn't know how to start it. And so the custom that has spread pretty well all over the world was established right here in Los Angeles' first meeting: reading a portion of Chapter Five. This Jewish boy says, "I don't know how to start a meeting, but there's a chapter in this book entitled 'How it Works' and it gives us this thing, and let's read it.'" And they read this portion of Chapter Five. And you'd be surprised how much of the world that's covered up until now. They do it in Australia, they do it in New Zealand, they do it in Canada, they do it in Texas. They read this all over, and it's beautiful. Every time I read it, it reminds me that my survival depends on this thing right here in Chapter Five.

Now a little bit later, this bunch, maybe a half dozen of them at this time, got ahold of an old boy off skid-row. His name was Whitey, and Whitey had been a little bit too close and too long with the vino. He babbled all through the meeting, he'd just sit there and babble, and he was bothering them. So they decided they ought to take him to the doctor and see what was the matter with him, and they did. They took Whitey to a doctor, and this doctor took a few quick passes at him and he said, "Boys, give him up. This one you can't help. Spend your time on somebody that's got a chance. He has such bad brain damage that you're just wasting your time.". So the next meeting, of course, they had a discussion about Whitey. And the whole gang of them wanted to dump Whitey and keep him from interrupting the procedure with his babbling. But there was one guy there that had read something in the book, and he said, "Wait a minute, boys. It says right here that the only requirement for sobriety is a desire to stop drinking, and Whitey wants to get sober. We can't kick him out.". And they said that was right, that's what it said, and they didn't kick him out. And it's a matter of medical record and AA record that one year later Whitey was accepted in the United States Marines. Last I heard of Whitey, he was running a newspaper in the Middle-West. So, there's a miracle here.

"There are those, too, who suffer from grave emotional and mental disorders, but many of them do recover if they have the capacity to be honest. Our stories disclose in a general way what we used to be like, what happened, and what we are like now. If you have decided you want what we have and are willing to go to any length to get it,"—*any length to get it*—"then you are ready to take certain steps."* Why are those phrases in there? You have to go clear

13

back to the first line of the second paragraph, Chapter Three, and read a line that says, "We learned that we had to fully concede to our innermost selves that we were alcoholics. This is the first step in recovery.".* Why? Why clear back there? The first word of the second paragraph, Chapter Three? The program of recovery is over here in Chapter Five! It's there in Chapter Three because if we be alcoholic we are caught in a trap we cannot spring. We have to have help, and we can't get help until we recognize the need for it. It's impossible. We're a peculiar breed of cat. We can't hear until we can hear, and we can't see until we can see. And it doesn't make a bit of difference who's talking.

For instance, a number of years back, in the state of Virginia, I spent a good deal of time with a great celebrity of films and TV, and he and his wife were both alkys, and I was very fond of them and I was very hopeful that something good was going to happen. We sat for almost all day in Richmond, Virginia, yakking. And everything I said, this guy's wife would say, "Why, that's the way I live. I've known that forever." Then I'd talk a little longer, and she'd say, "Well, that's the way we raised our kids. This is not new to us. We know the whole thing." And it went that way the whole morning. Well, they didn't know I knew that they'd just gotten out of Menninger's. Both of them! (Menniger's, for those of you who don't know, is a booby hatch.). But they had never heard it, and they didn't hear it when I said it, either. And you're going to hear a lot of things that you think you know this weekend; maybe you do. You may hear a lot of things that you disagree with. That's alright with me, too. If you disagree with them, and know why you disagree with them, maybe you should be up here, and me back there. But for now this is the way it's going to be.

Another condition, of course, is that sobriety has to come first. "If you have decided you want what we have and are willing to go to any length to get it...",*that's top man on the totem pole. I'm one who believes that unless and/or until sobriety comes first we can't have it. And unless it remains first we cannot keep it. That's what it says here. This is very positive stuff. "...and are willing to go to any length to get it—then you are ready to take certain steps. At some of these we balked. We thought we could find an easier, softer way. But we could not. With all the earnestness at our command, we beg of you to be fearless and thorough from the very start." This isn't a headache we're talking about. We're talking about a terminal illness, the disease of alcoholism. A terminal illness. That's why these things are in here. Because we have to have help, and we've got to recognize the need for it before we can get it, and it's got to be tops, top man on the totem pole.

"Some of us have tried to hold on to our old ideas and the result was nil until we let go absolutely."* It doesn't say half measures availed us 50%. It says half measures availed us nothing. Not a thing. "We stood at the turning point. We asked His protection and care with complete abandon."* We let go absolutely. Before that it says, "Without help it is too much for us. But there is One who has all power—that One is God. May you find Him now!"* It's beautiful. It's a beautiful thing.

Now this is our problem. We're caught in a trap we cannot spring. We've already been to human help. The first time I heard these steps, One and Two were a cinch. I know that I'd lost the battle of life. I didn't know anything about alcoholism, but I knew I'd lost the battle of life. And I knew that my life was unmanageable by me. I still know it, and it's never changed. It's still unmanageable by me. It's no problem to me. Two-fold admission of defeat in the first step, an admission that we're nuts in the second. Now these are two big steps for an alky, the first two. Lost the battle of life, number one; you're nuts, number two. So you need help and you need it bad, and if you're like me you'd been to the preacher, the priest, the doctor, and the guy that knows more psychiatry than there is, before you ever got to this place, to Step Three. And so you know you need help, and you can't get it from human power. So we make a decision to turn our will and our lives over to the care of God. Now this is one of the things that we're going to be spending some time on. This is the most fantastic thing on the face of the earth. There is nothing that will compare with this thing that happens to us when we do this. Not when we *read* it, when we *do* it. To abandon ourselves completely to this simple program. We make a decision to turn our will and our lives over to the care of God.

I don't suppose that there's a man in this room that analyzed himself and decided to turn himself in to Alcoholics Anonymous. I don't believe there's one of you in the whole bunch that did that. If there had been any way under Heaven for me to remain in left field, I'd still be out there. We are not the kind of people that run around surrendering on every other street corner. That isn't our way of doing things. We've lost the battle of life and we're nuts and we have to have help.

I told you a little bit ago that the greatest single event in my life, up until now, and I'm seventy-two years old, was when the bottle killed me in January of '46. I was forty-three. I had read Jack Alexander's article in the Saturday Evening Post in March of '41. Mrs. C. had found it, read it, opened it to the right place and put it on the arm of the chair I sit in right now. When I got home, I read it. I was four sheets to the wind when I read it, and I suspect I thought it was real good for you people that needed it. I imagine I did. But five years later I "came to" after a four week blackout. (My last drunk started on the Friday before Christmas, 1945, and I "came to" sometime after the middle of January '46.) I don't remember what the time was, what day the calendar said it was. But during that four weeks the thing that had stopped me was burned out. And I accepted the fact that everything dear to me in life was gone, and should be gone, and that I was not entitled to have it back. That was including my wife and my kids and my home and my job and my health and my sanity and my money. It was all gone and I wasn't entitled to have it back. I knew I was going to die, because I'd come within an ace of it the next-to-the-last time out. I'd fallen over on my face in the kitchen, turned blue, and they had to get the oxygen squad to wake me up. The doctor that was with them told me, after I "came to", that to all intents and purposes I was dead, that they'd had a hell of a time bringing me back, and that nobody would ever be able to bring me back again under those circumstances. And, said he, "If I were you, I wouldn't do that any more!" He said that right to me. But I did it again. So I knew I was going to die, and I accepted that, too. But I didn't want to die with a record.

Now I want you to listen to this, because this is a little bit different than a lot of things that happened. I didn't even want sobriety for myself, because I knew I was going to die. I didn't want anything for me, but I didn't want to die with a record. I didn't want Mrs. C. and the kids to remember me as nothing but a tongue-chewing, babbling idiot drunk. In the depths of this thing, I remembered that I'd read the article in the Saturday Evening Post, and the only two things I remembered about it was that drunks help drunks and didn't drink, and they called it Alcoholics Anonymous. And I said to myself, "If I ever live to get out of this bed, I will find Alcoholics Anonymous." And immediately the curtain dropped, just like that—bang!—it dropped. There was no more sanity. I was sick unto death, drunk and insane, and I had a lot of dying to do.

From the moment of commitment until right now I've never had a drink or pill. This is one of the reasons I believe so completely and totally that there is only one road block between me and you and me and God, and that's the human ego. The only road block there is. Because, you see, I sit in the same chair today that I sat in for ten years in Hell. The same chair, and I've sat in it for twenty-nine years in Heaven. Nothing happened to the chair. Nothing happened to my wife. Nothing happened to the kids. Something happened to me, and it proves that Heaven was always in that chair. I was in Hell, but Heaven was always in that chair. Nothing happened to that chair, and I'm still in it, still in Heaven. That's the reason these statements are so very, very positive. To abandon ourselves completely, to let go absolutely, it says. And to turn our will and our lives over to the care of God.

Now this is the problem. Something has to happen that we get rid of the obsession of the mind, and that's what this program of ours is all about. The American Medical Society (we have some of its most illumined members right here at this retreat) says alcoholism is a disease; it has symptoms, it is treatable, but not curable, and the only way an alcoholic can successfully live is not to take the next slug. But they cannot tell us how not to take the next slug. They can't tell us how. That's what this book* is all

---

* "Alcoholics Anonymous."

about, to tell us how to get rid of the obsessions of the mind that cause us to drink. That's what this whole program is all about. To rid us of the obsessions of the mind that cause us to drink.

Now why am I not drunk tonight? That's a good question! I'm a tongue-chewin', babblin' idiot drunk. Why am I not drunk tonight? This is Friday. Thursday night's kick-off night, right? You start oiling the machinery Thursday, you get in high gear on Friday, you pay Saturday, right? Sober up Sunday, taper off so you can go to work Monday. Some Sundays you taper off, so you can go to work some Mondays. Why am I not drunk tonight? Because I have the thing I was looking for in the bottle, and that's the only reason I'm not drunk. That's the *only* reason I'm not drunk. I have the thing I was looking for in the bottle. Now what is the thing? That king-size hurt is gone. You know the king-size hurt. The kids call it that hole in their guts when they're standing on the street corner and the wind's blowing through. That's what the kids call it. When I first heard them say that, I said they've been to a meetin' some place, they heard that. They stole it from somebody that knew what he was talking about. But that ain't right. I learned that that ain't right. They were the guys that coined it, standing on the street corner with the big hole in their guts and the wind blowin' through. The Big Hurt—that's gone. I'm not fighting me, or you, or life, or God or the devil. I am at peace with me and with you and with my very own God. That's the only reason I'm not drunk.

When I say I am an alcoholic, it means this: that I cannot live and drink, and of myself I cannot keep from drinking. And that's just as true right now as it was thirty years ago. Step One says we admitted we were powerless over alcohol, that our lives had become unmanageable by us. I've looked all the way through our book and through the manuscript from which it was written and through the most recent book that was printed, and there's nothing in any one of them that says that if I'm sober for ten or twelve or twenty-nine years, my life will become manageable by me. It doesn't say that—I looked—it's not in there!

And furthermore, there's nothing in my experience in twenty-nine years that would indicate that my life will ever be manageable by me again. But thank God it is no problem to me, because I have Step Eleven; I have lived by Step Eleven for twenty-nine years. "Sought through prayer and meditation to improve our conscious contact with God as *we understood Him*, praying only for knowledge of His will for us and the power to carry that out."* I have lived in total expectancy of guidance and direction for twenty-nine years, and I get it. And you might say, "How do you know?" I've got the simplest rule in the world: I never had it so good. This is the only good life I've ever known, the only easy life that's ever been mine in my entire lifetime. And I've got twenty-nine years to look over sober without a drink or pill, twenty-five years drunk or drinking, and nineteen years before that. And this is the only good life I've ever known, the only easy life that's ever been mine. So I highly recommend it. This is the way to get rid of the obsessions of the mind.

Here are the steps we *took*. We're sober. Now don't say, "Here are the steps we read, or heard read, or learned by heart." Don't say that. Don't say, "Here are the steps we interpreted." You can't find that in our book, so don't say that. Don't say, "Here are the steps we conned God into taking for us." There have been a few people around this neck of the woods that were experts on interpreting the steps. There was one guy out in the valley for a while that was selling interpretations of the steps and teaching interpretations of the steps, and then he got drunk! His measures went down the rat hole. It doesn't say that. It says, "Here are the steps we took...", and the reason we have to take them is because we're caught in a trap we can't spring. We have to have help and can't get help until we recognize the need for it.

The first three steps are decisions. The fourth and fifth are action steps. We "made a searching and fearless moral inventory of ourselves."* We write—the book says very, very specifically that it's good to write the things down. We're more apt to do it right if we're writing. It takes a little longer, but it's good for us, so we write it. Now it's a moral inventory, so we don't have to write every time we turned left when we should have turned right. It doesn't mean that we have to put down everything we ever stole, or every lie we told, or every time we got drunk. That is not what it means. It means to write down enough so that we can see the motivation for what we have done up until now. The motivating force in our lives. Of course, if we want to get real simple, the whole thing will boil down to obsessions of the mind, which is the ego. Every one of them will boil down to trying to satisfy the human ego, which cannot be done. So we write it down and then we share it. We share it with God, ourselves, and another human being. That other human being is the thing that really sets us up for the kill. I can admit to God and to myself while hidden in the privy! Nobody knows but me and God. But if I have to spread this dirty linen out before another human being, if I've got any ego left after that, I haven't done it! That's an ego-buster.

So we've written it and shared it and now we become willing to give it away, and we give it away. Now I find people all over the world beating their brains out trying to get rid of the obsessions of the mind, their defects of character. I bet you there've been a million hours spent in arguing over why Step Six says "...were entirely ready to have God remove all these defects of character."* and Step Seven says "Humbly asked Him to remove our shortcomings."* And there've been a million hours spent on "What's the difference between 'shortcomings' and 'defects of character'?". There's supposed to be a difference! I asked Bill, and he said, "I don't know, I think I didn't want to end two lines right next to each other with the same words. They mean the same thing." So that's going to knock a lot of arguments out, isn't it?

The main thing is that we become willing to give them away, and we give them away. If we could have done away with our defects of character, we would have done it before we came here. I wasn't just jumpin' up and kickin' my heels together, saying, "Goodie, goodie, I get to go to Alcoholics Anonymous!" I'm sure my mother didn't raise me to be a member of Alcoholics Anonymous. She's ninety-six and she doesn't believe it yet! I say, "I've had twenty-nine years without a drink", and she says "What's so hot about that, I've had ninety-six years!" So, we become willing to give them away and we give them away.

Then we have two more steps in the first ten, two of the greatest ones left. The most immediately effective steps in the whole program are Eight and Nine. We "Made a list of all persons we had harmed, and became willing to make amends to them all. Made direct amends to such people wherever possible, except when to do so would injure them or others."* If you haven't done that, do it. Do it quick. The weight of the world is removed from your shoulders when you honestly take care of Eight and Nine.

I'm going to tell you this little story, and it won't take long. Many of you have heard it, but it curls my hair yet. About ten years ago, I got a call on Friday night from a guy in Whittier, and he said, "Chuck, I'm sittin' here with a six-gun in my lap, and I'm going to blow my brains out. But Jim says, 'Don't shoot yourself until you talk to Chuck C.', and he gave me your number, and I called and I'm ready to talk. So what have you got to say?" And I said, "You called on a bad night! I'm talking tonight, tomorrow night and Sunday night, but Monday night's open. So if you want to see me, come down Monday night. But if you don't, blow your brains out." "That's exactly what I told him. And at 7:30 Monday evening the doorbell rang, and in came my boy. Now let me tell you a little story within a story. "Jim" was Jim W. who was Sybil's husband for many years. Sybil was fourteen years in our Central Office, and Jim was a compulsive gambler, and he started Gamblers Anonymous and wrote their book. He'd already done that, and then he became an alcoholic, and he called me one time and said, "Come and get me" And I said, "Where are you?" He was in his office on Pico, and I went and got him. And he got sober. Now, Jim is losing his eyesight, and he's a sick man, but he's sober. And I talked with him on the phone just the other day, and he's pretty happy.

Anyway, Jim had told this guy he not only was an alcoholic, but he was a compulsive gambler. And Jim had told him to talk to me before he blew his brains out. Well, here he was. And we started talking. At 2:30 in the morning we were right where we are now, at Steps Eight and Nine, and I was telling this monkey, "Now here's what you've got to do. You lost a lot of money that you didn't have. (And he had lost it to professional gamblers). And that ain't a very healthy situation; it don't do much for longevity." So here he sits, and I'm saying, "Now listen, here's what you've got do. You gotta go to these people and say, "Look,

I'm not the big shot I would have had you believe. I'm an alcoholic, and I've found a way to live that might let me live one day at a time without a drink for the rest of my life. And one of its conditions is that we've got to make amends and that's why I'm here. Now, I admit the debt. I owe you the money, and I'll pay you as soon as I can, but I ain't got no money now."

"Why," he said, "Chuck, I can't do that, they'll kill me!" And I said, "So what? You won't have suicide on your mind!" And the old boy started to laugh, and he's still laughing. And he's walking the streets a free man, he was laughing right over the hill ever since he left me, and he never quit. He paid them off, nobody killed him. It's a wonder, these things. So if you haven't done Steps Eight and Nine, do them. The weight of the world goes right off your back when you do them.

Now, to finish up. Alcoholism cuts across our society from the highest to lowest. We are peoples of all professions, all states of poverty and riches, priests and preachers, from all denominations. We have world scholars amongst us, and bankers. Not one would have come here if they could have stayed out. We have a problem that you and I cannot solve. We have to have help. And those first nine steps will roll away the stones, because those are the surrender steps. The surrender steps. Surrender is the thing that opens the door that allows us to get the help; because God, himself, cannot help us until we will allow it. The recognition of the need for help and the turning of our will and our lives over to the care of God, and clearing away of the wreckage of the past is the beginning of victory. It's fantastic. Don't be afraid of it.

I'm convinced that you and I have to do this without getting too serious about it. We get too serious and nothing happens. If we look too hard, we'll never find. I looked for this thing for thirty years before I got here, and I couldn't find it. I came here not looking for it, and it found me or we found each other. I wasn't looking for anything but a way to live one day at a time without drinking, so I could rub out as much of the record as I could. So I want us to have a lot of fun this weekend. Don't be too serious. You know, Rule 62. Some people put it on their license plates. Rule 62. It's a good rule. There's a little green book, and on the front cover it says, "Rule 62". And you open it up, and every page in the book is naked, except the double-truck in the middle. And it says, "Don't take yourself so goddamned seriously!" And that's what we want to do here this weekend; have a lot of fun, not get too serious, but realize the problem that we have that we cannot handle on our own. And to come to see totally before this weekend is over that what I can't do, *we* can do, with the Grace of God.

Chapter 2

THE GOLDEN KEY

I think maybe if we listened, we sort of established the fact that our problem actually is a living problem, and we have to have a living answer. It's my opinion that there isn't a living answer, for the non-alcoholic or the alcoholic alike, that does not include a personally satisfactory, conscious partnership with the living God that made us in the entire business of living. In the entire business of living. I don't think there's an answer that doesn't include that, for all people. Because if there's one thing that living with people like you for twenty-nine years has done for me, it has convinced me beyond any shadow of a doubt that all of us are God's kids. If one of us is God's kid, all of us are, and if one of us isn't, none of us are. Now this is whether we believe it or not, whether we like it or not. Even if we deny it, we cannot change the reality of our own being. We're God's kids. All of us.

Walking alone is not normal, is not natural. Most of us have walked alone for most of our lives. I walked alone for forty-three years, wanting so badly to be a part of, and always apart from. That is not normal. To be away from the Father's house is not normal. It's just as natural as breathing, to come home to the living God that made us. That's the normal state. Being away from home is not normal. So our problem is conscious separation and our answer is conscious unity.

Now I'm accused, sometimes, of being a water walker. Some people think I'm overboard on the so-called spiritual. I am not. I just happen to know that there isn't anything else but spiritual. That's all there is—there ain't no more. So I'm naturally a little bit prone to that direction. But I have never heard a speaker, including myself, from the podium of Alcoholics Anonymous so strongly affirm that as does the book, "Alcoholics Anonymous." For instance, here's a line in the second chapter; "There is a Solution." And here's what it says: "Each individual, in the personal stories" (in the back of the book) "describes in his own language and from his own point of view the way he established his relationship with God."* That's what it says right there. Second chapter. "The way he established his relationship with God." And so this is the answer. Conscious separation is the problem; conscious unity is the answer.

Now I've got a little diagram here, something that will show what I have been talking about. That circle I draw, in my thinking, represents the Universe and everything in it. All there is—there ain't no more. That's it.

Those three words in the circle, "Life, Good, God," insofar as I'm concerned, are synonymous. They all mean the same thing. So that's it—that's all there is, there ain't no more. The line represents the feeling of

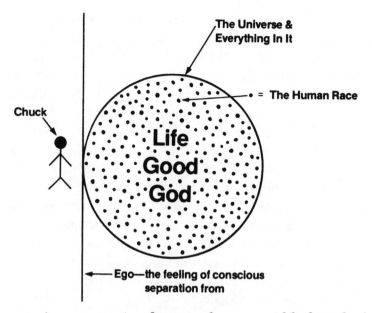

Chuck

The Universe &
Everything In It

• = The Human Race

Life
Good
God

Ego—the feeling of conscious
separation from

conscious separation from, and as we said before that's
human ego. That's the only roadblock between you and
me and me and God. And there am I out in left field, all
by myself. I spent forty-three years out there. Now that's
very real as an experience, but it is not reality. We also
said that the human ego could not be satisfied, but in
surrender ego goes by the boards, temporarily. Unfortunately, (but I believe fortunately) it doesn't remain gone.
We'll have to surrender forever, and as far as I'm
concerned there will never be a time when we don't have
to continuously surrender. When ego is gone, you wake
up right in the middle of the circle and you're now a part
of—not apart from—Life, Good, God. There is no life
apart from God. God is life and we are alive, so God is
that which we are.

In Him we live and move and have our Being. Now
that's the truth of life. The Carpenter said it like
this, "Who, by taking thought, can add one cubit to his

stature?" This means, I believe, you can't change the reality of your own being. You can only change your experience in reality. My experiences were very real for forty-three years, but they were not reality. And this is what happened to me in bed in January 1946, but I didn't know it. I had to discover, as time went on. Now the first time I talked with my wife, she knew that something had happened. I didn't know it; she did. Because I called her in, and I said, "Honey," (You know, she was divorcing me.) "it's no longer of any importance to me whether or not I live under this roof. It is of absolutely no importance to me at all. I'll never ask a thing of you as long as we live, but one. If I can ever add anything to your life, let me give it to you." And we closed the book, and it's never been reopened. She knew something had happened, I didn't. I called the kids in and I said, "Boys, there's no father in the household any longer. You don't need to love me, you don't need to obey me, I'll never ask a thing of you as long as you live, but one. If I ever have anything, be it money, counsel or blood that'll add to your life, let me give it to you." And we closed the book, and it's never been reopened. They were too young to know that something had happened.

I went to the office before I ever got into an AA meeting, because the boss had done something very nice for me on the Friday before Christmas, 1945. He'd called me in and told me (instead of shooting me), "You've had a lot of trouble this year." He didn't mention booze, but he knew that I knew what he meant when he said "trouble". And being a non-alcoholic, he said, "I think I know what's the matter with you. You're under too much pressure, and I'm going to take a little of the pressure off you." So instead of shooting me, as he had every right to do, he gave me three thousand dollars for a Christmas present the Friday before Christmas, 1945. If any of you have ever drunk any booze, you know that there's one thing that's worse for an alky than bad fortune, and that's good fortune. So I got drunk on the way home and I never showed up until the last of January, and he'd missed me. He'd sent word to the house that if I ever set foot in the plant again he was going to throw me through the window. And the window to which he referred doesn't open! Plate glass was there.

So I was down there before I got into the first Alcoholics Anonymous meeting because I didn't know where to find you guys, but I knew where the plant was. And I went down there knowing that I was going to be thrown through the window, but I couldn't help it because he'd paid me for something I didn't do. Had he come in to throw me through the window, and I couldn't have defended myself with a shotgun because I was puny; I was not well. I'd just come off a four-week blackout. Fortunately for me, I was on the phone when he came in and he had a little time, so he took my drafting boards and stuff out of the way so he'd have a clear shot at the window. As soon as I hung up (The phone was his. He was a frugal man; he didn't want to throw *it* through the window), he got ready to throw me through. I hung up the phone and he started to talk, and I said, "Victor, leave me alone. I don't work for you anymore. I'm down here to clean up this desk. I'm here to do the things you paid me for last year that I didn't do. And as soon as I get even with you, I'll get out of here on my own power and you'll never owe me a penny as long as you live. But for God's sake, leave me alone. I've got to get even with you." And he stopped in his tracks and said, "What the hell's happened to you, Charley?" I said. "I don't know." But he did, and he didn't throw me through the window.

So all of those people and many of my clients knew that something had happened to me a long time before I discovered it. I'd be sitting with a man at lunch, talking business with him, and right in the middle of a sentence he'd say, "What the hell has happened to you, Charley? I've known you for twenty-five years, and I don't know you." And I'd say, "I don't know.", and I didn't. But this is what happened: That thing called ego was gone, and eventually I woke up in the circle, a part of and not apart from.

Now there is no life apart from, there's only life a part of. So the circle becomes the whole human race. Inside the circle I am one dot and you are the other dots. The Good Book says God is Life, and you and I are alive. So God is that which I am, and God is that which you are. This is the meaning of the words "as we understood Him" in our book.* "As we understood Him" has no reference to understanding the infinite. It has reference only to the necessity of individual experience. My God. Your God. The necessity of individual experience. I hunted your God for thirty years before I got here, and I couldn't find Him. I came here not even looking, and we found each other. We have to find Him where He is, and He's right here in me and right there in you. So we have to find our own.

Now there is a man here that raises hell with me for quoting. He says, "I hate a man that quotes verses." And I joke with him, "That's because you don't know any verses." And then I explain myself. The only reason I ever quote verses is because some of those verses say things that I want to say better than I can say them, that's all. Because everything I say from here is my own experience. Everything that I share with you from this podium has happened to me in my lifetime. The bad and the good has happened to me in my lifetime. But there are some

---

* "Alcoholics Anonymous"

verses that I like. For instance, Paul said this, "Just as you have a body, and it's made up of many members, and all the members are different and all the members have a different function, and yet they all go together to make up the one body, so are we all in Christ." That's what this is. It takes every member of the human race to make up the Christ. Christ is the second of the Trinity: God the Father, God the Son. And it takes us all to make up the Christ, everyone of us. We're all God's kids, so it takes us all to make up the one Son, and that's what the circle is.

Now the conscious awareness of this is the difference between Hell and Heaven. Being born out of conscious separation into conscious unity I believe to be the rebirth, or the birth of Christ, in me, and the birth of Christ in you. I think it has to happen to everybody. We are the most fortunate of all God's kids, because we ran out of time and people and places and things and money and booze. There's no place else to go, so we come to Alcoholics Anonymous for sobriety. And we do the things that people like you, drunks who are not drunk, tell us that they have done. And they're sober. And they say, "If you want what we've got, do these things." And we want it, and we do them for sobriety. And a lot of things happen to us. We get sober. But all the related disorders disappear, also.

I have a fetish on this. Because we have so many experts now in related disorders, it's a little difficult to get anybody to talk to a drunk! I've got to share this with you, because I can't keep it. I shouldn't ever tell anybody, because I had no business doing it. I'd called on a person in the hospital, where they have an alcoholic rehabilitation thing, a fixing-up deal, and this guy wasn't in that. He's an alky, but he was in there for other physical troubles. I had visited with him a while and was going out and went through the alcoholic deal, and they recognized me and said, "Why don't you go in and visit the therapy section, we're having a therapeutic deal going on in here. Why don't you go visit it?" And I said, "Don't care if I do." So they took me in. And here was the therapist, one of us, who was quoting about a dozen drunks on how to handle such emotions as jealousy, anger and resentments. She was givin' em the therapy—how to work on these things. How to handle those things. I sat there and listened until I couldn't sit there anymore, and then I did a very bad thing. I just got up out of my seat and I said, "Just a goddamned minute! What makes you think that you can handle emotions like jealousy and anger and resentment. If we could have handled those things we would have handled them twenty years ago. There's no way that you can handle a thing like that. You've got to get rid of it. They're children of the ego. They're obsessions of the mind. And the only way to get rid of them is to get rid of the human ego, in surrender." And then I remembered that I wasn't supposed to be there, and I walked out. (Before I got thrown out!) They haven't asked me back, yet! So this being born out of conscious separation into conscious unity I believe to be the thing that happens that they told us had to happen to everybody: You must be born again. And we're so fortunate, because we *have* to have an answer in order to survive. It's quite a wonderful thing.

We talked a little about writing down our inventory and sharing it and then giving it away. Giving it away. We "Were entirely ready to have God remove all these defects of character. Humbly asked Him to remove our shortcomings."* And that I believe to be the only way that we can get rid of them. The *only* way we can get rid of them. How do I know if I've given them away? It's very simple: If I haven't got 'em! Now, that beats ya, doesn't it? If I've got 'em, I didn't give 'em away. So I've got to keep working on that particular act until its done, because when I them away, I haven't got them. They stay away for awhile and then they come back because ego comes back, and that's the reason for continuous surrender.

This program of Alcoholics Anonymous gives us a new motivation and a new action pattern in the entire business of living. Father Ed Dowling said it this way to me many years ago, twenty, I suspect it was. I'd talked at a St. Louis banquet, a yearly affair, and Father Ed was there, that was his base. Father Ed as you know, those of you who've read "Alcoholics Anonymous Comes of Age", was a Jesuit priest but he was not an alcoholic. He was sort of in our program, or with us, from the very beginning. I knew him very well, loved him very much and I think he loved me. He said to me one time, "Chuck, your cross was alcoholism, my cross was lack of faith. I went through all of my studies and was ordained and didn't believe a damn thing." Now that's a rough spot for a "Jebby". I think eighteen years he'd gone to school, and he went all through his studies and was ordained and didn't believe anything. And he said, "I came to believe by watching what happens to you people in Alcoholics Anonymous."

Now that's a tremendous statement. "I came to believe by watching the miracles in AA happen." And after this talk in St. Louis, we were going to get some coffee. Mrs. C. was with me and she said, "Chuck, maybe Father Ed would like to go with us for coffee." And I said, "Maybe he would, Honey, you ask him!" I didn't want to get turned down. I'm a sensitive alcoholic! So she asked him and he went. And we sat down in the booth and he started plying me with questions, and he never quit. I would say every fifteen minutes, "Father. You talk. I've been talking all

night. You talk. I love to hear you talk." But he'd ask
another question, and the last question he asked was,
"Chuck, tell me about the family. What's happened in the
family? And I said, "No, Father, I won't tell you. Mrs. C.'s
here; let her tell you." And so, she told him what had
happened in our family. And he sat there with his little
mouth perked up, looking out the window, seemingly
forever. That was a great habit of his; his mouth just
looked like a little ol' rosebud, and he'd look off into
space. He finally turned to me, and he said, "You know
something, Chuck?" And I said, "What, Father?" He said,
"Sometimes I have to believe that Heaven is just a new
pair of glasses." I think that's one of the most profound
statements I ever heard out of the mouth of anybody.
"Sometimes I have to believe that Heaven is just a new
pair of glasses." And that's exactly what this program has
been for me. I said to my wife, "Honey, where's the
difference?" This program is a new motivation and a new
action pattern.

Everything that I was taught as a child in home, in
school and in church has had to be reversed since I
became older. Everything. There isn't anything that they
taught me that is left except the multiplication tables.
That's all. Everything else has had to change. We talked
about the feeling that we had to get out there in the salt
mines and out-think, out-perform and out-maneuver in
order to eke out a miserable living out of an unfriendly
universe. And we're going to talk about that in "AA in
business", so we'll skip that for a minute. One side of my
family was Methodist Church South and the other side
was hard-shell Baptist, of which there is nothing
"whicher". We were taught that everything that happened
to us had to happen between the cradle and the grave and
that there is only one thing important in life. Life was
not worth very much; "This veil of tears", they called it.

The only important thing this life was good for was to prepare for death. Death is the big thing, and all of your rewards come when you get to heaven, or if you don't make it, in Hell. Hellfire and Brimstone. They taught us that we had to merit, to earn, to be worthy of the Grace of God. And that had to be reversed. You see, if we had to merit, be worthy of, earn the Grace God, the first alcoholic would not have gotten sober.

Bill Wilson was an agnostic and when Ebby talked to him, when Ebby got down to the God part, Bill removed his hearing aid and got a little bit more involved in his gin. (He was drinking a bit of gin that Ebby had refused). Ebby'd found sobriety in the Oxford movement, and they also had a God of their own. That's where "as we understood Him" came from, out of the Oxford movement and Jim Burwell.

So when Ebby talked about God, Bill just went ahead drinking his gin and first thing you know he's back in Town Hospital, and he heard Dr. Silkworth. Dr. Silkworth is the only one of that first gang that I never knew, and I'm very, very unhappy about that because he lived a long time after I got to the program. I never met Silky, but he must have been a helluva guy. Bill heard Silkworth tellin' Lois, Bill's wife, that the only thing she could do was to make his life as comfortable as she could because six months was all he had, and at the end of six months she'd either have to bury him or lock him up. Permanent insanity. Now Bill wasn't feelin' too good, he was comin' off a bad drunk and a withdrawal period, and he heard that pronouncement and he wasn't prepared for that. He said to himself, "Oh, oh... I have tried everything else but this God thing that Ebby was talking about." And being faced with permanent insanity or an alcoholic death, he didn't have much left to do except try what Ebby'd talked about.

37

In total and complete abandonment of self he said, "God, if there be a God, reveal yourself to me now." And *WHAMBO!* It happened like that! He had quite an experience, not unknown to many of us. And from that experience on he never had another drink.

When Silkworth made his next rounds, Bill told him what had happened to him and he said; "Now, Doctor, do you think this was real, or was it just another hallucination? The doctor said, "Well, Bill, whatever it is, hang on to it. This is the first sense you've made to me since I met you in the first place!" So Bill didn't have the time to earn, be worthy of, or merit. He didn't have the time to do anything but abandon himself. There was no "earning"instinct.

Had there been any requirement to understand the Infinite when I got here, I wouldn't be here. I had used every resource I had and I had lost. And I said to myself, "If I ever live to get out of this bed, I'll find AA." And from that second until now I haven't had to have a drink or pill. Just to become *willing* to come here was the key in my case. There was no earning or being worthy of or meriting anything. I had to live to be about sixty-five before I realized that the very word "grace", the meaning of the word "grace" is a free gift. A free gift. And there's no way that any of us can earn a free gift.

There is another little thing that is most important to me. When I discovered that I was sober, I started to try to do something about Step Eleven, and it said, "Sought through prayer and meditation..." and I thought I was going to have to "pray and meditate". And I had me a Grand Central Head; my Grand Central Head didn't leave early. A Grand Central Head is when ten thousand things are going through your mind at the same time and you can't hold a thought for a split second. But I knew I had to "pray and meditate" because it says "Sought through prayer and meditation. And I'm drinking my tea, sittin' in the same chair I sit in right now at home, trying to meditate. And it was a mess! Then two verses popped through my head and I wouldn't take a million dollars a verse for them. The first one was this: Seems like the Carpenter was walkin' off down the road one morning and somebody wanted something and yelled at him, "Good Master, Good Master." And the Carpenter walked over and looked down at the guy and he said, "Why callest thou me good? There is none good but one, and that's the Father." This is the Carpenter talking, mind you.

And a little later on some monkey came up to him and said, "Hey, Bub,you're doing some pretty fancy miracles. How do you do these things? And the Man said to him, "Go peddle your papers. I don't. Of myself I can do nothing. It's the Father within. He doeth the works." I wouldn't take a million dollars apiece for those two verses, because at that second I said to myself, "If it's good enough for Him, it's good enough for me." And it made it unnecessary for me to try to be good, or to try to be so damned accomplished. You know? If it's good enough for Him, it's good enough for me.

And so I've lived from then until now in total expectance of His guidance and direction. I changed Step eleven a little bit for me. The way I use it now, I get out of bed in the morning and I say, "Look, Dad, I'm reporting for duty. Now I'm going to move it around, I'm going to do the best I can with what I've got and all I want out of you is a little guidance and direction and the power to carry it out. Sure thank you." And I go about my business, totally expectant of His guidance and direction. This in business, AA, play, home, the works. And I get it. People say to me, "How do you know?" and I've got the simplest yard-stick in the world on that, too: I never had it so good.

This is the only easy life I've ever known, the only good life that's ever been mine in my entire lifetime. That's all the yardstick I need. The next thing that they say to me is, "I pray for His knowledge and will for me and the power to carry it out. I think I get direction, but how do I know whether it's my will or His will?" And that's a good question, and I have the simplest answer in the world for that, for me: If it's important to me personally, it's my will. If it is important to me personally, it is an ego satisfaction. If I am praying alright it is not for something for me. It's that I might be of some value to you.

Now, you might think, "You can call this a retreat. Why aren't you opening and closing these meetings with a prayer?" Because every one of these meetings is a prayer, as far as I'm concerned. Insofar as I am able to perceive, every serious thought is a prayer, even worry is a prayer for something you don't want to happen. Anticipatory anxiety tends to create the thing you're afraid of. Actually creates it. Ole Job says, "Lo, that which I've feared has come upon me." Anticipatory anxiety creates the thing we're afraid of.

Before we go any further I've got to tell you that I do not believe in a capricious God. I do not believe in a God of judgments, punishments, and rewards. I don't believe it, but many of you do. I do not, and I want to tell you why I don't. Number one, if there was anything other than God, God could not be infinite. If there were "otherness" God would not be infinite, He would be finite. The Good Book says, "In the Beginning, God..." God plus nothing leaves nothing but God. "In the Beginning, God." So insofar as I'm concerned, there is no "otherness". God's all there is, there ain't no more. Very likely the process of creation was something like this: God thinks and Himself becomes the thing he thinks about. You remember the little boy who said to the teacher,

"Where'd God stand when he created the earth?" That's a hell've a good question, isn't it? Where did he stand when he created the earth? He couldn't have stood on a ball of mud out of the Mississippi River. He hadn't made the Mississippi River, yet! He didn't have to stand. God thinks and Himself becomes the thing he thinks about.

Plotinus, eighteen hundred years ago, thought there were, I think, about a hundred and twenty stars in the universe. He'd counted them with his little telescope. A little while later Galileo thought there were five thousand stars. Presently they say there's an infinite number of galaxies. An infinite number of galaxies! So it's expanded a bit. Now when I look at these things I see God. The body of God is creation, just as you have a body. To perceive and say, "There's ol' Keith", that isn't "ol' Keith" at all—that's where Keith lives. When Keith moves out, that body goes back to the elements that make the mountains and the molehills. Same thing. So your body is just as real as it's supposed to be—in a state of constant flux. This is the reason that Einstein said energy and mass are equal, identical, and interchangeable. This is the reason that the Carpenter said, "That which is made is not made of that which it doth appear." It's the evidence of, or the body of, the Creator. And as such it's the most beautiful thing I've ever laid eyes on. I wish I had time to expand on that, too. It's a beautiful thing.

You and I duplicate God in our little world. We think and ourselves become the things we think about. For instance, something you and I know a little bit about is drinking whiskey and "muscadoodle" and Old Panther. I broke in on White Lightning—146 proof and from that up to 169. It's real good—I drank it out of a fruit jar. It's nice; you get a crease right across your nose. Take a big slug—Ugh, that's good!

But it got the job done. So, we think and ourselves become the thing we think about. After a while, every alky looks like every other alky. Every one of us looks just alike. We get a purple cauliflower on the end of our nose, all of our wiring is exposed, and we get a little bean belly sticking out. Every one of us looks just alike. When you see one, you say, "There's a drunk, there's an alky." Every gourmet looks just alike. You get fat, rolly-polly, and get a very nice disposition because you can't whip anybody. We all look just alike. So, we think and ourselves become the thing we think about.

For instance, I drew the plans for every market that I put in. I drew the plans for all my clients with my own hands. Laid them out, put the departments where they should be and allotted the space to them. I put the back rooms where they should be and allotted the space according to the operation, whether the man had his own warehouse or twice-a-week deliveries from someplace else. I spotted all the plumbing and wiring that it took to operate the thing. Then we gave it to the architect, who in collaboration with the builders built a building around it and I built the fixtures that went in it. Then the operator put some canned goods and some meat in there and had a store. But that store came out of my head before it was ever on paper. We think and ourselves become the thing we think about. That's the way it is with our lives. We duplicate the Creator in our little word. And that's the reason that it behooves us to know what this thinking apparatus is.

Now I told you I didn't believe in a God of judgment because I don't believe that an Infinite can think comparatively. I don't think that God knows the difference between a molehill and a mountain in size because God is both the molehill and the mountain. He doesn't have to think comparatively. He's both the molehill and the mountain. To compare there has to be "otherness", you hear me? This makes it unnecessary to have a God of judgment. We have a God of love and a great law of justice without judgment. The law says, "What you sow you reap." You can't plant radishes and get cucumbers. What you sow you reap. "As a man thinketh in his heart, so is he." It's a great law of life. And it's just as cold as any law in the universe. It's as cold as the law of electricity. That law of electricity will light that light, fry your bacon, or fry your fanny, and it's just as comfortable frying your fanny as lighting that light. It's the nature of the law. The nature of the law of life is that if I pour in slop I get back slop. And it's just as comfortable giving me back slop as it is giving me back love.

Now I taught that law to others forty years ago and I thought people could live by it, but they can't. If you're an alky, you can't live by it. You know it intellectually; you know you can't plant radishes and get cucumbers. But you think you are above the law and you try to do a little controlling job on your thinking. You're not getting back what you want, but you think you can *think* your way into getting it.

You've got to have some heat (love), which you don't have in the cold law. Where's the heat come from? There were two pillars in front of the temple of Solomon, they were called Jachin and Boaz. You had to walk between those pillars to get in to the temple, the holy of holys. Jachin and Boaz, now that means law and love. Law and Love. And the ancients put it like this: "On the one hand all is law." The way it works. Law. What you sow, you reap. "And on the other hand all is love, and love is the fulfillment of the law." Love is the fulfillment of the law. Now what does that mean? That means sooner or later you and I can have only one motivation for any act whatsoever, and that's love. The only reason for doing anything is because you love it—for free and for fun. That's in work, play, AA, home, the works. Love is the fulfillment of the law. It is axiomatic that if the only thing I pour into life is love, the only thing the law can give me back is love. Love is the fulfillment of the law.

I love you, period. Why? In the beginning because you were drunks and because you rocked me to sleep, and you gave me the program of Alcoholics Anonymous and helped me do it. So I had to love you. Before I got here I hated you more than any part of the whole human race. Before the thing happened to me I thought the entire human race was a cosmic mistake. God's kids were too damn mean and too stupid to merit my attention. I was interested in God. I learned a lot about Him, and the more I learned the drunker I got. Now that wasn't because I knew more, but because I didn't do anything. I knew so much, I didn't have to do; I told you guys what to do. But I didn't have to do these things because I already knew them, you know. So it took me pretty nearly seventy years to learn that you can live yourself into right thinking but you cannot think yourself into right living. All you've got to do is do these things and something happens; don't do them and nothing happens, regardless of how much you know about the program of Alcoholics Anonymous.

We had a guy here when I first got here and we called him The Coach. His name was Paul C. Some of you guys were here long enough ago to know him. Paul had two vocabularies. He had an under-the-bridge vocabulary (and I thought I had a pretty good one, but he could lose me), and he had a Notre Dame vocabulary. And he knew the AA book practically by heart. He could stand up here and almost quote Chapter Three in its entirety and Chapter Five in its entirety, without cracking a book. And we had to watch Paul die. We had to watch him die. He came to me at our meeting in Beverly Hills just a short time before he left us, and he fell on my neck and cried like a baby and said, "Chuck, look at you and look at me. Just think, I was going to throw you out of my own house when you came to see me." And he had to die because he forgot to do these things. He knew them but he didn't do them. We can live ourselves into right thinking, but we can't think ourselves into right living.

I love you. It's none of my business what you think of me. It is none of my business. It's my business what I think of you and I love you. Now if you happen to love me back it's a plus. So you can add to my life but you can't take away. Did you hear me? This is one of the greatest things that you ever heard tell of. You can add to my life but you can't take away, and everybody that lives can add to my life, but they can't take away, because I'm not trading with you—I love you, period. First because you're a drunk. Second because I know who you are, whether you do or not. You're God's children, every one of you, and for that reason I love you, and for no other.

Now I want to throw this in. As many of you know, I do a few things in Alcoholics Anonymous and I have been doing them for twenty-nine years—like maybe having as many as eight talks in a row. I don't do it because I want to hear my voice, I've heard me before. And I don't do it because I want your applause, because I've had that before. The only reason I'm here is to share me with anybody that wants me in love. That's the only reason I'm here and that's the only reason I can do what I do. If I was concerned about saving your souls I wouldn't be here, because if any of you have a lost soul I wouldn't have the slightest idea where to look for it. Not the slightest. And I am most certainly not here to make Christians out of you, because as I understand or misunderstand Christianity, I just might not be a Christian myself. (You priests take note!)

I've never had a sponsor in this program. Never. When I got here I didn't know anything about a sponsor, and when I'd learned about a sponsor I didn't figure that I was entitled to that much consideration from anybody. I never even asked any questions for a long time. I became an eavesdropper. When I got well enough to hold a cup of coffee, I'd get me a cup of coffee, pick out somebody that seemed to be talking pretty good AA and back up to him and stick my ear into the conversation. I became a helluv' an eavesdropper. If they caught me, I'd take off, back up to somebody else, and if they caught me and included me in, I couldn't take it. I couldn't believe it, and I'd go out under the pepper trees and cry like a damn baby. A little later on, when I might of been able to accept a sponsor, I had a few hundred of them. Everybody that I see in Alcoholics Anonymous is my sponsor. Those who are in the program and those who are not in it, every one of them is my sponsor. I feel that every man is my teacher, some teaching me what to do and some teaching me what not to do. And I think the one that teaches me what not to do might be just as important as the one that teaches me what to do.

As I have told many of you, I went through two deaths last year with people that I'd known, one of them twenty-eight years, and one of them twenty-five. And they both left by their own hand. One of them was only forty-five years old, and he'd been sober twenty-five years, and I'd been instrumental in getting him in here. And his image got between him and his program and his God. He had to die. And the other one let something get too important to her, and she had to die. Twenty-eight years. So, those that teach us what not to do are just about as important teachers as those that teach us what to do.

Now why does this law and love do away with the necessity for a God of judgment? It's quite possible, gentlemen, that the only bondage there is in this life is absolute freedom under law. Absolute freedom under law. For instance, there is no law of God or man that says I can't drink whiskey. You can't find a law that says I can't drink whiskey. And by the Grace of God through the miracle of AA, I have enough money in my pocket right now, if you won't tell anybody, to get us all drunk and keep us drunk for quite a little while. Without even going to the bank I can do that. Why don't I drink whiskey? The priest says, "You ought not." And I say, "I don't know what you're talkin' about, Son" I don't know what that means, "You ought not." Who says, "I ought not?" But I know what this means: "I can't afford it." I cannot afford it. When I drink whiskey it robs me of everything I like about me and you and life. So I cannot afford it and I don't drink it. There's no law of God or man that says I can't hate you. I can hate the b'Jesus out of every one of you if I want to. No law says I can't. Why don't I? Again, the priest says, "You ought not." And again I say, "I don't know what you're talkin' about." But I know this, I can't afford it, because whatever I pour in, I get back, and I've gotten back enough of that slop. I don't want any more, so I don't do it.

There's no law of God or man that says I can't judge you. I'm perfectly free to judge the Hell out of you if I want to, and I'm very capable along those lines! For many years I inventoried everybody that I ever knew and lots of people that were just walking by! Why don't I judge you? I can't afford it. The Carpenter told me what would happen to me if I did, but He did not tell me I couldn't. He said, "Judge not that

47

you be not judged, for with whatsoever judgment ye judge, ye shall be judged. And with whatsoever measure ye meet, it will be measured to you again, heaped up, pressed down, and running over." That's what happens to me if I judge, but He didn't say you can't. If I'm willing to pay the penalty I can do it. But I'm not willing to pay the penalty, so I don't do it. No law of God or man says I can't resent you. Why don't I? Can't afford it. Envy. Can't afford it, so I don't do it, because whatever I pour in, whatever I sow, I reap. The only bondage there is, perhaps, in this entire life is absolute freedom under law. You can do anything your imagination conjures up if you're willing to pay the inevitable consequence of your thought and act. I am not willing, so I don't do it.

Now, we've got to take a little moment and do away with something that many, many of us think about. People were telling me for years, "Chuck, you can't drink. You've got to quit." I could look around me and see a lot of people that were drinking and not getting into trouble, and I couldn't understand why I couldn't drink like they did. I sit up there in my room, now, in that same chair, and I look down on the little town of Laguna Beach and there are fifteen thousand, one hundred people in Laguna Beach at the last count. And fifteen thousand of them can do things I can't do. And they're all God's kids. How come? They can eat a little and drink a little, love a little, hate a little, judge a little, resent a little, lie a little and cheat a little. They're God's kids, same as I am. How come they can do that and I can't? Simply because, as yet, they have not run out of time. They can eat a little and drink a little. You and I never could do that. We've always figured that anything that was worth doing was worth doing to excess. We ran out of time and they haven't run out, yet. And it is my opinion that it doesn't make any difference to the universe when they run out of time. Whether it's now or five hundred years from now, it doesn't make any difference. Sooner or later every one of us has to come back home, to the Living God that made us, because we're all God's kids.

Timing doesn't count with the universe, it counts with me. Life is pretty good, living it with you guys. It isn't worth a damn living out there in that jungle where I used to live. So that's the deal. Our motivation is to add to, to go about our Father's business doing things for His kids that they need to have done, because we want to. And that's what our twelfth step tells us to do: "Having had a spiritual awakening as the result of these steps, we tried to carry this message to alcoholics"—to God's kids—"and to practice these principles in all our affairs."* With God's kids, in every department of our lives; at home, in business, in play, in AA. And so if our motivation is love and we do these things for free and for fun, the only thing that the law can give us back is love. This is the motivation, this is the way it works, and it totally does away with the necessity of a God of judgment. It's built in. What you sow, you reap. As a man thinketh in his heart, so is he.

Now I can go right down the middle of the road with a God of law and order, a God of love, a law of justice without judgment. I can go right down the middle of the road with that. But I can't go a foot with the God they told me about when I was a kid. You see? They told me that God would take my kids away from me in death, to punish me for my sins. I said, when I was four feet tall, "If there's a God like that, I'm going to get me a pitchfork and join with the Devil. If I ever catch Him, I'm going to stick that pitchfork through Him." I could not accept a God of that kind, and I don't now. My insides wouldn't hack it, and they still don't. But a God of love and a great

49

law of justice without judgment, I can go with. It's a fantastic thing. I don't happen to believe in good or bad. I don't happen to believe in right or wrong. I don't happen to believe in two worlds. I believe in one world. I believe that this is an experience, but it's not reality.

The Carpenter said, "Judge not according to appearances, but judge righteous judgment." That means that pretty soon we see ourselves in all men and all men in ourselves, and we look through the condition to the thing behind it. I haven't seen a drunk, now, for twenty years. It's been twenty years since I've seen a drunk. When I was in business my plant was at Fortieth and Alameda, every time I went downtown, if time permitted, I went to the head of Fifth Street and drove west. It drew me like a magnet. And every time I ever went in to Fifth Street the black paddy wagon was just ahead of me. And I knew that black paddy wagon inside and out; I'd ridden in her in chains. And all the boys on the street knew her, too. And here's a little wino, you know, with his bottle in his brown paper bag (So nobody'd know what he's got! There's nothing that looks so much like a bottle of wine in a brown paper bag as a bottle of wine in a brown paper bag!) He sees these rag pickers coming, you know, and he tries to hide and he goes flat on his ass (Strike that!) about four times, runnin' for the alley. But he doesn't break that bottle. He breaks his fanny, but he doesn't break that bottle. And he gets into the alley, and I say, "Thank God, thank God." Because that's me, that's me but for the Grace of God.

So I'm going down the street and here's this ol' boy in the doorway; it's July and he's got on two overcoats, a black one and a gray one. There he sits in the doorway. His bottle's right out in the open and it's half full (Red Eye). He's sittin' there laughin' and talkin' with his friends and havin' a helluva' time—but his friends aren't there! I can hardly drive by him, I want to leave that car of mine right in the middle of Fifth Street and go over and pick him up and set him on my lap, because that's me but for the Grace of God. You see, I used to wear my overcoat in July and I used to meet the people and talk to them. They'd talk to me and we'd have a helluva' time. But they weren't there. I think that one of the things that made the biggest impression on my family, of all the things I did drunk, was when we'd all be in the same living room, and I'd have company and they wouldn't have any! They couldn't understand it. So, we don't judge according to appearances. We look through the appearance and see God's kid, right under that crud, and we share with Him. We share our experience, strength and hope, one with another in love, and that's the reason our program works and nothing else does. Without the sharing, without the caring, there would be no recovery in Alcoholics Anonymous.

Now I told you a little bit ago it's my business what I think of you and it's your business what you think of me. What you think of me is not my business unless you want to make it my business. It never concerns me, I never even wonder. I don't have to because I love you and love is a complete thing within itself. It's like virtue. When virtue recognizes itself as virtue it immediately becomes vice. Virtue is its own reward and love is its own reward. The fulfillment of the law. I don't have to wonder about it. In personal relations this has the greatest meaning on the face of the earth because, you see, all of us are God's kids. All of us do what we have to do because all of us have obsessions of the mind. In my early experience in Alcoholics Anonymous, I thought that obsessions of the mind were a part of my disease, that the other people didn't have any right to them.

They're not alcoholics—"alcoholism is a disease of a twofold nature, an allergy of the body coupled with an obsession of the mind."* They haven't got an allergy of the body, so they can't have the obsession of the mind. That was just for drunks. But in living a while, I had to come to see that we're all God's kids and every one of us is doing the best we can according to our understanding of our life.

People don't do what they do because they want to but because they have to. Just as I drank and you drank against our own will, we have to come to see that obsessions of the mind, whoever has them, are greater than will power. When the will and the imagination and/or the emotions are in conflict, the emotions and the imagination always win. We drank against our own will. And so people don't do what they do because they want to, but because they have to. The man never lived that disliked me enough to have to tear me down. The only reason that anybody tries to tear me down is to build himself up. And when we come to see this, people can't hurt us. There's no way that they can hurt us.

When we know better, we do better. Now this fools a lot of people because they think that since they know these things intellectually, they know them. They don't. Forty years ago, I knew everything I know now that is of consequence in my life except one thing: the disease of alcoholism. I didn't know anything about that. Forty years ago I believed everything that I believe now that is consequential to my way of life. I was born believing in God and I never got drunk enough not to believe in God. Belief in God is good, but it's not good enough. If you are a drunk, living in God is the only answer there is. The consciousness of the *living* presence of the Almighty. The only answer there is. In Him I live and move and have my Being. So when we know better we do better. I knew it from the neck up, forty years ago. I know it all over, now. And I don't sow what I'm unwilling to reap too often, but I still do it sometimes.

I have a little trick that I wouldn't trade for a million dollars. I share everything in life with my God. Everything; the good, the bad and the indifferent. I share it and dump it. For instance, when I do a lousy stunt, which I do, once in a while (too often), I take it into my closet with me and I say, "Look, Dad, look what I did yesterday. Isn't this a lousy thing for a guy like me to do? I knew better when I did it but I had to make an impression. Now I don't like it and you don't like it and I'm going to do better, and with your help I'll do a lot better. Sure thank you." And I dump it and never pick it up again. When a good thing happens, I do the same thing with it. I say, "Look, Father, isn't this beautiful? It couldn't happen to a bum like me, but it did. And I know where it came from. Sure thank you." And I dump that. I think it's just as tough on us to try to carry the so-called good as the so-called bad. We don't need either one of them, because this life should be spontaneous. We don't need any impediments. Get rid of the whole business and start each day anew, with no yesterdays and no tomorrows.

Spontaneous life. There's a Golden Key to this thing called life. My friend Harold's been waitin' on it for twenty years. Just follow'n me around—he and ol' Doc R.— follow'n me around for five years, waitin' for me to drop the Golden Key. They knew that sometime, by mistake, I'd spill it and they'd be there to get it. And every time they'd come down and take up the whole night, yakkin' in my living room, I would tell them, "Look, I've given you this key every time you've heard me talk. I've given it to you. All you've got to do is these simple things. But they knew there was something else. So I'm giving them that Golden Key, now, after twenty years.

The Golden Key to this thing called life is rigorous self-honesty. Rigorous self-honesty. Why? Because we have a monitor within us. We didn't put it there, and we can't dislodge it. The religious call it conscience. (This is another thing I don't understand—don't' know anything about.) I call it God. God in me, as me, is me. I'm not God, but God is me. Infinitely greater than I because He's all of you, as well as me. Not different from, or other than, or apart from, but a part of. I am consciously aware of the living presence of the Almighty. So the Golden Key to this thing called life is rigorous self-honesty. The pattern is right here. When I perform according to the best I know, the pattern's right here; it's not in the mountain, it's not in the temple, it's not in Jerusalem, it's in your own mouth, that you might know it and do it. It's right here in me. When I perform according to the best I know there seems to be a nod of approval from the universe, and they call that "peace of mind." When I perform less than my best the ol' sausage grinder's right here, too, and it starts chewing me up: "Uh Oh, Chuck, why'd you do it, why'd you do it? The only way I can get rid of it is to see for what it is and decide to do better, with the Grace of God. And it disappears, and I'm back in the King Row. To keep our priorities where they belong, this is the great secret to this thing called life: rigorous self-honesty. And the pattern is right here within me and within you.

Again, talking to you guys is a lot fun for me—it's the greatest joy in my life. There's nothing that I like better than to talk about these things, because they happened to me. To me, in me, and through me. And I love to talk about it, to share. And that's what we're going to be doing again, and we're going to talk a little about the greatest power in this life. Greater than any hydrogen bomb, greater than all other power, is the simple unadulterated truth. It's the greatest power there is. And the seat of it is right here in us.

Chapter 3

THE POWER OF TRUTH

"**A**nd practice these principles in all of our affairs." Step Ten says, we "continued to take personal inventory, and when we were wrong, promptly admitted it."* Now I do not believe that this means that we go back through our lives and redo Step Four. I think this means that we look at our day. How closely are we living according to these principles today. How're we doing today. Step Ten has been very, very important to me because up until the time I got into this program there was no way that I could say, "I don't know." There was no way I could say, "I don't know" particularly in business. You don't say "I don't know" in business. They ask you anything and you answer! No way you could say, "I don't know." I'm quite sure that if you'd asked me to explain Einstein's theory, I'd have explained it. If you asked me how God created the earth I'd have told you and I very likely would have said, "Now on the third day, *we* did thus and so...." I couldn't say, "I don't know." I came to the program, and I learned by doing the things that the program told me to do, that the truth was the   most powerful thing on earth.   Just by doing them.   In business I learned to say, "I don't know, but that question's important.   Tomorrow I'll know the answer to it."   And tomorrow I did.   As to anything I didn't know, I said, "I don't know."   And that's very easy, because you don't have to remember what you said when you don't tell them something that you don't know.   You don't have to remember.   Tell them the truth and you don't have to remember.   Another thing to remember is, "I was wrong."   Hell, I didn't used to go around saying, "I was wrong."   I think I told you this morning; once I thought I was wrong, but I was mistaken.

The twenty-fourth day of June of this year, if we live and if Mrs. C. doesn't divorce me between now and then, we'll have fifty years in double harness.   (With a little time out for bad behavior!)   And now I catch myself saying to my wife, "I was wrong.   You were right all the time".   I would have sworn that I was right but I was wrong all the time."   Now that's awful!   You've been married to the same broad for fifty years and tell her you're wrong!   Isn't that awful?   But it's good, it's real good because you're comfortable.   When you do it that way you're comfortable.

The most powerful thing on the face of the earth is the simple unadulterated truth.   So much so that somebody said one time, "Know the truth, and the truth will make you free."   The *truth* will make you free.   And in all of our affairs this holds true—in business, in play, in family, in AA, the works.   I've known many over the years, particularly those who have become and maybe still are so-called "circuit speakers", who have thought that a little embellishment might make their story more interesting.   So they've got to build it up a little, and first thing you know they're drunk.   Or they get to think they're big in the program, they're experts in this program, because people tell them how good they are. And they believe their press, and the next thing you know they're drunk. You can't get big in this program of ours. No way.

If you and I could have handled this deal we would have done so, and we would not be members of Alcoholics Anonymous. We had plenty of time. I had forty-three years to run my life, during which time I was the star of the show and the director of energies. I gave it my best shot. All my wit and my wisdom I put in and I lost. I lost. As I told you, at the ripe old age of forty-three I was a failure as a husband, a father, a businessman, a man and a drunk. And that's all the departments I had. If I'd had any more departments I'd have been a failure in those, too. I take credit for that, but the last twenty-nine years I take no credit for at all. I thank God and you, and maybe I should put it the other way, I thank you and God. Because it's people like you that rocked me to sleep on my first night. And it was living with people like you that I came to see that I had a God of my very own. I didn't even know what had taken place. So in my thinking, maybe I should say first that I'm grateful to you, and then I'm grateful to God. It doesn't make any difference to me, because I have come to see God is people. God is people, so it doesn't make any difference.

Now, "in all of our affairs" means at home. You see the thing that makes this program work for us is a fellowship of men and women who share—*who share*—their experience, strength and hope, one with another in love. *Who share.* There are very few people in Alcoholics Anonymous that'll *tell* you anything. We don't tell, we share. I've a guy that calls me his sponsor, who tells. And he makes it stick pretty good. I say to him, "You're not even a member of Alcoholics Anonymous. Alcoholics Anonymous is made up of people who share. You don't share with anybody. You tell them. But whatever you do, keep doin' it!" Because I go over there on his birthday and there're sixty-five sober kooks in his backyard. Sixty-five of them, and every one of them are his babies and every one of them are people I couldn't touch with a ten-foot pole. And they're sober. "So whatever you're doing, keep doing it." The Society could not do without one Clancy, but if it had two it would have one too many!

I shared when I discovered I was sober. I started sharing with drunks. I like to think of it like this—many of you have heard me say this before—I like to think of me as a glass of dirty water, a dirty glass full of dirty water. And during my drinking days I was always knocking it off, quittin'. Every time it got too bad, I quit. And when I quit it was like pouring out the dirty water, and then I had an empty glass, dirty and empty. It could only be empty so long, and then I had to fill it again, and I filled it back up with dirty water. When I came to the program, I didn't quit. I hadn't quit drinking yet. I came with a dirty glass full of dirty water. At the first meeting a little stream of clear water started running in, and I liked it and I came back and came back, and the little stream of clear water kept running in. After a while I discovered that the glass was clean and the water was clean, and the glass was full. And then I had to start trying to give it away, and it was only tipped to the drunk because the drunks had given it to me. And I shared with more drunks. And as time went by the glass started straightening up, and eventually it was straight and the water was still running in because I was still going to meetings. And the clear water was spilling in all directions, to whomsoever will. And it was good. And I shared with lots of people, Jews, Gentiles, and Greeks; blacks, whites. All kinds of people. I shared.

But my youngest son I told; I didn't share with him. I told him, because, you see, when he came along he was born with greasepaint in his ears. And I was born with a pitchfork in my hand, and I couldn't understand him. I just couldn't understand him. When he was about six, we lived over in Beverly Hills and we had alleys behind the houses. They picked up the garbage and stuff from behind the alley. Old Dick used to run in the alleys, and he'd find where somebody'd thrown away a colorful dress or something, and he'd get it and he'd bring it into the garage and he'd make a costume out of it. And he'd get himself some earrings and he'd paint himself all up, and have this costume, and he'd come out and put on a show. Six or seven years old. And I'd look at him, and I'd say to myself, "What the goddamned hell have I got, here?" And I started trying to make him over after my design. Tried to put a pitchfork in his hand. He didn't know what a pitchfork was.

When he got to be a little older (He was ten, I guess, or eleven, when I sobered up.), we sent him to school in Pomona, and he got pretty much the whole package. The kid can paint and draw and play and sing and dance. He was taking art, art and philosophy as a matter of fact; art was his major and philosophy was his second. I'd go out there and take him to dinner once in a while, and he'd tell me the values of modernistic and futuristic painting, and he shouldn't have done that! Now mind you, I'd share his talents with everybody else. But he tells me about the values of modernistic and futuristic painting, and I says, "The very idea of a guy with my blood in his veins thinking there's value in that stuff!" "Why," says I, "I've seen a better picture than that when an ol' cow slapped her tail up against the side of the barn." Now that's not a good way to win friends and influence people, especially if they happen to be your son. The boy also talked with his friends about philosophy. He's got a painter friend by the name of Martin, who's doing a good job—has his own shows now. And they were talking philosophy in my house, and I sat and listened to them for a while, and it was obvious to me they didn't know what they were talking about. So I had to straighten them out! I made them sit there and listen to me for an hour and a half. It's a wonder they didn't kill me, but they didn't.

I couldn't understand why we couldn't get along. I was trying my damnedest to get acquainted with that kid and I could not understand why I couldn't. We had been living in the house we live in now for about ten years, and we have a tremendous view from every room in the house, particularly out of the living room. People had been telling me for ten years what they saw out of my window, and it gradually dawned on me as people kept telling me what they saw, that nobody ever looked out of that window and told me what I saw. And eventually I came to see that nobody sees what I see out that window, and something started a'clickin' in my mind. Up until that time, it had never occurred to me that nobody sees what I see. It had never occurred to me. I grew up thinking that white was white, and black was black, and a cow was a cow. Anybody that looked at a cow saw a cow, and if they were looking at the same one I saw, they saw the same cow. But they don't, and the way I found it out was people telling me what they saw out of my window. So I started thinking, "Something's wrong with me. It isn't the kid. It's me. He sees things that I don't see."

Then I got thinking about this philosophy deal, and I saw that I was trying to make the kid cross the street in St. Louis when he was in Chicago. You can't do that, kids. You've got to be in St. Louis to cross the street in St. Louis. So I said to my wife, "We're going to London. And she asked, "Why?" I said, "To get acquainted with my kid." And we went to London. And we went to dinner, and I told this kid how blind I'd been. Totally unaware of the fact that people don't see what I see. How blind I'd been! And how I came to see, by people telling me what they saw out of my window, what he was talking about when he'd talked about the values in these things. And I'd come over to apologize to him, to make my amends. And then I talked about his philosophy, and I apologized for that. I made amends, and the first thing you know we pretty nearly got thrown out of the restaurant. We were laughin' and hollerin' and having a picnic. They pretty nearly threw us out. Because, you see, the dam went out and we shared with each other.

After that we went pretty well all over Europe, and when we came home he came with us. Mrs. C. and I were due in Roanoke to talk on the way home. We got off the plane in Chicago and visited some of my people. He'd never wanted to do that, but now he wanted to go. Then we got down to my Mother's place. Mother is ninety-six and still going. She's not mobile, but she's as keen as a whip. We were visiting there and then we were going to drive on down to Roanoke, and the kid said, "I've got to go back to New York, but I'll be in Roanoke on Friday. I've got some business to do in New York." When he went I said to my wife, "He'll never be in Roanoke." Because, you see, both Mrs. C. and I were talking there, and I knew he wouldn't come. But Friday he was in Roanoke. I had told him before he went, I said, "Dick, these people down there are our people, they love Mrs. C. and I, and they won't leave you alone. You can't be anonymous there because they won't leave you alone." And he said, "I don't care." He was there and he listened to his Mother talk on Friday night, and he listened to me the next morning. And the tables were round, and there were about ten people at each table, and he told me afterwards that he would sit there, listen a little bit, and then he'd say, "I never knew, I never knew." And a little later, "I never knew."

Now what are we talking about? We're talking about taking this thing at home; to *share* our experience, strength and hope. At home nobody likes to be told anything. We think that we're old enough and smart enough that we should be able to tell our kids. They don't want to be told, they want to share. They don't want to know how smart we are, they want to know how we beat ourselves to death, and what we did to get out of it. They want to share with us. The language of the heart has no age. One of the great experiences of my life, I guess it's pretty near two years now, was when they carried me up to North Battleford, Saskatchewan. It was the inner provincial Alateen meeting, and we had twelve or fifteen hundred kids for me to share with. It was a fabulous weekend. Don't think that they can't understand you when you share with them, because they can, if you share and don't tell. It's fantastic.

These women that we married! If the shoe had been on the other foot, my wife wouldn't have lasted sixty days. Not sixty days would I have put up with the performance out of my wife that she put up with me. And she put up with me for twenty years. Twenty years! Now you and I (I suppose you're like me) sort of dreamed all our lives about getting up every morning and having a new woman across the table from us. I thought that was a great deal. I thought a guy ought to have that, you know. You definitely shouldn't get in a rut. Being married to the same broad for fifty years—that's indecent in California! But I came to see that every morning I have a new woman across the table from me, because, you see, we're changing people. We're changing people. You've never heard me before. I'm not the guy I was yesterday. I'm the guy I was yesterday plus yesterday's experience and it's lesson. So we're always new, and that woman that you're married to is always new.

One of the greatest handicaps we put on ourselves is categorizing each other, and particularly the members of our own family. When we live close to them, we come to think that we know everything they're going to do, the way they're going to react to everything. We've got them categorized. But we really haven't, you see. Because they're changing, too. And this is one of the jobs we have in Alcoholics Anonymous. Particularly it's one of the great jobs that we have for our mates, whether they be the lady who is in Al-Anon or the man who is in Al-Anon (or who isn't the alcoholic—maybe they're not in any program). When a guy gets sober in Alcoholics Anonymous and does these things, he grows like a weed. If he does these things, he can't keep from growing, growing like a weed.

My wife went to meetings with me for six years before Al-Anon was born, and she thought she knew this thing real well. She knew all the words, but she listened for *me* for six years. (She liked to have me where she could punch me, and when I was there, she punched me!) She was listening for me. Then Al-Anon was born, and she started a meeting in Beverly Hills in our living room. And it grew and prospered, and she thought she was doing great because she was the mother hen, and she *told* them. Then we moved to Laguna when I was eleven years sober, and here she was with nobody to tell. Weren't any Al-Anons in Laguna. And my business was still in town, and whilst when we had lived in Beverly I could go get her and take her to meetings with me every night (have dinner at home and take her to a meeting), when we got to Laguna that couldn't happen. And so she got very, very depressed. She put the bee on me to slow down. I must stay home a little bit, because she wasn't getting the attention that she ought to have. She had no friends down there.

I lasted from February to Thanksgiving, trying to slow down, and I got so uncomfortable I couldn't live. So after a Thanksgiving dinner on this year, the kids and Mrs. C. were there, and I told them, "Kids, and Mrs. C., I have an announcement to make. From now on, when that phone rings I've got to go. I can't pick and choose what I'm going to do. I can't tell this guy, 'Yeah, I'll talk to you.' And this one, "I won't talk to you.' There'll be drunks in both places, and I can't do it. When that phone rings, I've got to do what they want me to do, within my power. And if you don't like it, get yourself another husband and get yourself another father." I had to do it, because I couldn't live any other way. "Suppose a guy hadn't been there when I went." Then Dick came into the picture. He said, "Mom, why don't you start another Al-Anon group?" Because his mother was deeply depressed. So she started another Al-Anon group and the next thing you knew she was going to town, because this time she started for her. She started growing like a weed and she's found the same thing I've found. And she's a beautiful thing. And we share, we share all the time. We don't always agree, but it isn't necessary. We've learned how to disagree and not be disagreeable. And it's a good thing, you know. We share, we don't tell. I don't tell her anything, she doesn't tell me anything. We share. Now this is what we're talking about to practice these principles in *all* of our affairs. All of our affairs. We said this morning that when we learned why people did what they did, they couldn't hurt us, and that people do what they do because they have to, not because they want to. When we know better we do better.

One of the things we didn't speak of yet was this—that in simple psychology they told us that the two great needs of the individual are to be needed and to be loved. Everybody gets that in psychology, I guess. The two great needs are to be needed and to be loved. That's just as backwards as everything else they told me. What about business and about God? Totally backwards. The two great needs of the individual are to love and to do. These are the great needs of the individual, to love and to do. A certain doctor called me one night at midnight and asked, "Chuck, what's your definition of love?" I said, "It's the same at 10 o'clock in the morning as it is at midnight! What the hell are you calling me at midnight for?" But he repeated, "What's your definition of love?" and I said, "You won't like it." Again he asked, "What is it?" I said, "Action!" He said, "What do you mean, action?" I said, "Action. If you love somebody, you do things for them." You do things. You don't trade with them. There's no barter in love. There's no barter in love. You do things because you want to, with no strings on it at all. Marriage isn't a fifty-fifty thing, it isn't a seventy-five/twenty-five thing, marriage is a thousand to nothing. You don't barter. You don't barter with God, and you don't barter with each other. That's the simple, unadulterated truth. The motivation is love, and love is the fulfillment of the law. You do it because you love it, for free and for fun. It's a fantastic thing. Yes, you do have a new woman across the table from you every morning, and it's beautiful. How much more interesting life is!

I have one more thing that was fantastic in my life that I want to share with you. It came out of total collapse, total failure. The fact is that I'd already practically ruined my body and my mind. Many of you have heard me say that when I got here it took me over six months to put the Serenity prayer together in English. Not spiritually—in English. I couldn't make that thing make sense. That's the kind of a mind I brought. And it took me three-and-a-half years to get over falling on my face, after my last drunk. That's the kind of a body I brought. I guess I had as many related disorders as you usually have. My wife was divorcing me. I believe that to be a related disorder! My kids wouldn't come home when I was around. I think that's a related disorder. My boss had sent word to the house that if I ever stepped foot in the place again, he was going to throw me through the window. I think that's a related disorder, because that means that you ain't got nothing coming in. I'd no health, no sanity, no job, no nothing. I came here merely for sobriety. Just for sobriety, so that I might rub out what I could of the record before I died.

As I told you yesterday, I knew I was going to die because I'd come so close to it the next-to-the-last time out, and this was worse. So I'd accepted the fact that everything dear to me in life was gone and should be gone, and I wasn't entitled to have it back. And I had accepted death. So I wanted nothing for me. Not even sobriety. And incidentally, this is the greatest freedom on the face of the earth. Freedom is to not want anything at any time for yourself. This is total freedom. Now my first surrender, brought on by the bottle, lasted three and a half years. It's the greatest period of miracles through which I ever lived. And it was a period of total non-expectancy. Total non-expectancy from God or man, my wife, my kids, my boss, or anyone else. The greatest period of miracles through which I ever lived. Every little piece of the jigsaw puzzle of life fell together in that first three and one-half years. But a bad thing happened. I became somebody again in those three and one-half years, and when you're somebody you've got rights, and when you've got rights you have to defend them. So here I find myself, after three and one-half years of peace, freedom, and having to consciously surrender. And it griped the hell out of me. I couldn't make sense out of it at all. Here for three and one-half years, I'd been free, and now I had to start consciously surrendering and I'm saying to myself, "Why does this thing come back? Why? Why? Why?" I looked at it for the next fifteen years, and I was sixteen years and six months sober before I got an answer that was satisfactory to me.

After sixteen years and six months, I got an answer that's totally satisfactory. I found something good in the human ego. It's the burr under the saddle. It's the thing that keeps us walking. And when you and I have committed ourselves, namely, we "made a decision to turn our will and our lives over to the care of God,"* when we have made this commitment, there's no way that we can stop walking. When we get fat and complacent and stop walking, we're in trouble. We find that we either have to surrender again or get drunk. And so we start consciously surrendering. I did. But I didn't like it, I never liked it during the sixteen years before I got the answer. I am convinced that we will never reach a point where we will never have to surrender. That time will never come. An infinite Father, an infinite Child and an infinite Journey.

Now it took me seventy years to learn that it isn't what we know that makes this life so consumingly interesting; it's what we don't know. The thing that makes this life so fantastic is the discoveries as we walk up these stairs. There'll always be as much ahead of us as there is right now. An infinite Father. Infinity; I don't even know what it means. Infinity. An infinite Father, an infinite Child,, and an infinite Journey, no destination.   An infinite Journey, and there'll always be as much ahead of us as there is right now. It's fantastic! And that's the wonder of this thing called life.   That's what makes it so consumingly interesting. It's not what we know, it's what we don't know. Sharing our experience, strength and hope, one with another in love, in all the departments of our life. The language of the heart has no age. And when we see that this life does not contain barter, even in the business world, it's amazingly wonderful. Amazingly wonderful.

We're going to talk about the business world. We won't get through with this, but we're going to talk about it a little. On the Thursday before Christmas, 1945, I hated my job. I hated my boss. And I hated the people that worked for him. The job was beneath my dignity. Anybody with my ability should be at least a Senator, if not President of the United States, and here I was in the fixture business. It was obvious to me that I was the only one around there that had any brains, but the boss had all the money, and he was telling me what to do. The very injustice of the situation caused me to do a little drinking. That was the Thursday before Christmas. The Friday before Christmas, he called me in, gave me that little talk and gave me three thousand bucks for a Christmas present. And I got drunk on the way home. "Came to" after the middle of January, finally went down there about the end of January, and he came in to throw me through the window, but he didn't. Being in the state I was in, physically and mentally, it took everything I had to do the simplest things. To dress myself was a major operation.

This forced me, by necessity, to give my entire interest, attention and love to the thing I was doing, or I couldn't do it. And this is one of the greatest lessons I ever learned. Of course this too, was out of absolute necessity. I hadn't figured this out; that anything that we give our entire interest, attention and love to is the most interesting thing in the world, even if it's nothing but shaving and dressing. It's the most interesting thing in the world. I had gone down to that office to clear up my desk; the office and the home were the two things that I'd fouled up the worst. And so there's where I had to do my stuff. Mainly, that was my big job, to rub out the record. And I started rubbing out the record in the business. Helping people do things that they needed to have done because I wanted to, and by necessity giving my entire interest, attention and love to the thing at hand. I got lost in doing that. And as I told you yesterday, after maybe two years, I discovered that I was still trying to clean up my desk.

Lest I forget to mention it, when I was eleven years sober I bought the business, and I owned it until three years ago when I sold out. And when I sold out, about fifty men worked for me, and many of them had been with me for many years, and they had an eighth of an inch of skin inside their hands; they were mechanics. They were machine men, they were metal men, they were carpenters, they were installers, and they worked with their hands. And when I sold that business, every one of those monkeys bawled, every one of them cried, and I cried. I had learned to love that business and love the guys that were working with me. That was the business I hated on the Thursday before Christmas. This is what we're talking about. When you give your entire interest, attention and love to the thing at hand, it becomes the most interesting thing in the world.

A few years before, I wouldn't have drawn a plan for Jesus Christ. I was too big a man. I had a guy working for me and I told him what to draw. If he didn't draw it like I told him he got hell ... (you know!). But when I went back down there the last of January, 1946, I didn't have anybody working for me and I started drawing those plans myself. And I drew them until I got out of the business. I never again had anybody draw the plans. I drew them, and it was amazingly interesting. It's beautiful.

Now what are we talking about? We're talking about rubbing out a record. You can't rub out a record thinking, "I want, I don't want, I like, I don't like, I – I – I – I." You rub out a record by doing something for somebody without a price tag on it, and it's amazing what happens. It's amazing! For instance, after I had been sober a while, there was a Jewish gentleman who had been in the food business for a long time and he'd retired. He'd made a lot of dough and he'd retired. He had two sons-in-law, and he was going to build a building for his kids, for the two sons-in-law; set them up in the market business. At that time it was the biggest single floor operation in the country. It was Panorama Market—some of you have seen it. When it came time for me to go see him, he was off seeing the Palace Market on Sepulveda just south of Manchester. One of his sons-in-law was running that market. Over the meat department there were a series of offices and a little balcony, and there were a lot of people on the balcony waiting to go in. I waited my turn, and by the time I got ready there were a lot of other people waiting to see him. The door into the office was open, and I went in.

This guy's name was Morris Weinstein, God rest his soul, he's gone now, and Morris sat there looking like an accident going some place to happen. He told me what I was going to have to do to get his business. It took him about five minutes to tell me and when he got through I said, "Morris, I think you've got me wrong. You're talking like I came out here to sell you something. I didn't. I came out here to help you, if I can, and if I can't, you're busy and so am I." And he leaned back in his chair and he said, "I know it, Charley." And I put in his market for him, some seventy five thousand dollars worth. When his market opened, a bunch of those people that were on that balcony were out there to see the opening, which all the vendors did in those days. And I showed up and they grabbed me and they took me off in the corner and they said, "Charley (I was 'Charley' in business), that was the greatest piece of reverse psychology that we've ever seen. We've been talking about it ever since." And I said, "What are you talking about?" "Well", they said, "We heard you. You went in there to see Morris, and you said, I haven't got anything to sell.' And you come out with a seventy five thousand dollar order. Greatest piece of reverse psychology we've ever seen!" And I said, "What the hell are you talking about. If that guy was subject to reverse psychology, he wouldn't have the two million dollars to put the thing in!" He'd heard more about reverse psychology than all of us put together. I told him the simple unadulterated truth, and he knew it. That's what I'm talking about. He knew it. I said, "I think you got me wrong. You think I came out here to sell you something, I didn't. I'm here to help you if I can, and if I can't, you're busy and so am I." And I meant every syllable of it, and he knew it.

You see, this thing we call the truth is a very powerful thing. It's the most powerful force on earth, and there's no barter in it. People sat across the desk from me for twenty-five years. First they would tell me, "You're a damn liar. Business cannot be done this way! You're a damn liar." And they didn't even make me mad—I just laughed because they didn't know something I knew: I'd been doing it that way for ten years, and it was alright. So I just went ahead doing it and pretty soon they were coming in, everybody in like businesses. We would call them competitors if we called anybody competitors, but I didn't have any competitors because I wasn't competing with anybody. I was just helping my people do things they needed to have done because I wanted to.

The last few years everybody who was in like businesses (the ones that told me I was a damn liar) came in, and they'd sit down and they'd say to me, "How do you do these things?" They couldn't even bid the business I was working on. They'd go to see Von's and say, "Look, you're putting in this new market. We want to bid on it." But Von's would say, "Charley is going to put it in." Then they'd say, "What do you mean? How do you know he's not going to take your eye teeth? You've got to have some bids to compare!" But Von's would reply, "Charley's going to put it in. It costs money to bid one of these jobs. Go see somebody else." And so they started coming in to see me and they'd ask. "How'd you do these things?" And I'd take two hours out and I'd tell them. I'd tell them exactly, and they'd leave thinking. "I've got his number, now, I'll fix him! I know how he does it. I'll get him." But they didn't get me, neither did they get the business. Because you see, they weren't motivated as I was. They weren't motivated that way. They thought you had to out-think, out-perform and out-maneuver. I knew better because I had done it that way for thirty years, and ended up in the bottom of the snake pit. After that, for twenty-five years I did it for free and for fun, helping God's kids do things they needed to have done because I wanted to, and I got rich. I wasn't even trying to get rich, they made me rich.

Now I'm going to tell you a couple of other things because nearly all you guys are still in business, and you'll know very well that what follows is impossible, so you can say when you get through, "Well, I heard that mutt, but he's a liar." A couple of my Jewish friends had a market at Crenshaw and Highway 101, called Foods Company. These boys were a couple of youngsters about your age. I had done business with their Dad years before, when they were little bitty kids running around the store, and I did business with them. They wanted to change the fixtures in the liquor department and they had an architect design some fixtures, and then they called me and said, "Come down and take a look at this. Tell us what they're worth." I went and looked at them and I said, "Hey, this guy's drawing up some pretty fancy stuff. I've never drawn you up anything that fancy because it's very expensive." "Well," they said, "What do you think it's going to cost?" "My guess is they'd cost $4,500," I replied. They said, "Put them in." And I put them in, and they were in the store, and they were doing a good job for them. After I had my costs in, I saw I had $5,700 in it. My money. Fifty-seven hundred bucks. So I called Abe and said, "Hey, do you remember what I quoted you for those fixtures?" He said, "No, but I suppose I have written down here someplace on my desk." "Well," I said, "Don't look for it. I'll tell you. It's $4,500. And Abe, you can have them for $4,500. They're in your store and they're doing a good job. And you can have them for $4,500 because that's what I guessed on it, but I was wrong. I have $5,700 in those fixtures." He said, "Charley, add a profit and send the bill." But I said, "I don't' want that. I made the mistake, but I would like to get my money out of it." He repeated, "Charley, put a profit on it and send me a bill and I'll pay you." I said, "No, but I'll bill you for $5,700, if that's alright with you." He replied, "If that's the way you want to do it." Now, you know better than that! Nobody would do that.

But I billed him $5,700, and he paid.

I had another outfit that I did business with, and the last unit I put in for them was at Fallbrook & Victory out in the West Valley and it was a big deal. We put it in and it was opened and it had run about ninety days. It did a good job, a beautiful thing. Dave Shore called me one day and said, "Charley, you haven't billed me." And I said, "No, Dave, I didn't know what to bill you, but I've got the costs in now and I can get it together for you pretty fast." He said, "How fast?" I said, "I can probably call you back in an hour." "Well", he says, "Please do. We want to finance this thing and we have to know the amount, so call me back as quick as you can." And in an hour I had the dope for him and I called him and said, "Dave, are you sittin' down?" And he said, "Yeh." I said, "Are you alone in the office?" He said, "No, Charley's sittin' across the desk from me." I said, "Is your heart alright?" And he said, "I've had no trouble with it." "Well", I said, "Here it comes. You owe me $225,000." And he said, "Well, isn't that too bad? I just wrote on a slip of paper $225,000' and handed it over to Charley, across the desk. You ought to hire me as an estimator. Send me a bill." Now you know that's wrong. He's got to say, "Well how about the sales tax? You are going to take off the sales tax?" All he said was, "Send me a bill."

I was in trouble in 1958. Pretty bad trouble and I had to have some business. I had a vacant plant and it cost me $13,500 a week to keep the doors open, and I had to get some business. So I went out to get it, and I had five deals that I thought I could get. Deals that I'd worked on, and they looked like they were mine. I went to get them, and one after another they evaporated. But the last one could not evaporate because the two owners of the deal were members of Alcoholics Anonymous. Forty-eight of their high-echelon were members of Alcoholics Anonymous. So that was my deal. It couldn't be anybody else's deal because I'd done all their thinking, all their planning everything. I'd gotten the deal together for them, and it was mine. So I went down to get it, and about four or five of us went to lunch and had a good time down there at Welch's on Atlantic. We came back and everybody left, like rats from a sinking ship! There was nobody left but Harold and myself. We went into his office, and he said, "Chuck I thought you could never get yourself out of that mess you were in up there, and I gave the deal to Hill." It was the last one! There weren't any more. Five minutes passed and he said, "Chuck, why don't you say something?" I said, "Harold, there's nothing to say."

And I went out and started to drive back to town— their office was in Long Beach, my plant was at Fortieth and Alameda. But I couldn't drive, so I pulled off the road and I sat there and looked at myself for a while, and I couldn't get myself together. Here everything had just evaporated right in front of my eyes. I finally came to see that I had gone out for the first time in years for the sole purpose of getting some business. Twelve years before, I'd started making twelve step calls in business; helping people do things they needed to have done because I wanted to. And here there was a pinch and I had to go get some business, and I went out there to get it and everything evaporated. Then I said to myself, "Can't get any worse. Why don't you start making twelve step calls in business like you did twelve years ago. Let the chips fall where they may." So I gave the business back to my Partner and started making twelve step calls. Then something happened that every one of you will know is impossible. (Even those who aren't in business—the Jesuits—will know this is no good.) I got back to the office and either that day or the next I got a call from a guy in San Bernardino, and he said, "Charley, I have the feeling you're in trouble and I have written out a check for $50,000 in your name, and it's lying here on this desk of mine. You don't sign a note, you don't pay any interest, we'll apply it the next deal we have. Come and get it if you need it. I don't know whether you do or not, but I have the feeling." And he said, "I'm going to Miami tonight, I'm going to be gone a week to the SMI Institute. (That was the Supermarket Institute). You can either come and get it now or you can come after I get back." Boy, I'm tellin' you something; that was something! I said, "Milton, go ahead to Miami, and if I need it when you come back, I'll come and get it. But I want you to know that I'll never forget what you just said to me. It's beautiful." And by the time he got back from Miami, I didn't need it. The place had filled up and it was full until I sold it.

Now gentlemen, what am I talking about? Am I trying to tell you how good I am? No sir. I'm trying to tell you how good this is. The gift of God was made at the foundation of the earth. In my book, God hasn't got anything to give me. Not because he hasn't got anything but because he already did. The gift of God was made at the foundation of the earth. He gave us the universe. He gave us Himself at the foundation of the earth. When I was sitting in that same chair I sit in now, with everything gone, at the blackest moment of my life the universe was mine. God was mine, and all that He had was mine. He knew it, but I didn't, I had to discover it. And being an Alcoholic, I had to discover it in my own way and in my own time. God loved me just as much that day as He does now. Just the same, no different. But He never kept me from making mistakes. He's a Gentleman, God. He doesn't intrude where He's not wanted, so He never kept me from making mistakes. He loved me enough to allow me to make my own mistakes, that I might the sooner run out of my own resources and come back home where I belonged.

So my business is to go about His business, and it's His business to take care of me. That is not my business, that's His business. Now what is His business that I'm going about? Helping His kids do things they need to have done because I want to. A twelve step call in business, a twelve step call at home. A twelve step call in AA, a twelve step call in play. Just going about our Father's business, that's my business. It's His business to take care of me, and He's done an infinitely better job than I ever did, and I'm most grateful.

We talked about prayer, a little, wondering why we didn't start and close these meetings with a prayer. And I told you that as far as I'm concerned, this is a prayer. *This* is a prayer. My life is a prayer. If you asked me, "What's your religion?", I would say, "It's the way I live." That's my religion. It doesn't make any difference what I call myself, it's the way I live. That's my religion, so that's my business, to go about His business because I want to. There are a couple of little things that I learned many, many years ago that fit right into this picture. There's an old Upanishad that comes out of India. (Most of you scholars know about the Upanishads from the country of India). I had a guy down in Palm Springs when we were down there last, who was a pedantist. He was telling me what a bunch of butchers we were in AA, as far as spiritual things were concerned. He was telling me that we had to purify our hearts so we would be worthy to see God. We had to purify our hearts! I said, "Yeh, I went through that route myself. I purified the hell out of my heart, and the purer I got, the drunker I got." I said, "You know something, bud, I'm sittin' here looking at you and I see God." And he didn't know what I was talking about. He couldn't know, because he thought there were four different things you had to do. Yogi this and Yogi that and Yogi these two things, and you Yogi yourself right into a purified spirit! Then you can see God. I'm sure glad that that isn't the way it is. I'm sure glad that the God that there is is not anything like the God I was told about. I'm most happy about that.

Now this Upanishad says this: "The whole world is the garment of the Lord. Renounce it and receive it back as the gift of God." What does it mean? It means that as long as these things were important to me, I couldn't have them. I beat my brains out for thirty years to get the things I thought I was born without, and ended up in the bottom of the snake pit. I wasn't a fast buck artist nor was I a confidence man. I worked hard to get, and I ended up in the bottom of the snake pit. Then I put in twenty-five years trying to add to and all the things I beat my brains out to get are mine, and infinitely more so. When they're unimportant to me, they belong to me. "The whole world is the garment of the Lord. Renounce it and receive it back as the gift of God." It's beautiful!

They say another thing. They say that anything that's worth doing is an end in itself; that anything that's done as a means to an end is self-robbery. Now what does that mean? I had, we'll say, fifty men working for me. Thirty-five of them worked for a paycheck. They lost five days and lived two out of every week. They worked for a paycheck. Fifteen of them worked for fun. They had a picnic! They never lost any time and they were my premium men. They got more money than anybody else and they lived seven days a week; lost no time. Anything done as a means to an end is self-robbery. Even to be good for something is self-robbery, even if it's being good to go to Heaven. It's pretty good motivation, but it's self-robbery because there's no barter in this deal, no barter at all. We do it for free and for fun because we love it. Fascinating. To be good for nothing, this is the freedom of life. Just to be good for nothing; That's not self-robbery, that's for free and for fun.

I said a while ago that in my opinion, the gift of God was made at the foundation of the earth. I'm not the first guy that's ever said that. It's written, "Fear not little flock, it's the Father's good pleasure to give us the Kingdom." It doesn't say you've got to earn it. It is written, "Take no thought of the morrow what you shall eat, what you shall drink or wherewithal you shall be clothed." The Heavenly Father knows what you have need of before you ask him. It is written, "Whatsoever desire when you pray, believe that you have it and you'll receive it." Now how in the world are you going to believe that you've got something that you haven't got? How're you going to believe it? There's a trick to it. You've got to *know* that the gift of God was made at the foundation of the earth, and that God's will for you, his child, is fulfillment, peace and joy; and that every good and perfect gift is from His hands. When we recognize this, we then know that what we might pray for is already ours. It's already ours. The Gift of God to his kids. No barter.

Now for a last thought. The easy way is the right way. The tough way is the wrong way. There's an easy way and a hard way to do this program. The hard way is to try to do it yourself. The easy way is to know that you can't, to know that you can't and to recognize the need for help. I have never asked God one time, in twenty-nine years, to keep me sober. Never asked Him once. I've thanked Him a million times, but I've never asked Him once to keep me sober because that's not the way I read my book. The way I read my book, it says, "Here are the steps we took." When we take them something happens, when we don't take them, nothing happens. So as I told Father Barney, "I've never asked God to keep me sober."" He asked, "Why not?" I said, "I think that's not His business. I think it's my business to do these things, and His business to take care of me. And He does it. I don't have to tell him what to do about His business.

You guys told me what to do about my business, and I do it. I take the steps and I'm sober. And many, many good things have happened in my life, including the disappearance of the related disorders, which I didn't spend five seconds on. Not five seconds did I spend trying to get my wife back, or the kids, or my God, or my health or my sanity. And somehow or another it sort of all fell together. So God's will for you and for me is fulfillment, peace and joy. The Gift of God was made at the foundation of the earth. What you came here looking for, you came here looking with. What we have to find is where it is, and it's right here inside us. It's an inside job. Uncovering, Discovering, and Discarding is Alcoholics Anonymous. It's a fascinating way of life and it gets better for twenty-nine years to my certain knowledge, and I suspect it's going to get better forever. "A world without end, Amen."

Chapter 4
SOBRIETY—A SPIRITUAL REST

We have talked about the fact that ever since we grew up a little bit, we have had to reverse everything that we were conditioned to believe that was true about life in home, school, and church. And, of course, this includes getting out of our own way. Self-discovery. It includes surrender, even though we were conditioned to believe that surrender was for the weak. "Strong man wins, weak man surrenders." Thus we thought we had to run our own lives, we had to win the battle. But in this new way of life we have nothing to win, nothing to prove, and we're not going anyplace. Nothing to win, nothing to prove, and we're not going any place. I'm either going to run my life and take the consequences thereof, or I'm not going to run it and take the consequences thereof; one or the other of those things I must do. We cannot do both. It is written that you can't serve two masters. Either you cling to the one and despise the other, or vice-versa. A house divided against itself can't stand. So either I'm going to run my life and take the consequences thereof, or I'm not going to run it and take the consequences thereof, and they don't mix. But I can't run mine. As I have said, I had forty-three years to run the show, during which time I was the star of the show and master of ceremonies. And after forty-three years I had accomplished failure in every department of life.

So I can't run my life, I can't run anything. I can't run my business, can't run my wife, can't run my kids, can't run anything, and I know it. I knew it when I got here. I came here knowing that I had lost the battle of life, and I'd given it everything I had. I gave it my wife, my kids, our home, my job, my health, my sanity and my money, and I lost. So I can't run my life. It's no big deal as far as I'm concerned, however, because I don't need to. I've lived for twenty-nine years in total expectance of guidance and direction. So I don't need to run my life. It isn't necessary, and I can't, and I accept it.

Now the next premise is that God is either sufficient unto all of my needs or He is not. One or the other. If He is not sufficient unto all of my needs there's nothing to worry about, because in that case life is not worth a candle. The sooner it's over, the better. We might as well knock this thing off and go down with the bus and fill it full of liquor, and shack up and drink 'til we die! If God is not sufficient unto our needs, the sooner it's over the better. There's nothing to recommend life. So if He is not sufficient, there's nothing to worry about. But if He is sufficient unto all my needs, there's nothing to worry about either, so I've got you both ways! Got you both ways, because all I have to do is act like His kid, and prove that I am. And that's written like this, "Act as though I am and I will be, sayeth the Lord." Act as though I am, and I will be. So that's all I have to do; to act as if it were true and prove that it is true, that's what we do in this program of ours. There's nothing else to do.

There's nothing else to do, because we've already lost. We've already tried with human power.

I went to the best: the priest, the preacher, the doctor, and as I've said, to the guy who knew more psychiatry than there is. And every one of them talked to me about will power, backbone, about standing up and being a man. Every one of them! Because, you see, prior to twenty-nine years ago almost nobody knew anything about alcoholism. The people I went to see, the authorities, did not know anything about alcoholism and they couldn't help me. And I didn't know anything about alcoholism, so I couldn't help myself. I had to keep right on drinking until the bottle killed me before I could even come here to investigate. Now I knew that my job and my problem was not the lack of will power, or the lack of backbone, or the lack of being able to stand up and be a man. I knew that. I was born with a pitchfork in my hand! I can't remember when I wasn't working. I always worked. And I was a pretty good athlete in my day, and I can say that without fear of successful contradiction, because there's nobody here old enough to remember! My backbone had never given me the slightest trouble, and you know something? It hasn't yet. My backbone does a hell of a job for me. If everything I had worked as well as my backbone, I'd be in top shape! So it isn't backbone.

It most certainly isn't will power. If there was ever a group of people on the face of the earth who has will power, it's the drunks of the world. Boy! We've got will power to burn. I could get whiskey in Kansas on Election Day if it fell on Sunday! How long it took depended only on how high I was walking off the sidewalk. Anyplace in the country, if the need was great, it didn't take long to get a jug. Every time I hear these earth people talkin' about backbone, will power, I want to ask them one question: "How many of them ever crawled a mile in the mud after dark just to get a bucket of ice?" It's par for the course for a drunk, you know. We've got will power to burn. And in the standing up and being a man department, we can give them hearts and spades. If there was ever a bunch of philosophers on the face of the earth, it's the drunks of the world. We have all the answers for everybody but us. One of our great assets, one of the things that really endeared us to the non-alcoholic world, was that we always knew exactly what was wrong with them and we didn't mind telling them. And that's not a good way to win friends and influence people. We're a great bunch of philosophers. You could go, right now, into any bar in this part of the country, and ask the first drunk that you bumped into any question that popped in your head, and he'd tell you. He wouldn't stammer and stutter, he wouldn't say, "I don't know." He'd tell you. Great bunch of philosophers!

So I knew all the time that my problem was not will power, backbone or standin' up and bein' a man, but I didn't know what it was. I had to keep right on drinking until I died before I could come here and find out. Now this isn't any criticism of the doctors or the preachers or the priests or the psychiatrists, because they didn't know. Back in those days they did not know. It's comparatively recent thing that doctors and priests and preachers and psychiatrists, a great percentage of them, have made it their business to find out something about the disease of alcoholism. Now they can tell us about our disease and tell us where we can go for help, but in my day this was not true. Thank God there's so much more known about it today than there was then; that many people can find out and come, without having to destroy themselves as some of us did.

Even so, we each must do what we have to do. Mrs.

Sobriety–A Spiritual Rest

C. says to me quite often, "Supposing I had known something about Al-Anon back in the days when you were drinking. Supposing Al-Anon had been here and I was in it, and I was knowin' a little bit more about how to handle you or how to treat you. Do you think that it would have hastened you into the Society, before you came? And I say, "I don't really believe it would have." In my case, I don't really believe it would have because I am one who certainly could not hear 'till I could hear, and could not see until I could see. As I told you the other day, I read Jack Alexander's article in the Post '41, and five years later I remembered that I'd read it. I was four sheets to the wind when I read it and I remembered only two things about it: that drunks help drunks and didn't drink, and they called it Alcoholics Anonymous. And that's why I said to myself. "If I ever live to get out of this bed, I'll find AA." From that decision until now, I haven't had a drink. So I don't know. In my own case, up until my last drink, it was never my fault that I drank.

I got drunk for twenty-five years and I was a periodic for the last ten, and during those last ten I was physically as sober then as I am tonight between every two drunks. I could look at my record with physically sober eyes for that whole ten years, and yet until my last drink it was never my fault that I drank. It was your fault, it was my wife's fault, it was her mother's fault. Now there was a kingsize reason for getting drunk, that mother-in-law of mine! Reminds me of a little story I picked up from Al B. in Dallas. Al has gone to the Big Meeting. He was a helluva' guy. He was about three or four months before me in the program and he was sober until he died a year or so ago. He was a great storyteller, and he told this story. He said there was two drunks who met on the street, and one of them says to the other, "How's things?"

"Aw," he replies, "Not good." "Well," says the first, "That's bad." He replies, "Not so bad. I got married." "Well" says the first, "That's good." He replies, "Not so good. I got my mother-in-law, too." And the first says, "That's bad." He replies, "Not so bad, she's got money." And the first says, "That's good." He replies, "Not so good, she wants to boss everything." The first one says, "That's bad." He replies, "Not so bad, she bought us a house." "Well," says the first, "That's good." He replies, "Not so good, the house burnt down." And the first says, "That sure is bad." He replies, "Not bad, brother, she burned, too!"

So the last excuse has got to go by the boards. It's got to burn up. If you and I have one excuse left that is still acceptable to us, we have another drunk left. Nobody is going to do what is necessary to obtain and maintain sobriety if there is any way to pin this onto anybody else; your mother-in-law, your boss, anybody else. We're not going to do it.

In my own case, as I may have said, on my next-to-last drunk, I went to the kitchen after a glass of buttermilk, Dick and Mrs. C. were sitting in the living room. They heard me let out a beller and heard me hit the floor and came running out, thinking that I was in an alcoholic convulsion, but I wasn't. I was just lying there on the kitchen floor as peaceful as anybody ever saw, doing nothing. But they couldn't wake me up, and they tell me I was a peculiar color. I was blue. They got all exercised and called the oxygen squad, who came down and, after a while woke me up. They told me that to all intents and purposes I'd been dead; that they'd had a hell of a time bringing me to, and nobody would ever bring me to again under those circumstances. And they told me if they were me, they wouldn't do that any more!

I did do it again, but the thing I want to tell about is this. About twenty-four or thirty-six hours after they'd brought me to, I was able to get the old dirty bathrobe on and start walkin' off this drunk. That's the way I had to sober up. I never heard of an easy way to sober up until I got to Alcoholics Anonymous. The only way I could sober up was to die until I could live, and I did it mainly by walking. Now I've got the old bathrobe on, and I'm walkin' up and down the living room floor, back and forth; sweatin', freezin', shakin', dyin' and walkin'. Mrs. C. was standing over at the fireplace, and I was walkin' away from her and she said, "Chuck, don't you think you might get a little help if you'd read the book, "Alcoholics Anonymous?" I turned on her like a lion and said, "You! My very own wife, suggesting that I read a book written by a bunch of drunks! I, who have read all the good books by the good authors. And you want me...Why," I said, "You wound me deeply." Now, I'd just been dead forty-eight hours before, yet she wounded me deeply! Then I polished her off completely by saying, "And besides, I can write a better book than that myself." That was just ninety days before I came crawling into this program. Just ninety days, I'd been getting drunk for twenty-five years, and she wounded me deeply by suggesting that I read that book.

So I doubt very much if there was any way that I could've gotten here except the way I came, and that was through being totally burnt up, which happened to me my last time out. Now many times people hearing a guy like me, or like some of you, who had everything happen to him that can happen to anybody, say, "Well those things didn't happen to me. I've never been to jail. I've never had DT's. I've never had convulsions. I've never had trouble with elephants." (You know, I had a lot of trouble with elephants. I may be one of the few people that ever lived in Beverly Hills that were charged by a herd of elephants! That almost never happens in Beverly Hills. They were running me right out of the town!) So they say, "Well, those things haven't happened to me, therefore I'm not an alcoholic." Now we believe that there are no degrees of alcoholism; you can either drink well or you can't.   One or the other. Alcoholism is a great deal like pregnancy: a gal don't get any more pregnant in eight and a half months than she was fifteen seconds after conception. It just shows more. Same thing is true with us. I don't think we get more alcoholic. I think it just shows more as time goes on. And it doesn't make any difference how many of those things you've missed. You know whether or not you can drink well, and if you can't drink well you might be an alcoholic. We say in this deal of ours. If alcohol interferes with your personal life, your business life, or your social life—any one of these three, maybe; any two, perhaps; and the three of them, you're a cinch. But there's another little question that I like better than all three of those. And it's very, very, simple. Is it necessary for you to wonder whether or not you're an alcoholic? If you do, sign up with the secretary before you leave. In twenty-nine years I have never caught a nonalcoholic wondering whether or not they were an alcoholic. It's always been an alky that's trying to figure out some way to beat this rap.

So it isn't how much, or where or when. It's what it does for you. I'm mindful of a number of years back. We had a doctor in San Francisco who was quite a member of Alcoholics Anonymous. As a matter of fact, he was five times a doctor. He was a doctor, a surgeon, an obstetrician, a gynecologist and a psychiatrist. He was qualified in all those fields, and he told this little story. He said he was operating on a lady who was getting pretty well along in years, past sixty. He had determined in her examination that her arterial tree was very weak. And he had also determined that she'd never had a drink of liquor in her life. So for post-operative care he prescribed a little brandy, and they started giving this lady a little brandy. And he said on the third day after the operation, she stole the keys from the nurse and got into the brandy. And she'd never had a drink in her life up until that time!

So, it's not how much or how long, it's what it does to us. You can either drink well or you can't, and if you can't, this program is for you. The quicker you embrace it and the quicker you do something about it, the better, because alcoholism gets worse, never better, in its manifestation. I'm actually twenty-nine years worse off, so far as successfully drinking liquor is concerned, than I was when I got here, and I know it. I know it and I don't have to take a drink to prove it. I've been close to and active in this program the whole time I've been here, and when you're close to and active in, all you have to do is keep your eyes open. Your friends are forever taking that drink for you, and you don't have to take it. They do your experimenting for you if you keep your eyes open.

Now there are two or three little things that I want to add. When I first got here, I was quite sure that people who had not suffered as much as I had suffered couldn't possibly love this thing as much as I did. I felt a little bit sorry for those who came and hadn't had some of the things happen to them than I had happen to me, because I knew that they couldn't feel anything like I did. And then I got to working with a priest who'd never been kicked out of anything, he was still serving the altar. But he was a priest, and it gradually dawned on me that when I was a drunken nobody, nobody gave a damn whether I drank or didn't. (Half a dozen people, maybe). But a priest, how much he must suffer in doing a bad job.

And I got to working with my banker and he was one of the biggest bankers in the country. He was an internationally known banker. He taught banking and he was a dollar-a-year man with the United States government for quite a while. And he'd never been kicked out of anything. He belonged to everything in town! He'd never been kicked out of his home. He lived in Fremont Place; you can only get in there and out one way. No cross streets, no out-the-other-end. You go in and out the same way. It's private. That was where he lived and he'd never been kicked out of home, never been kicked out of anything. But he couldn't drink well and he wasn't doing his job well, and he came to Alcoholics Anonymous.

When the time came, when he felt that he had to start trying to give this thing away, he went to his committee (He was chairman of the executive committee of one of the biggest banks in the city.) and he said, "Look, I have an alcoholic problem, and I have found a way that might let me live the rest of my life without drinking. And one of the things we must do is to work with alcoholics, and I'm going to have to start working a bit with alcoholics because they've worked with me and now I'm sober. And I'm going to have to talk a bit, and people might know and it might be damaging to this bank, and so I'm submitting my resignation to this committee right now, for your action."And they said, "Go to your office." And he went out, and he was almost to his office when they opened the door and called him back. And they said, "Whatever you feel that is necessary for you to do, do. And we're with you a thousand percent." Now, isn't that beautiful? And this was one of the most humble men I've ever known in my entire life, up until the time he died. (He's the guy that allowed me to buy my business.) Beautiful, beautiful! We used to sit, between Christmas and New Years every year, and have lunch in the California Club, which he belonged to. I didn't, but he did; he belonged to everything. He'd sit there and tell me that lunch with me between

Christmas and New Years every year was the high point in his year, and I'd sit there and bawl like a baby. Fabulous man. Never got kicked out of anything, but how he must have hurt. So I had to come to see that it's not possible for you and for me to decide how much somebody else is hurt. I didn't know what was going on inside of somebody else. They might have hurt ten times, a hundred times worse than I, and here I was pitying him because he couldn't love this thing as much as I did!

Also, I knew very well that when people didn't practice these principles like I thought they should they couldn't stay sober. Our book tells us we cease to fight anything and anybody, or everything and everybody; we cease to fight. We had an old boy in our group in Beverly Hills that fought everything and everybody. He was a year and a half-sober when I got here, and he's a year and a half older in the program than I am right now. He never did quit fighting. He still fights, and he's practically a dead man. Back in the old days I used to try to make him speak to me, and he wouldn't do it. Maybe a whole year'd go by—we're in the same group—and I couldn't make him speak to me. And I'd do stuff like this. I'd walk up to him in the middle of a sentence while he was talking to someone, and he'd have to do something, and he did. He turned on his heel and walked off without even finishing the sentence! I couldn't make him talk to me. But when I got my twenty-first birthday, he gave it to me. And this roughneck kissed me on the neck when he gave me my birthday cake. He may be one of the guys that loves me the most in this town, now. So we have to come to see that it isn't where you are, it's where you came from. Eddy just might have grown ten times more than I did in this program, but he didn't start even with me. He started down the ladder a ways. So we have to come to see these things, and it makes for a much, much more beautiful living experience in Alcoholics Anonymous.

There's a little verse in the Book which says this: "Blessed is he who condemneth not himself in that which he alloweth." What does that mean? I believe it means that if you can do a thing without condemning yourself, it's not so bad. But if you condemn yourself for it, you better jolly well quit or it'll kill you. And I think this is the one of the greatest differences between a good ol' Saturday night drunk and an alcoholic. You and I condemned ourselves from the beginning. If we were raised in a religion that did not condemn us for moderate drinking, maybe we didn't condemn ourselves for moderate drinking, but we condemned ourselves for a bad performance. So from the beginning we condemned ourselves. I knew better than to drink before I ever took my first drink. I condemned myself from the first drink and as time went on, the condemnation became hatred, and I ended up hating my guts. We can hardly look in the mirror to shave because of self-loathing. "Blessed is he who condemneth not himself in that which he alloweth." Now again, this tells us this: that there's no particular way that you can classify so-called sin amongst those people around you. Many people can do things that I can't do and don't condemn themselves at all. Personally, I could do many things five years ago that today I cannot do. And so it depends on where we are as to what we can do, and what we have to get rid of. And it's a continuous process because the higher we go the more we have to discard, and the more we discard the freer we become. It's amazing.

There's no such thing as the meaning of a word. Now this blows my mind, and the way it came about was that I got to thinking some time back about this: the first two and a half pages in Chapter Five add up, at the end of "C", to about four hundred and fifty or sixty words. That's all there is (I never counted them, but I figure that's about it.) I have gone through that section not less than twenty-five and probably nearer thirty thousand times, in twenty-nine years. And you might say, "Well, that must be the driest reading on the face of the earth. It's not last week's dishwater, it's last year's dishwater." But it isn't. The words are always new. Every time I hear them, they're always new. Every time I read them, every time I talk about them, they're new. The words remain the same, but we don't. And it depends entirely where we are what they mean. They will always be more meaningful. They always take a new meaning, depending on where *we* are. And we'll be walking up this ladder forever. A world without end, Amen.

Here's another thing I like to think about, sitting up there on my hill. I believe that I'm right in this and if I'm not, one of you sailors can correct me. I think that when you're sitting in a boat at water level on a clear day, the horizon is seven miles. I think that's as far as you can see when you're at water level. Now I'm up maybe a thousand feet above the water level, and on a clear day my horizon is almost limitless. A hundred and fifty miles I can see. Sometimes Catalina Island, San Clemente Island and Point Fermin are all close enough that it seems like I could skip a rock to them. Just that little bit of elevation changes the horizon from seven to, maybe, a hundred and fifty miles. And we'll be walking up these stairs forever. The only thing we can't change about our lives, the only thing that cannot be changed by us, is that we're stuck with ourselves forever. World without end, Amen. Now this is a bleak prospect, isn't it? We could get to thinking about committing suicide, you know! You can't make it; you're stuck with you forever. Everything else in life you can change, you don't even have to go home from here if you don't want to.

You can go someplace else. You don't ever have to see your wife again if you don't want to. You never have to see your kids again if you don't want to. You don't have to stay in California, you don't have to stay in the United States, you can change everything in life but one. You can't get away from you. You're stuck with you forever; I'm stuck with me forever.

Now you would think that when we arrive in this world, they would try to teach us how to be friends with ourselves, but they don't. They teach us how we have to work with other people, be sure that we make a good impression on the neighbors and the people around us. We have to show respect to our elders, particularly the priest and the preacher and the mother-in-law. But they don't tell us how to get along with us, how to become friends with ourselves.

In my opinion the definition of sobriety is the ability to live comfortably, peacefully and joyously with me. This is sobriety. Things short of it are partial sobriety. When I got here, I didn't think of those things. When we got to the program, all of us thought if we hadn't had a drink that day, we were sober, and we talked much about puttin' the plug in the jug. Puttin' the plug in the jug. I never had any problem putting the plug in the jug. I was a periodic for ten years and after every drunk, I put the plug in the jug. Periodics have to get sober—there's no way a periodic can keep from getting sober—because we're pigs. We drink everything there is that's too thin to chew! And we drink it all. The time comes when we can't get it down, we can't get it up, and we can't live and we can't die. So we have to get sober. So I never had any problem putting the plug in the jug. I quit forever, with and without a solemn oath! Put the plug in the jug.

My problem was not puttin' the plug in the jug, it was taking the plug out of the jug. Because when my time came, I took the plug out of the jug, and I was off again. Physical sobriety is absolutely important. To me it's synonymous with life. I cannot live and drink and of myself I can't keep from drinking. So I have to be physically sober, lest I die. I'm not selling physical sobriety short, it's the foundation under sobriety. But sobriety is physical, mental, emotional and spiritual. Four parts of the same thing and it adds up to the ability to live comfortably, peacefully, and joyously with me. That is sobriety.

This program is more important to me today than it was twenty-nine years ago, because twenty-nine years ago, if I could have just died and had it over it would have been the greatest thing in the world. I was born knowing that suicide wasn't an answer, but it never occurred to me that drinking yourself to death was suicide until I was sober five years. So I tried my damnedest to drink myself to death but I couldn't make it. You can't drink yourself to death if you want to die. The guys that die of alcoholism don't want to die. If we want to drink ourselves to death we just go nuts and stay nuts, but we can't get over the brink. I want to make this point.

One of the great big insurance companies of the country was built by a man whose son got sober in Alcoholics Anonymous. The son was an attorney and he was never going in the insurance business, he was going to stay an attorney. It was a beautiful impasse. I don't know how much affect I had on him, but I talked with him for a long, long time about getting on in that business and taking over, because his dad was a long way in years. And he eventually did. Here was a man that built his empire, and he was pretty old, and he'd been doing a bit of drinking and his son talked to him a little about it, and his father says, "I can drink myself to death if I want to." But his son says, "No, you can't." "Why," says his father, "So-and so did." (Mentioning another big man in the insurance business who had drunk himself to death.) And the lad says, "Yes, but he didn't want to." And it hit me like a ton of bricks because that's what I was trying to do, but I couldn't make it.

The thing that hastened me into Alcoholics Anonymous after twenty-five years was that I knew I wasn't going to die. I was going to stay insane. I'd sit there in that chair of mine, dreaming about my boys when the kids in the block said, "Where's your dad?" And they'd say, "He died." And they'd turn and walk off, because they couldn't tell them I was in Patton with just enough left to know how to tie my shoes and why I was there. That kind of dreamin' drives you nuts! It drives you nuts and that helped drive me in here. We can't make it if we try, and it never occurred to me until I was five years sober that drinking yourself to death was suicide, which of course it is.

How am I going to stay sober? I have to be sober. Sobriety and life are synonymous. How am I going to stay sober? I'm going to perform so that I'm comfortable, right here inside me. That's the only way I can stay sober. When I get to feelin' a certain way right here, I get drunk. Now I hear many people say that if you've been in Alcoholics Anonymous a while you have to think to drink. I don't believe it. I don't think you have to do anything but quit doing the things that keep you comfortable, right here. And you wake up drunk because, you see, you and I know a way to stop that Big Hurt. And if we allow it to hurt like it used to hurt, we'll be just as drunk as we were in the old days. And we don't have to think about it at all. Just quit doing the things that keep us comfortable right here.

I believe with the doctors that alcoholism is a disease, and I believe that it's terminal. I believe that it's a disease of a two-fold nature; an allergy of the body coupled with an obsession of the mind. I accept all this but I do not believe that that's all there is to the disease of alcoholism. If it were merely mental and physical, a good internist and a good psychiatrist could take me apart and put me back together and I'd tick. But this doesn't very often happen to us. Once in a while somebody gets sober and stays sober, but it doesn't often happen. So there must be something else to this deal. A living problem to which we must have a living answer. Inasmuch as there has never been a mass recovering program for alcoholics that did not include a basic spiritual rest, it seems kindergarten to me that the problem behind the problem must be a basic spiritual unrest.

I say often, when I'm about ready to quit talking, that the time has to come in our lives when we come to see that if there be fault, it's ours. If there be fault, it's mine. And I say, "If there be fault" because I don't believe there is fault. I believe that you and I are the victims of a combination of characteristics which came with us that make it impossible for us to integrate ourselves into the life that we're born into; into the so-called civilization that we're born into. And I look at myself and a few thousand of you people, and it seems that there're three characteristics that are common to all of us, so common that they're so easy to see in every one of us, regardless of race, color or creed, religion or the lack of it, education or the lack of it, which side of the tracks we were born on; doesn't make any difference.

Every alcoholic that I've ever known, almost throughout the world, is a perfectionist. An idealist with the terrific drive for excellence that goes with perfectionism. It is this drive for excellence that brought about the cliche that you've heard ever since you were a little guy. "This is the best mechanic we

99

ever had in the shop, but..." "The best lawyer that ever hit this part of the country, but..." "The best stenographer we ever had in the office, but she can't get down 'til about of a Tuesday or Wednesday. Drinks too much." Terrific drive for excellence. Perfectionism. Now perfectionism is a beautiful characteristic, or attribute, when we learn how to live with it, but until we do it'll kill us. It makes us set goals for ourselves that we cannot attain, and we're forever disappointed in our own performance. And it makes us demand more of those around us than they can put out. It makes it necessary for us to make them over; our wives and our kids and the people that work with us, and so on. It's a killer until we learn how to live with it. Perfectionism, idealism. It's very evident in all of us.

The second thing is that to a man we were born with the interior awareness that life should be a good and a big and a beautiful thing. I knew when I was six years old that life should be like it is now. My insides proclaimed it but I looked at it and it was cheap and it was dirty and it was ugly. And that was one of my biggest problems. I couldn't integrate myself into the life around me because I didn't like it. There was a scene, if you remember, in the "Days of Wine and Roses," that just tears the heart out of me, and I haven't had a drink for twenty-nine years. Every time I think of it, it does me in. This gal had come back to her ex-husband's apartment to try to talk him into rejoining her in the drinking world. He'd gotten into Alcoholics Anonymous and he was begging her to join him in this new way of life. She was standing, looking out the window high above New York City, and she finally said to him, "I can't, I can't, I can't! When I look out of this window sober it's cheap and it's dirty and it's ugly. But when I look out drunk it's beautiful." For twenty-five years, the only way I could stand what I looked at was to be half in the bag. And this was one of my big problems, and yours.

Lastly, (There're many more, but we'll just use three.) and this is the most incongruous thing you'll ever hear coming out of the mouth of an alky, and I caution you not to speak of this to your psychiatrist. We are a highly sensitive people. Now isn't that something, when there we lay in the gutter, "and the pig got up and slowly walked away?" We're a highly sensitive people. That's the reason that the psychiatric world, from one end of the world to the next, has labeled us as being "emotionally immature." Every one of them. We're emotionally immature. I don't believe it! I think that we have several times the capacity for feeling that the psychiatrist has. If a psychiatrist came in and found me lying there on the floor in front of my big window, so drunk I couldn't even get up, crying my eyes out over a beautiful sunset, he would say, "emotional immaturity." He wouldn't know it was so damn pretty I couldn't stand it. I haven't had a drink for twenty-nine years, but a year ago I was down on the knobs above Louisville, Kentucky, along the Ohio River. It was in October and the leaves had turned, and it's the most beautiful sight on the face of the earth. All those beautiful colors! And miles of it—it's so beautiful. I sat there all alone in my car and bawled my eyes out. So pretty I couldn't stand it. We're not emotionally immature, we are highly sensitive people.

As I've told many of you, I've been in prisons practically all over the world, mostly as a guest. I could leave after a while. And amongst them is Folsom. Now Folsom is for habitual criminals. You can't get into Folsom for murder if it's the first time. You have to be a habitual criminal to get into Folsom. They tell me that the swallows that build up there in those rocks used to build in Capistrano, but they're four-time losers so they build up there in the stone wall around that place. Now, I've stood there and talked to twice or three times this many people, watched them cry right along with me. The tears are bouncing off their bellys and they make no attempt to hide it, and it isn't because they're emotionally immature. It's because of the identity. They feel right here inside exactly like I do. And they cry with me and they laugh with me, and it isn't because they're emotionally immature.

I'm convinced that people like us, when we get here, have all the characteristics for alcoholism except alcohol. All we have to do is to add a little alcohol and we're off. Very few things can happen to us; from the time we're born we're either going to be priests, preachers or nuns, or hopheads or alcoholics, because we cannot integrate ourselves into the life around us. And it's not because we don't want to, because we do. We want so much to be a part of, and we're forever apart from. So this is our problem, a basic spiritual unrest. Unfortunately, the teachers don't know the answers.

I buried a few people, I think I told you I had two this week; Monday and Tuesday I had funerals. A few months ago I was asked to give a little eulogy for a sixteen year old girl who had taken an overdose of cocaine. That's the "in" thing down in my country now, cocaine. And she died. I got out there to the place, the cemetery. There was no chapel, it was just a graveside service, and that whole hill was covered with kids. I don't know how many, just a whole parcel of kids—teenagers—on that hill. And I said to myself, "This can't be just a regular deal. I've got to talk to these kids." And I talked first for a little bit with the parents and with a few older people that were there, and I told them that I didn't believe in death and why, and then I started talking to the kids.

I told them I had great empathy because I too had been born into a society that I couldn't swallow, I couldn't integrate myself into. I had to find a way to be comfortable because I was not comfortable in the society in which I had to move. But when I was nineteen I found a way to get comfortable in that society, and for the next fifteen years I used this chemical for an answer. It remained an answer for the first fifteen years, but after fifteen years my answer turned on me and became the problem. The next ten years made it necessary for me to find the right answer, and I did. Then I told these kids that if they could just come to see that, there was an answer that stayed with us. I said, "When you're behind the acid you've got all the answers, but when the acid's gone you ain't got none. The answer's gone, too, you see. But there is an answer that stays with you, and it's so much better than any chemical that you can put in your body, that then you can sing about your business. The business of living. And you don't have to repeat a dosage of chemicals. And if you just decide that you want to find this answer, and make an effort, you can find it. There are many people that'll help you. And if you do this, maybe this death will be justified."

Her mother called me the early part of the week, the first time since I had been there, and she said there was quite a movement amongst the teachers and amongst the students to find an answer to replace this stuff. She told me about some guy that had thrown his house open to kids in Laguna Beach, and they wanted me to go down there last Friday. But isn't that beautiful, that they might now be looking for something that might take the place of this chemical deal?

I want to close with this little story. Before Alcohol-

103

ics Anonymous was born, there was a chap by the name of Rowland, and Rowland was an alky. Rowland was doctoring with Dr. Carl Jung, who might possibly be the greatest psychological mind that the world has produced so far. (If I was learned that would be a good opinion, but I'm not.) To me, he was tops. He was the same vintage as Freud and Adler, but it seems that Jung had a personal answer, he had a living answer that maybe the others didn't. And Rowland was doctoring with him, and every time he came back to him he was worse. He finally came back and the doctor told him, "Medical science has done everything in it's power for you, and it can do no more. Psychiatry has done everything in it's power for you, and it can do no more. And now it's my duty to tell you that your only hope is to find a spiritual experience that might save you. It's your only chance."

This was some little time before Alcoholics Anonymous was born. Eventually Ebby called on Bill, and eventually Bill heard the pronouncement that we've talked about already. That he might have six more months to live and then his wife would have to either lock him up or bury him. And he called out, "God, if there be a God, reveal yourself to me now." And something happened and he got sober. And he shared this thing pretty well until he died. Never had to drink anymore. Bill and Dr. Bob and some of the rest of them worked out this formula, and proved that it worked if you and I work it, and put it in the book, Alcoholics Anonymous for us. Then Bill heard about Rowland and what Dr. Jung had told him about a spiritual awakening or a spiritual experience being his only chance.

So Bill wrote to Dr. Carl Jung in Zurich, Switzerland, and asked him how he had known enough about alcoholism to so counsel Rowland as he had done. And Dr. Jung wrote back and he told Bill, in essence, that he had always known that the alcoholic's problem was his search for unity. His search for unity, and he couldn't find it. He even quoted one of my favorite verses: "As the hart panteth after the waterbrook, so panteth my soul after thee, Oh God." He'd always known that this was the alcoholic's problem; his attempt to find unity with the life around him and with the God that made him. And when he found the bottle, it seemed to be the missing ingredient. It seemed to let him live a little bit more comfortably with himself and in the society around him. He had found chemical unity, and it did a pretty good job for him until it became the problem that only a spiritual answer could solve. Now that's a beautiful thing, and most of us agree with it.

Now here's what happened, and this just curls my hair. This is fantastic—it's a beautiful, a beautiful thing to me. Rowland, having heard this, affiliated himself with the Oxford Movement and got sober. Then he ran into Ebby, and he got Ebby into the Oxford Movement, and Ebby got sober. And Ebby called on Bill, and Bill got sober. And so the finger of God. Oh, this is so beautiful! In our entire history the finger of God is so evident all the way through. From Dr. Carl Jung to Rowland to Ebby to Bill, Bill to Dr. Bob, Dr. Bob and Bill to us. What a beautiful thing it is. And how fortunate we are. I believe this to be the most fortunate segment of humanity, of God's kids. Because, you see, we have to—*we have to*—find an answer lest we die. We come here not looking for God, or to get our wives back, or to get the love of our kids back. In many cases (like my own) we are not even looking for health, but just a way to live one day at a time without drinking, so that we might rub out a little of the record. And we find that the formula for sobriety and the formula for the good life

105

and the formula of God is all the same. And we find an answer that makes the chemical unnecessary, and it's an answer that doesn't just stay in the meeting. When we leave it goes with us, and we're never alone anymore. How fortunate can a man be!

Chapter 5
THE PRODIGAL SON

All good things have to come to an end, I guess. But in thinking again, this might be just the beginning, not the end. I want to thank you gentlemen for coming down here. I don't' believe that we could have hand picked a group of men that would have been more to our purpose than the ones that are here. This is a fabulous bunch of guys. It's been a most amazingly beautiful weekend. There's been a lot of love on the grounds and in the meeting rooms and in the hospitality rooms. A lot of love—the spirit has been excellent. As far as I'm concerned, I've never been to anything that has been more nearly right than this has been for me, and I thank you very much for coming.

I can think of nothing that I might have wanted to say when I got down here that I haven't said sometime during these hours that we've been together. Of course, we could talk about this thing from now until Christmas, and never get through, because there's no way that you can get through talking about this. One of the greatest things about getting older in the program of Alcoholics Anonymous is the memories that build over the years. The memories, the tremendous experiences that we have, one with another, as we go along. I remember when we went to Toronto in '65 for the International up there. There was an old boy by the name of Frank M., from Edmonton. I'd met Frank a number of years before and I had a beautiful experience with him. I was hoping that Frank might be there, and he came. When I spotted him we immediately went for coffee, and we sat down there and talked. And I told him how I so wanted him to be there, and I said that all the way up here I was thinking, "Supposing five years ago, I had said to myself, 'I've done enough, I've done my stint. I'm going to take it easy—I'm going to retire. Let the other guys have it, now. I've done my thing.' And I was so happy, coming up here, that I hadn't done that, because I feel that the last five years have been the greatest period of my own growth." And the tears came into ol' Frank's eyes, and he said, "I drove down here from Edmonton, and all the way down I was thanking God that I had remained active in Alcoholics Anonymous, because I felt that the last few years had been my greatest period of growth."

I'm sure that one of the great spiritual values of things like this is the memories that'll go with us through the years. Sharing our experience, strength and hope, one with another in love. It's a beautiful thing. And as we said a while ago, this ain't no big deal. This ain't no big deal. People don't get sober on profundities, they don't get sober on intellectual knowledge, it ain't no big deal. It's a little deal. The little things are the things we remember. There was a guy that came up to me twenty-some years ago, in Claremont, and I believe he was the ugliest man I ever saw. He was tall, six foot four or five, and he had kinky hair, and it was standing straight up. He had big ears, a great beak on him, and no teeth. He didn't have a tooth in his head. After the talk, he came up to me and he smelled like two breweries. Not one, two. And he said, "Chuck, I heard what you said, and I'm not going to have to drink anymore." And every Christmas from that time, wherever the guy is, on Christmas day I get a call from him. I answer the phone and he says, "Don't take that first drink. If you don't take that first drink, you can't get drunk." It's been twenty some-odd years, and he's called me every year. "I heard what you said, and I don't have to drink anymore." Little things that make this thing so big.

I want to share a few more little things with you, before we go into the last business of the day. Many of you have heard me say this, but it's more real to me today than it ever was. Twenty some-odd years ago, I talked on Sunday night in Highland Park, and after the meeting there were four or five of us standing in the middle of the room with our arms on each other's shoulders. And we were saying to each other, "How lucky can a man be? How fortunate can you be? That a tongue-chewin', babblin' idiot drunk could have a life like this. How fortunate could we be?" And one kid wasn't saying anything, and pretty soon he looked to me and he said, "Chuck, I'm ignorant. I ain't never read no books. There's no sense in me reading books because I don't understand them. I don't know nothin' about God, I don't know nothin' about the Bible, but this program no man can take away from me. When I do these simple things, one day at a time to the best of my ability, I feel clean inside, and good things happen in my life. And when I could talk, I said, "Son, don't ever read no books, no time. You said the very essence of all the books that were ever written. That's what we want—that we might feel clean inside and have good things happen in our lives."

About three or four years ago I was talking to a group, and Eddy H. was there. And I got to thinking that Eddy was in that meeting that night, when this monkey said, "I'm ignorant." So after this thing was over, as soon as I could sneak away I caught Eddy on his way out and I said, "Eddy, do you remember who it was that said, 'I ain't never read no books. I'm ignorant.'?" and Eddy said, "No" and started to walk away, but then he came back and said, "It was me." And it was, it was Eddy, and he's had twenty-five years or more, sober and happy in this program. It's beautiful!

A little earlier than that, I'd yakked someplace and a kid came up to me and he said, "Chuck, do you know why it's so hard for us to find God?" And I didn't want to answer him. I was too tired. I wanted to get the hell out of there. I thought to myself, "I'm going to have to listen for an hour to some explanation of why it's so hard for us to find God." But I couldn't get away from him, so I had to say, "No, why is it so hard for us to find God?" And he said, "Because He ain't lost." Because He ain't lost. Isn't that fabulous? Because He ain't lost. He said, "You see, all we've got to do is come back home, and we find God's always been there. We've been away."

And there was another old boy, his name was Big Smith. Big Smith was from Flint, Michigan, and he was my kind of a drunk. He was the kind of a guy that drove his car off the end of a pier and through brick buildings. He'd sort've shriveled himself up a bit. One leg was about two inches longer than the other, and he'd walk like he was sneaking up on somebody. Smitty came into the meeting in Hawthorne twenty-seven years ago, I expect it was, and he had a little ol' plaque under his arm that he'd picked up in a hospital down in Texas. And here's what the plague said, "If you are not as close to God as you once were, or as you would like to be, make no mistake, you are the one that moved." And Smitty said, "You see, all we've got to do is come back home." We find that God's always been there. We've been away.

There's another little thing that I have treasured over the years. I don't know where it came from. I don't know where I got it, but it's a fish story, too. (You remember—we had a fish story already.) This is a story about three little fish that were swimmin' around there off the coast of Laguna, just playin' around. They'd had breakfast, they weren't even hungry, they were just playin' around there. A big, wise fish swam by and he said, "Good morning, boys. Isn't the water fine, this morning?" And he swam on off. As soon as he got out of hearing, these little fish got together and they said, "Wait a minute, wait a minute. That boy spoke about water. What's water? Did you ever hear of 'water'?" And one replied, "No, how about you?" "Never heard of it!" "Neither did I." So they swam all over the Pacific Ocean, hunting for water, *in which they lived and moved and had their being.* Fascinating!

Now, I'm going to tell you a little story, and I'm going to use my own interpretation of it. Some of you might not think I have the right to change it a little, but I'm telling the story! And this is my story, and it's your story. It does more to explain me to me, and you to me, and our relationship to God than pretty nearly anything I've ever heard. It's the story of the Prodigal Son, and it goes something like this. A certain wealthy man had two sons. And the youngest one of them came to his dad and he said, "Dad, I've got me some ideas. I'm going out to Hollywood. They do a lot of things out there, there're big deals out there. The motion picture industry's big, and you can do big things out there. So, give me my inheritance." And the father gave it to him. Now that father didn't say, "Wait a minute, son, we're wealthy, we have everything you need right here. Stay home. You'll get out there away from home, away from your family, and you're liable to get in trouble—You might run on to a blonde with a bottle of muscadoodle, and get into a hell of a lot of trouble! Stay home." He didn't say that. He didn't say anything. The kid said, "Give me my inheritance." And he gave it to him. And the kid went away from home into a far country, and wasted his substance on riotous living. Now that might not fit you, but it fits me pretty good! Sounds suspiciously like me. He wasted his substance on riotous living. And when he'd spent all, there arose a mighty famine in the land.

And as serious as this is, it tickles the hell out of me. If there were ever a bunch of people that should understand a famine, it's us! How many times have you come off a drunk, found everybody that you knew looking for you (ninety percent of them just to tell you they never want to see you again), and the other ten percent trying to bank one of your checks with a tennis racket! I don't think they make famines like that anymore—that's a famine.

So after the kid had spent all, there arose a mighty famine in the land, and what'd he do? Did he go back home? No, he didn't. He did just like you did and like I did. He went to a man in that country. We did to. We went to men in that country: doctors, psychiatrists, priests, and preachers. He went to a man in that country and the man put him to work. And of all the things he might have put him to doing, he didn't. He gave him a job tending the pigs. Now this is very significant, because this was a Jew boy telling this story, and Jews don't like pigs! There would be nothing so obnoxious to a Jew than having to tend pigs, and there he was, tending the pigs. Meaningful, it is, because that means the guy was down. Low. He was low-down. We have a name for it: we call it low bottom. Tending pigs. And while he was in the pig pen with the pigs, he got hungry, and he fain would eat the husks that the pigs did eat. And no man gave unto him. He was beyond human help. And *no* man gave unto him.

"Probably no human power could have relieved our alcoholism." * Same thing.

And while he was there, with everything gone, it occurred to him that in his father's house was plenty to spare. They were wealthy, and here he was, totally done in. But he said to himself, "I can go back there and say to my father, 'Look Dad, I'm your boy. Do you recognize me? I'm your son.'" He couldn't do that, just couldn't do that.

The self-condemnation that goes with the disease of alcoholism! How we condemned ourselves! How we hated ourselves for the failure that we were making in the business of living.

And so it was with him. But he also remembered that the servants back there, the hired servants, were pretty well taken care of. They were living a lot better than he was, and so he said to himself, "I'm goin' back home. And I'm not going to say, 'I'm your son, how about takin' me back on.' I'm going to apply for a servant's job. A hired servant." So he made a decision, he said, "I will arise and go to my father."

We, too, made a decision. We made a decision to turn our will and our lives over to the care of God. It's very parallel to my life, all the way through. It's my story, and your story, I think.

So he got up and started home. The kid had made his decision and started home, and the father saw him a long ways off and came to meet him. Ah, this is fantastic!

Now here's the miracle of Alcoholics Anonymous. Here's the thing itself. This is the essence of our program. The Father saw me a long ways off. And as I walked through the door of my first AA meeting, the man said to me, "Mister, were you looking for somebody?" And I said, "No sir." And he said, "What were you looking for?" And thinking he was a Veteran, I said, "Well, if it would interest you, sir, I was looking for sobriety." And everything about that man changed in a twinkling of an eye. I was hooked before he ever opened his mouth again, because it was obvious that he was glad I was there, when everybody that knew me wouldn't even spit on me. My own flesh and blood wouldn't have anything to do with me. And here was this stranger, so glad that I was there that he lit up, and when he spoke again, this is what he said. "Why, take off your hat and coat. You're in the right place." And he took me and rocked me to sleep. God came to meet me, through you, who had already found your way. I didn't know you, but you knew me, because I was an alcoholic and it didn't make any difference. You didn't ask me if I was hot, if I was in bad with the law, if I owed money, if I had turned over a new leaf, if I was sorry for my sins. You didn't say any of those things to me. "Have you quit drinking?" You didn't say that. You said, "Take off your hat and coat. You're in the right place."

And so the father saw the kid a long ways off, and he came to meet him. And the kid started trying to tell him what a bum he was, what a failure he had been in the business of living. But again the father didn't hear him. He didn't argue with him at all. He didn't say, "Look, I've got the record on you right here, and you sure are a bum. You're no good. I've got it right down here. I know every time you turned right when you should have turned left. Get the grubbin' hoe and get back here on the back forty, and grub out those persimmon sprouts and sassafras bushes. And maybe, if you do a good job, twenty-five years from now I'll invite you in for lunch." He didn't say that. He didn't say anything. He fell on his neck and kissed him! And he put a ring on his finger, the symbol of eternal life: no beginning and no end. And he called to the servants, and he said, "Kill the fatted calf. We're going to have a party. The boy was dead and he's now alive. He was lost, and now he's come back home, so let's have a party." No condemnation, no reprimand, no argument. The love of the father for his child.

You and I, having run out of our own resources, have been privileged to wander in to an Alcoholics Anonymous meeting, and to stay, and to find this same experience as the Prodigal Son. We've come home. It's not normal to walk alone. It's normal for us to walk down the high road of life with our arms around each other, sharing our experience, strength and hope, one with another in love. This is normal—it's as normal as breathing. It's not normal to be away from the Father's house. We're like little kids that are lost in the woods, and darkness has come on, and we're scared to death. And we wander in to an Alcoholics Anonymous meeting and find ourselves in each other and God. What a deal it is. What a fabulous thing it is.

Now I recognized my problem ten years before coming here, and that's thirty-nine years ago. Thirty-nine years ago. And in this thirty-nine years millions of men and women have died of the same disease that I have, the disease of alcoholism, because they didn't find this place. There are many dying now, almost in rifle shot of right here, dying of the disease of alcoholism. And they don't know, they don't know.

115

We might say to ourselves, "How come we were so fortunate?", and there's no answer to that. We were. I have had over ten thousand, six-hundred days, one day at a time, of the finest life that anybody ever dreamed of—from a tongue-chewin', babblin' idiot, to a personally satisfactory, conscious partnership with the Living God that made us, in the entire business of living. What a transition! What a miracle of life! What a thing to keep us practicing these principles in all of our affairs!

And carrying this message to the alcoholic who still suffers. How fortunate are we that we have a lifetime job outlined for us in Step Twelve. As I have said on many occasions, I don't know who to be most grateful for, or to. I don't know. Because I didn't come to you to find God. I didn't come to you get to my wife back, or my kids, or my health, or my sanity. I'd looked for God for thirty years and I couldn't find Him, because I had Him located someplace else. I came here to find out how to live, one day at a time, without drinking. And guys just like you took me in and shared their experience, strength and hope with me, but more than that—much more than that—their love. Guys that I didn't know, but they knew me, you see. And so, insofar as I am capable of doing it, I will be attempting to share this thing with drunks as long as there is breath in me. And again, and again, and again. You guys get dearer to call me all the time. All the time, because you are the guys that nursed me back to health. You helped me do that which I could not do alone, and showered enough love on me that I became, I hope, aware of the fact that God is love. God is love, and he that abideth in love abideth in God, and God abideth in him. I'm so grateful to you that I can't see. I love you. It's my joy to have had this time with you, and I shall never forget it, because some part of everyone of you is going to be with me for the rest of my life. So I thank you again. All I have to do is to look into the eyes of a bunch like you, to see my God. God bless you! Thank you, very much.

Chapter 6

QUESTIONS AND ANSWERS

In 1923 I was in the real estate business in Los Angeles. I had a picture on my desk of an old man with a white beard down to about his navel, and the caption was "I'm an old man and I've had many troubles, most of which never happened." I like that! This is to be a question period.

Should we work with practicing alcoholics before we have taken all the steps ourselves?

I think that the very moment that a guy decides he wants what we have and becomes willing to go to any length to get it, he is ready to work with alcoholics. Not that he tries to carry the message to alcoholics, but that he tries to carry the alcoholic to the message. As soon as we have decided that we want what's here, we could tell anybody, "Look, I've found a place that seems to manufacture sobriety; a bunch of guys that are doing something about their drinking. They have impressed me very much, and I'm going to a meeting. How about going with me?" So you carry the alcoholic to the message. The book says, "Obviously, we can't transmit something we don't have." That's what you're referring to, but you don't have to be anything but kind to carry a message. Really, that's all. A little love.

In our sobriety, how do we deal with our emotions and the emotions of others we work with in the program?

Sobriety. I got into that, I guess. I said sobriety was four-fold: Physical, mental, emotional and spiritual. Emotional would just be one of the areas of our life that has to become stable. For instance, if we're going to work with alcoholics, we can't afford to become emotionally involved in their problem, or we lose all of our possibility for help. You've got to stay above the problem. Now it seems like, maybe, that would be a cold attitude. It is not. You have to love more to stay emotionally uninvolved in the problem than you do to become involved in it. The answer is not in the problem, the answer is in the answer. I worked on my problem for ten years, and the more I looked at the problem and the harder I worked on the problem, the greater the problem became. It was just like fertilizing and watering and cultivating a weed. It grew out of all proportions. I think we have to be able to live above the problem to be of value to those that have it. We don't get emotionally involved in the problem. It's not that we love less, it's that we love more. I think it takes much more love to release than it does to hold onto. Emotional stability comes, I am sure, out of this thing we call self-discovery.

Physical sobriety comes from not drinking. We don't drink today, and after a while we are physically free from the effects of alcohol. But until we become emotionally stable and mentally stable and spiritually somewhat stable, we're not sober. Sobriety is the ability to live comfortably, peacefully and joyously with oneself. I find much confusion in this area of becoming emotionally involved in the problem of our so-called babies. Many people think you've got to be emotionally involved in them, and I think we completely stymie ourselves when we do.

What about sex after sobriety?

Is there anybody here that wants to cover that subject? What's that, you say, you could be arrested for assault with a deadly weapon? I'm delighted to be able to report that, as we said yesterday, love includes possession but not the necessity to possess. I think that it's perfectly possible to live very happily in a marriage relation without emphasis on that particular deal. I also know it's quite important to many, many people. It's strange how important that it gets at times and then, in a little while, how unimportant it is. We used to call it the biggest "enough" there is! I realize that this is a problem in many, many families. I believe that sex, as such, should be just as spontaneous as everything else. I think it should come as the result of love, the givingness of self to self in love. And I think that's the only way it has any value at all. I think that we as a sex are very, very lacking in this area. All men. Because we are inclined to want what we want when we want it, and we want to explode, and that's what happens. When the explosion's over, the job's done as far as we're concerned but I feel that's a totally selfish approach. I think that the love and adoration, both before and after the act, is far superior to the act itself. In other words, I find nothing wrong with sexual intercourse as a result of love. But as an objective, I think it's self-robbery. It's a beautiful thing when it's the givingness of self to self in love. Otherwise, I find no value in it.

121

A New Pair of Glasses

What is the value of patience when counseling with another alcoholic?

If we had all the alcoholics in the world in this room, right now, we would have ninety percent of the impatience of the human race. We are a very impatient lot. We want everything to happen yesterday. Patience is certainly a virtue.

I doubt very much if our value as a counselor equals our value as a listener. If you can get the guy or the gal talking, if you can get them talking—this is the deal. In my own case, if I'm talking to somebody new, the one thing that I listen for is the first attempt at a belly laugh. This ain't no big deal; you can't get serious. An alcoholic cannot take a preachment or lecture. We know all about the preachment and the lecture; we've given them to ourselves a thousand times. We know exactly what they're going to say before they say it. And so the sharing, and getting them to talk and being a good listener, gives the counselor more value than talking himself. We're not experts on anything. It's the simple little thing that opens the door, it isn't the profundity. Nobody ever got sober on profundity. It's the little things.

Many of you've heard me tell this. I was talking at the Bob White group many years ago on Santa Barbara and Van Ness, and there was a drunk in bad shape sitting right in front, and it came time for him to light a cigarette and he couldn't do it. He couldn't get the things to mate. He struggled and he struggled, and after a while a little old lady that was sitting next to him reached over and took his cigarette and his match, and lit it, and put it in his mouth. The next year I was there at the same time and this guy had his first birthday, and I thought, "Well, I must have done pretty well!" So I was prepared to get a nice compliment, you know, when he got up to take his birthday cake. But he said the reason he was back was not what was said or done in the meeting, it was the fact that this little old lady had lit his cigarette for him. This thing doesn't depend on profundity or expertise. It's love, and love is patient. Love is patient.

Another one that I love to think about happened at the La Habra Group. I talk there on Friday before Christmas every year, and ten or twelve years ago there was a guy sitting along the wall—there were benches along the wall. And he was leaping—he wasn't shaking—he was leaping! I went over and sat down beside him before the meeting started, and I put my arm around the guy and said, "Son, this ain't no big deal. If you don't drink, if you don't take that next drink, in three days you'll be pretty nearly well, physically. Just put it off, don't take that next drink—it ain't no big deal. Make a game out of it, and go for three days without a drink. See what happens to you." And for years, at least once a year in some meeting, he's gone by me and he gets right up to my left ear, and he says, "Son, it ain't no big deal." And then he goes on about his business. So yes, if you love them, you're patient.

How do we surrender and turn our will over to God, when after asking for guidance, we still flounder at times?

There are many times when even prayer is like praying up a chimney. No way can you seem to make any conscious contact with anything. Everything's futile. You have no purchase at all up there on the end of that line. That's what the book means when it says, "When everything else fails, get you a wet drunk." Because, you see, when we're feeling futile, we want something and it isn't happening. But there's no way that you can want something when you're working with a wet drunk. No way. You can't think about yourself when you're working with a wet drunk. That's one place where you give all your attention, interest and love to the person at hand, even if it's just simply to outmaneuver him. To neither be the pukee or the pukor in that case! So we've got to get ourselves off our mind.

I have a theory of my own: I can't solve a problem. No way can I solve a problem, and I haven't tried it much in these last twenty-nine years because I've expected guidance and direction. If I wake up to the fact that I'm all tied in a knot, working on something, and I'm just completely rigid and I recognize it (subconsciously I've been messin' with this thing and beatin' my brains out), then this is my little deal, and it works for me right along. As I said to you, I share everything with my own God—the good, bad and the indifferent—and in this case I say, "Look, Dad, I'm beatin' my brains out over this problem and I don't know the answer. You do, and when you get ready to give it to me I'd certainly be glad to have it. Sure thank you." And I dump it and never look at it again. I just dump it. That's it. And in a very short time I'd find out that it either wasn't a problem in the first place (which was about fifty percent of the time), or I had the answer. It's the self-concern and the impatience that bring about this sort of an impasse in our own lives, and to get ourselves off our mind there's nothing more highly recommended than to sit down with a wet drunk.

With self and ego taking over periodically, do I analyze and look for answers too much?

You're a mess! If I were you I'd just give up. I find so many of our people in AA, even in the Grapevine, writing about self-esteem, building self-esteem. I hear people get up here and talk all the time about "You have to learn to love yourself before you can love anybody else." I am most grateful that isn't the case. I never spent any time trying to build up self-esteem or trying to love me. I wouldn't have taken me with a large dowry. I hated my damn guts. But I got busy doing things our book suggests, and it wasn't trying to learn how to "self-esteem" me, or to love me so I could love you. I don't think that's the way it is at all. Francis says, "For it is better to love than to be loved. It is better to understand than to be understood. For it is in giving that we receive, it is in forgiving that we're forgiven, and it is in dying to self that we awaken to eternal life."

That's exactly what we've been talking about ever since we've been down here, exactly what we've been talking about. I don't believe that an image of me would add anything to my life at all. I haven't any more an image of me than I have of a walrus. I'm not interested in an image of me, that's not why I'm here. I'm here to share me with anybody that wants me in love, and let the chips fall where they may. I'm not even interested in your opinion of what's happened, except when you want to give it to me. That's not my deal. I love you, and that's all I have to do. That's what I'm interested in, that's my deal. It's not my deal who you love or what you love, or what you think. That's your deal. I love you, period. I don't even have to concern myself with what you think about me. I've got no image at all of me.

I think of myself exactly as that big window up there in front of my chair. To me, that window *is* me. And when there is no obstruction the light comes through, but the window is not the light. And I think of that drape as my ego, and when that drape's closed the light doesn't come through, but just as the window is not the light, the drape is not the darkness.

It just shuts out the light. So my business is to keep the drape open and let the light shine. I don't furnish the light, I'm a channel. I'm a channel. You and I are necessary to God as channels through which He goes forth into his creation. We're channels. And we get ourselves out of the way and let it be. As we said last night, and as I say to me all the time, I'm either going to run my life and take the consequences thereof, or I'm not going to run it and take the consequences thereof. I can't run mine, I don't get involved in running my life. I get involved in living.

I think losing yourself in life guarantees finding yourself in God. Guarantees it, because all you've got to do is to get rid of the roadblocks. You lose yourself in life and find yourself in God. And so I wouldn't, if I were you, spend another five seconds trying to find self-worth or anything else. To find yourself, yes. To realize that whatever it is you're looking for is right here inside you—what you're looking for you're looking with; what you came here to get came with you. Everything you've ever wanted to know you've always known, and everything you've wanted to be you've always been, but it's covered up. It's covered up, so we uncover and discover. Forget about you—to hell with you. Maybe you've got a little better break on that than I have. Maybe you have, and maybe you haven't. Let the chips fall where they may. The beautiful thing about this deal is not to get serious about yourself, to make the whole deal a game. A play of life upon itself. And to have fun at it. I have more fun with God than just about anyone. I have a hell of a lot of fun with God. I think that the guy has a tremendous sense of humor, or he wouldn't have hid himself in the last place we'd ever look! I think it's terrific! The very last place we'd ever look, there He is. I can just see Him! Here I am try-ing to find a bottle, off hours, and I've got to have a drink and He says, "Look at that son-of-a-bitch, he's huntin' Me, and I'm with him!" I love it! It's a fun deal. You're too serious, Phil, make a fun deal out of it.

Should members of AA work professionally in the field of alcoholism?

I do not really care much to comment on it, but I would say this. It's awfully hard for amateurs like us to get mixed up with professionals and stay amateurs. We're a strange bunch. All we have to do is rub elbows a little with a doctor, and we become one. Maybe some people can retain their amateur standing in working for money in the field of alcoholism, I don't know. But in my personal life I've met only one that seemed to do it, and he wasn't around long enough to really see whether it was going to work out or not. His name was Warren S. Warren died about a year or so after he started working for money in the field of alcoholism.

The one thing that would seem to be furthest from a paid twelve step call would be working with the National Committee on Alcoholism, because the National Committee on Alcoholism has no recovery program at all. They are educational and referral. That's their business, and that's not the business we're in, so it would appear that there would be no conflict to work for the National Committee on Alcoholism. They have no program of recovery. But those of my friends who work with them somehow become professionals. I'm mindful of one gal I love very, very much, who ten years ago made one of the finest AA talks I've ever heard in my life. Then she became Secretary of the Committee on Alcoholism, and she talked at our group a year ago and she made just as fine a talk as she'd ever made, but it wasn't an Alcoholics Anonymous talk. It was a professional talk, and the one thing about us that we must maintain is caring and sharing. We're not experts on anything, we share our experience, strength and hope, one with another in love. So I haven't seen anybody be able to do that kind of thing without seeming to get lost in professionalism. Incidentally, it wasn't three months after that talk that she was in the hospital herself. Not, I'm sure, for either pills or drinking (I say I'm sure—I'm not sure of anything.), but for a breakdown of some kind.

I can't do it. Personally, when I talk for organizations that have an honorarium for, say seventy-five or one hundred and fifty dollars, I won't take it. Because, whilst they don't know it, I learned what I'm telling them from you guys, from drunks who don't drink. And I can't any more take an honorarium than I can fly, because you guys didn't charge me a thing. You didn't even ask me if I had anything. The only thing you said to me when I came to my first meeting was, "Mister, were you looking for somebody?" And I said, "No, sir." And you said, "Well, what were you looking for?" And I said, "If it would interest you, sir, I was looking for sobriety." And you lit up like a Christmas tree! Took me and rocked me to sleep. Now any alcoholic is totally free to make a living. I think we're entitled to make a living, but if I were a preacher, I would want my business on the side, because I would not want to get up here and try to tell you monkeys what you want to hear. I would not want my gas and water in your hands. If you didn't like me, you'd turn off my gas and water, so I'd have to try to please you. I can't do that. I'd want my business on the side. I'd want my money coming in from somewhere else, so I could tell you what I think. I can't talk without saying it as I feel it, as I think that it should be. So I can't work in that field.

But if I were a captain in the marines, and they wanted me to head up a program of alcoholism for the Marines and I could set up my own staff, as certain marines have had the privilege of doing, I might do what a captain in the Marines (who asked this question) did. He turned blue and he said, "What am I going to do?" I said, "Get your staff to handle the related disorders. Get all those people that you have working with you to handle the hopheads, the pill heads, the sex maniacs, and you deal in Alcoholics Anonymous, the drunk in Alcoholics Anonymous." And that's what he did, and it's worked out beautifully, and I don't see it's doing him any harm.

Should members of AA attend meetings of Al-Anon? Are we missing anything?

Well I think you are, because most of them are women! I have a lot of fun, of course my wife is quite an Al-Anon, and I have a lot of fun with her. I got by for many years by saying to her when she got a little out of line, "Look, sister, you people wouldn't even have a program if it hadn't been for us." Because we loaned them our program, you know. And after a while she got smarty pants, and she said, "We wouldn't have needed your program if it hadn't been for you!" Now I don't see why I should go anyplace else, or have to go anyplace else, to find out how to work my program in Alcoholics Anonymous. As far as I'm concerned, I don't see the need for it. Long before Al-Anon was born, when people were coming to me and saying, "You've got to get this guy sober, or this gal sober," I was saying to them, "Maybe, just maybe, this is the best time in your life to find yourself. Maybe the only chance you've got to help this alky is not to come to me, but to apply these principles to yourself, find your own peace, and maintain your own peace in your own household. It might be the only good thing you can do for that drunk." This was a long time before Al-Anon was born. But now that's what they're trying to do. They're trying to find living answers in our program, which *we* must find, along with sobriety.

I don't mind going to Al-Anon meetings, I talk before Al-Anon meetings a great deal. As a matter of fact, you people don't know it, but you're looking at the greatest Al-Anon speaker there is! A few years ago, somebody from Dallas called me, and it was Thursday, and he said, "Chuck, when can you leave for Dallas?" I said, "I'm not comin'." And he said, "Oh, yes you are." I said, "I'm not comin' to Dallas." He said, "I asked you when you can leave." And I said, "I'm not comin'." And he said, "I don't want that kind of an answer. When're you leaving?" And I said, "Who let you down? What's the matter with the speaker you had? Why didn't you ask me first? Who ran out on you?" He said, "None of your goddamned business!" Well, to make a long story short, I flew to Dallas and talked at the Al-Anon luncheon. And I was a substitute for a substitute! The first one that had agreed to talk to the Al-Anon luncheon was the late Liz, you know, the gal that wrote the book, "The Late Liz." What was her name? Gert, Gert B. Gerty and I don't get along too well, anyway. But she was the gal that was supposed to talk, and she pooped out. And the next one was Adel S., and she pooped out. So I'm a substitute for two broads, a substitute for a substitute, and they still say down there that I gave the best Al-Anon talk they ever heard. (I just threw that in.) No, there's no reason you shouldn't go to an Al-Anon meeting if you want to.

How do you prove love?

I don't think that you prove anything. I don't think we've got anything to prove. Nothing to win, and we're not going anyplace. I'll have to tell you again, I said this already, but I'll spill it again because I love it myself. This certain doctor called me at midnight and he asked, "What's the definition of love?" I said, "It's the same as it is at 10 o'clock in the morning. What the hell're you calling me at midnight and asking me what the definition of love is?" But he asked again, "What's your definition of love?" I said, "You won't like it." He said, "What is it?" I said, "Action." To talk about love is like talking about humility: you can't. Action. If you love somebody or something, you do something for them. You just do it, and you don't make a big deal out of it. You don't make a big deal out of it.

I wouldn't spend five seconds trying to prove anything that I've said from this podium to anybody here. That's not why I'm here, to prove something. I wouldn't spend five seconds trying to defend anything I've said. I have a right to my own opinion and you have a right to yours. You have my approval if you want to disagree with anything I've said or the way I've said it. It's perfectly alright with me. And the same thing is true with people every place. I love you; it's none of my business what you think of me, unless you want to make it so. So quit trying to make something out of it, to prove it.

Upon waking with negative thoughts, how does one establish a relationship with God?

I think this is what we've been talking about all along. Praying without ceasing. I find no difference in a prayer and a serious thought. They're the same thing. As we've said since we've been in here, fear or worry is a prayer for something you don't want to happen. To live in the conscious awareness of the living presence of God. I don't even much like (I talk about it an awful lot) the "Our Father..." prayer. Our Father, God. I talk about our Father a lot, but this relationship that we've been talking about this weekend is much, much closer than a father-son relationship. As I said, I've got two sons someplace in Southern California, I don't know where either one of them is. That is impossible with my relationship with my own God, because God is that which I am. God is that which I am. I couldn't breathe, I couldn't be, there would be nothing, I would be extinct, but for God. Because God is life, and there's no way to be separated from God in reality.

The only separation there is is conscious. The feeling of conscious separation from—left field. Very real as an experience, but not reality. So I don't think that we ought to wake up feeling any different than when we went to sleep, or feel any different than ten minutes after we get up. Now is the deal. How is it with me, right now? If I had to get up and start praying right quick to feel good, I don't think I'd feel good when I got through praying. I think you ought to feel good before you start to pray. Again, I don't know when my prayers start and stop. I feel like Brother Lawrence a little, in that deal. Because I like to live in the conscious awareness of the Living Presence, God, in a relationship with everything around me. Everything around me. So I think that's the thing to get through your head: that now is the time. You see, this is so very vital to me, because tomorrow was always the day I was going to straighten up and fly right. Tomorrow I was going to do'er, you know? But tomorrow never got here. Every time I came to it was now, and I was thirsty! So I took a drink. Tomorrow never got here. Again, I don't think I have to be in any particular position to retain this feeling of the Living Presence of God. I don't think that it happens in a church or in the mountain or in the temple or in Jerusalem. It's in my own mouth, that I might know it and do it. So that's the only answer I have for that.

When did you really start trusting God all the way?

I don't know. I don't know, because I just discovered that it had happened, you see? I think it happened when my ego was burned out the first time. I think that's when it happened, because I was in that circle which is Life, Good, God. To be born out of conscious separation into conscious unity makes it a reality. A belief in God is good, but it is not good enough for alcoholics. We have to live in God. To *live* in God. That's what this whole thing is all about—to get us out of our own way, so that we can go about our Father's business. That's the only business I've had for twenty-nine years. I haven't any other business. I go about my Father's business, and that's my business, and it's his business to take care of me. It's just as natural and normal as breathing. I expect it, not that I'm sittin' around in expectancy and waiting for somebody to pick up the phone, or to ring it, it's just by my being. I know that every good and perfect gift is from His hand.

Father Barney said something to me ten years ago when I was taking him home with me from the office. Just as we went under the freeway, he said to me, "Chuck, how in the hell do you fulfill your commitments?" I said, "What're you talking about?" And he said, "You've got three lives, and any one of them's enough for anybody, and you do all three of them. How do you do it?" And I said, "Father, you ought to know that better than I do. You've been studying all your life! Why'd you ask me that question?" And he said, "Why, how do you do it?" And I said, "There's no division in my life, there's no division at all."

So when we practice these principles in all of our affairs, gentlemen, there is no division in life. There is nothing that is more or less important, and there's nothing that is more or less spiritual than another.

Your business is just as spiritual as your AA, your AA's just as spiritual as your church, your home is just as spiritual as both of them. Substance is just as spiritual as "Ha, ha." Every good and perfect gift is from His hand. And to live in this, to be aware of this, constantly aware of it, that's what I have been saying: to trim the sails; some ships ply east and some ply west by the self-same wind that blows. It is the set of the sail, and not the gale, that determines where it goes.

So I trim the sails, saying to myself maybe fifty times a day. "God is my refuge and my strength." Now why do I do that? I'm not afraid of anything. I'm not afraid of you, I'm not afraid of God, I'm not afraid of the Devil, I'm not afraid of tomorrow or yesterday. Why would I be saying, "God is my refuge and my strength"? "Lift up your eyes unto the hills, from whence cometh thy strength." I love the hills. I love God. And I trim the sails, reminding myself that in Him I live and move and have my being. The conscious awareness of the Living Presence of the Almighty. Now that's what this retreat's all about. There's nothing else here so far as I'm concerned. I'm either going to run my life and take the consequences thereof, or I'm not going to run it and take the consequences thereof. *And those are not just words.* That's the way I live. I cannot live any other way. I tried to for forty-three years, and that was forty-three years too long.

I've always been a competitor. How do I remove competition from my life?

I have been a competitor all my life. I could do anything with my body up until I got hurt in football. I could do anything with it. Football, basketball, baseball and track—the whole business was just duck soup. Old Walter Kemp said years ago that the only way I could keep from being an all-American was to get hurt, so I got hurt. Got removed from football. Competition was my life.

I had a brother that was three-and-a-half years older than I, and we were competitors. From the time I could walk until I left home at twenty, we were in a fight. It lasted twenty years on the installment plan! He was three-and-a-half years older than I and three-and-a-half years stronger, and up until I was eighteen or twenty he could whip me, but he could not make me believe it. He could never make me believe it. We'd start a fight a good two miles from home, and every time he got off of me I'd dog him. And when we did that in the living room, Mother'd whip us both.

I left home at twenty thinking I could whip that guy. He never did make me believe that he could whip me. So yes, competition was my life. Now, I do a lot of lawn bowling, and if I go down there to beat somebody, I'm like a wash woman. It's just like I never had a bowling ball in my hand. But if I go down there to do the best I can with what I've got, and enjoy my competitor's shot just the same as my own, I can beat anybody in the place. In 1957 I was singles champion of the Beverly Hills Lawn Bowling Club, and I only bowled twice a week. I bowled Saturday and Sunday, and all the rest of them bowled every day. And you know that's a delicate, delicate game, lawn bowling.

So, I can't compete with anybody. And again, it is not because I decided not to compete. You see, I'm lucky because I didn't want anything when I came here, not even sobriety. I just wanted to rub out as much of the record as I could, but you can't rub out a record thinking in terms of competition, you can't do it. You just help people do things they need to have done, because you want to. I had to do that to rub it out, and when I finally woke up to the fact that things were going good, I was in the habit of it and I just kept doing it, and I'm still doing it, and I believe this is the thing that we're talking about. Our civilization has laid so many things on us that are totally extraneous; you have to be this, and have that, and be known as, before you can live. The only thing you can do with life, gentlemen, is live it. Being is the only thing that counts. The reality of the now is the *only* thing that counts in this life. "Take no thought of the 'morrow, what you shall eat, what you shall drink or wherewithal you shall be clothed." The Heavenly Father knoweth what you have need of before you ask. Now I learned it's so much more fun to get as much fun out of your opponent's shot, as your own. It's so much more fun—it's twice as much, and if you're in a foursome it's four times as much. It's so much more natural that you wish your so-called competition well. Wish him well. They do their thing and you do yours, and there's no competition if you're doing it right. There's no competition, there's no feeling of competition in it.

Now while I've got it on my mind, all you've got to do, everything that this thing's about, is a shift in the motivation in your life. That's all you've got to do. Shift your motivation from taking something from, to giving something, to adding to. Even when you're going to a meeting in Alcoholics Anonymous, shift your motivation from going to get, to going to add to. From the time I discovered I was sober, six months after I got here, until right now, I have never gone to a meeting to get anything. And I can't go to a bad meeting. I can go to a meeting and disagree with everything that's done in it—the speaker, and everything he says and the way he says it—and come out with a full cup. If you go hoping that somebody just seeing you might get a lift, or that it might do somebody good just to see you there, it always happens. Maybe somebody will ask you a question that you can answer, that you can share. You can't come away from that thing without a full cup. It's just shifting your attitude from taking from to adding to. And you do it throughout your life, everything in life. It's not a "Do-gooder" attitude. God damn the Do-gooders! (Excuse me.) It's not that you want to be a Do-gooder. As we said yesterday, to be good for something is self-robbery, even if it's to go to heaven. To be good for something is self-robbery. Be good for nothing! That's the fun deal, just to be good for nothing!

How do I overcome the insistence of my family and business associates, who say that I should make plans for tomorrow and the future?

I don't think I told you guys about having to walk off from a half-million dollars in 1957. I want to tell you this, because this is the answer to your question. When I was a year sober, I ran into a piece of property at the corner of Gardena and Normandy that was owned by some very good friends of mine. Jackson brothers, builders. Very good Mormons. Did you hear this one? The Pope got the College of Cardinals together, and he said, "Boys, I just got a phone call, and I got some good news and some bad news. Which do you want first?" They figured it out and they said, "We want the good news first." So he said, "Well, the phone call said that the second coming of Christ had already taken place, that Christ was at this time walking the earth." They thought that was great, and they said, "Now, what's the bad news?" He said, "The telephone call came from Salt Lake City."

So anyway, I knew this property was ten acres on the corner down there and I knew it was a tremendous buy, and I thought it was a good place for a

137

market. In my early years in the market business, I got all of my business from promoting markets. I found who owned properties and talked to them either about leasing them or building a building, or whatnot. And if they wanted to do something I'd get a tenant for it. Or I'd buy the property for them. All that was just to get a fixture order. I wasn't in the real estate business at that time at all, I was in the fixture business. Now I knew values, and was pretty familiar with what would make a good market site and what wouldn't. I liked this property and I thought, "Who'll I get to buy it?" Then it occurred to me that my boss might want it, because his father had started the business and he was a wealthy man before he took it over. In 1908 his dad had started, and he was very wealthy.

And so I went in one morning and I said, "Victor, I found something that you might want." And he said, "What is it?" And I told him about it, and he listened and then he said, "Go buy it for yourself, Charley." And I said, "No, I'll show it to you, but I won't buy it." "Why," he said, "you like it, go buy it." I said, "No, Victor. Get in the car and we'll go down. We can go down and back in an hour." So we did, and we looked at it and he said, "Go buy it." I said, "No, let's find out if anybody else in town likes it. Let me bring a couple market operators down here and see if they like it. Let's see if they'd like to have a building on it." But he said, "Charley, you like it. Go buy it." And I went out and bought it.

After it got through escrow, one night after everybody had gone but his secretary and myself, he called me in. The two of us were with him. And he said, "Charley, I didn't want that property. I don't want it, I don't need it. I want to get you in the same position I'm in, and as soon as I get you in the same position I'm in, we'll retire together. I'm giving you twenty-five percent of this deal. Twenty-five percent of this deal is yours! Now go out and get us a tenant and we'll build him a building and we'll go from there. Twenty-five percent of this deal's yours." And I went, and I got Von's to take a deal on it. They didn't like it, but said they, "This is the first time we've ever had any chance to do anything for Charley, and he's never given us a bum steer yet on location. So let's take it. It can't be that bad, it can't hurt us much." So they took the deal because of me, and they knew about my twenty-five percent, not only from me, but from Victor.

And we built them a building. Gatson Brothers built it, and they built it for half a fee: five percent instead of ten, because I'd known them since they were labor contractors—the two boys and their father and an uncle. I had contracted with them to build duplexes over there between Highland and La Brea and North Third Street in Hancock Park, and I was the duplex king. We worked together often and we knew each other well, and they wanted to do something for me, so they built a building for half fee. To build the building, we needed a loan. I went to Vern Jenkins, who was Chairman of the Board of Occidental Life. I'd called on his son, and he'd gotten sober, and Vern thought the sun rose and set on me. So I went down to see him, and I said, "Vern, we need a loan to build a building." He said, "What do you want? You can have anything we've got down here, including the company. Just tell me what you want and you've got it." And everybody in the deal knew all about the agreement between Vic and me.

We built the building and Von's opened, and it was a bonanza. From the very beginning it was a bonanza. We were getting from $1,700 to $2,100 dollars a week in rent. (We had a percentage lease.) A week, Gentlemen! And the idea had been great. $100,000,

A New Pair of Glasses

$125,000, $140,000 a week volume they were doing in that place. And everybody was real happy. And then they got into department stores, and we built them a department store and that went the same way, and everything was just beautiful. To make a long story short, ten years later, in my eleventh year, Victor was going to retire and I was going to retire with him. All this time we had talked about this thing, we talked about what I was doing, and we laughed and cried together as one man. Up until the last year. By my eleventh year it seemed like the guy was growing away from me, but I just thought it was because he was retiring and his mind was on something else. I was retiring right along with him—we'd talked about it for ten years! I bought that house, where I live now, because I was going to retire with my part of the deal, which was worth $500,000, a minimum of $500,000. So that was my security, you see. I was going to retire, and I had a very good and commendable motivation. I was going to retire and spend my whole time working with bums like you at my own expense. Nothing wrong with that motivation, huh? So I bought that house to retire in.

Then it came right down to the wire, and Victor couldn't do it. He could not do it. It was too much money, and he had to deny the whole thing. It was impossible, because we had been so close! We had laughed and cried for ten years, and we'd discussed this thing time and time again. We were going to retire together. But he couldn't do it. It was too much dough, and he had to deny the whole dad-blamed thing. Now I was naturally destroyed, because I could not believe that this man would do that. I couldn't believe that he could possibly do it! My insides said, "You can't let him do this! For his own sake, you can't let him do this to himself." And my toenails and my hair knew I was right, and my insides said, "This is for your family, your kids and your wife. This is their thing! And this just can't be!"

I talked to counsel, good counsel. Legal counsel. And they said to me, "Charley, you can take him to court and beat him hands down. You've got every witness in town, everybody in town knows about that thing, from him and from you. You can take him to court and beat him, like that." So I considered taking him to court, but I couldn't. Why not? Because in 1946 he came in to throw me through that window, but he didn't. He didn't throw me through that window and I couldn't take him to court. I couldn't judge him, I couldn't resent him, I couldn't hate him. If I did, I'd get drunk, and if I got drunk I'd die. So there I was between a rock and a hard place. Suffering the tortures of the damned, because I couldn't see through this damned thing. It was just a reversal of everything that we had built on for ten years. It was interesting, too, because his secretary had heard everything, and I would talk to her about it. She heard things that she wanted to hear, but when she didn't want to hear anything, she didn't hear it even if she heard it. She had a hearing problem, and she would tell me, "Charley, I didn't get it, I didn't hear it right." Well now, the reason she said that was because this guy's dad had set up a $30,000 thing for her, and Victor hadn't paid it. She had $30,000 coming, and she couldn't take sides against the guy! So she had to tell me, "I never heard it."

It took me a whole year of the most excruciating pain, thinking about this whole thing. You can see what a thing it was, because I had subconsciously come to believe this was my security. The only thing that was good about that pain period, except what came out of it, was that there wasn't one instance in the whole year that it ever occurred to me to take a drink. Now that's something, because I suffered the tortures of the damned. Finally, along toward the end of the year I came to see that there's only one security, and this is the answer to your question. There is only one security, that's my own relationship with my own God. There are no values out there. The values are here inside me. There's evidence of value out there, but no value. The minute we put a value on a million bucks, we've tied a noose around our necks because we're liable to lose it, just like that $500,000. So there's evidence of value out there, but the actual value's right here.

Remember, the Man said, "Don't lay up to yourself treasures on earth where the rust corrupts, and thieves break through and steal, but lay up to yourself treasures in Heaven where rust does not corrupt, and thieves don't break through and steal. Because where the treasure is, there will be the heart, also." I had to come to see that there's only one security, and that's my own relationship with my own God. After that happened I called Vic in one night—everybody was gone again but Vic and I—and I said, "Victor, I want to go through this deal with you once more, and I don't want you to let me make one mistake. If I say anything that isn't exactly as it happened, stop me, and we'll iron that out or we will stop talking." And I went through the deal step by step, and when I got through, I said, "Victor, you didn't stop me." And he said, "No, Charley, I didn't." And I said, "Is that exactly the way it happened?" And he said, "Yes, it is." Then I said, "Victor, you take it. You need it, I don't. God bless you. Go about your business." And he slipped off my back, and the $500,000 slipped off my back, and everything slipped off my back. And I became a free man.

Instead of retiring in 1957, I bought the business. I worked in it over fifteen years, and I commuted from Laguna Beach to Fortieth and Alameda every day.

People would say, "How can you do that, how can you do that?" But it became the best time of my day, because it was the only time of the day when I was alone. Not alone by myself, but alone with God. And that's when I did my yakkin' with my Pappa, so that was good. And after the fifteen years, I had all I had wanted and more.

Now what am I talking about? I'm talking about the only security there is. When you and I think that we are secure because we have a job, or because we have some dough in the bank, or this, or that or the other thing, don't you believe it. That became one of the greatest living lessons I have ever learned, because there's never been a day or an hour since then that I haven't known where my security is. It's my own relationship with my own God. And so one day at a time, one second at a time, the "isness" of the now is the only thing. It is not that we do not make appointments for next year. (If you saw my calendar, you'd know what I'm talkin' about.) It's not that we don't know what we're going to do tomorrow when we're in the business world, but rather it's that we do today's job today and tomorrow's job tomorrow, and we don't get them mixed up. Again and again and again I can stand up here and tell you gentlemen, "God is sufficient unto all of my needs," and He is—I'm telling the truth. But if I don't do something about it I starve to death. It's a true statement, but there's something for me to do. The gift of God was made at the foundation of the earth, not on my terms but on His. And His terms are that I act like His kid and go about His business. When I do that, I come into my inheritance. And it's that simple, it's that simple. It's my business to go about His business, and it's His business to take care of me.

EPILOGUE

Probably the most comfortable corner in Chuck C.'s active life—and where he could most easily be approached—was the big chair in his living room. Facing a large picture window, he found much pleasure and relaxation in the lovely Laguna Beach coastline far below.

It was especially appropriate, then, that he had just been seated in his chair on the morning of December 14, 1984 when his eyes closed and his gallant and indomitable spirit "moved into the next room."

His passing was mourned by tens of thousands throughout the world. In a real sense, however, he remains among us—the testament of his life will be honored whenever and wherever men and women gather together in that fellowship of the spirit known as Alcoholics Anonymous.

**IN LOVING MEMORY
OF
MILTON E. PICKMAN
1909-1993**

For the unselfish effort and labor
that he put in making
this book a reality.

Alcoholics Anonymous

The following section is from the 1955 Edition

ALCOHOLICS ANONYMOUS

ALCOHOLICS ANONYMOUS

The Story of

**How Many Thousands of Men and Women
Have Recovered from Alcoholism**

NEW AND REVISED EDITION

ALCOHOLICS ANONYMOUS WORLD SERVICES, INC.

New York City

1955

FOREWORD

The copyright of the original book "Alcoholics Anonymous" is registered in the U.S. Library of Congress as authored by William G. Wilson and published on April 10, 1937 by the Works Publishing Co. A Second Edition was published on June 20, 1955. A renewal of the 1937 copyright was never applied for and therefore is no longer in force.

As Chuck C. refers to this book so often in "A New Pair of Glasses" and credits it with his success on the AA program, we felt that it would be helpful to the readers of Chuck's book to have a handy copy of the main body of the original book.

All printings of the official "Alcoholics Anonymous" book contain personal stories of recovering alcoholics after the first 164 pages of the books. We feel that these stories are important to one who is in recovery and therefore the official book should be acquired and read. This volume is not meant to replace it.

A "New Pair of Glasses" was published because in the opinion of so many, his application of the information in the first 164 pages was so well demonstrated in his lifestyle that his opinions and life story would be valuable to others.

The Publisher
February, 1998

CONTENTS

APPENDICES

PREFACE

THIS is the second edition of the book "Alcoholics Anonymous," which made its first appearance in April 1939. More than 300,000 copies of the first edition are now in circulation.

Because this book has become the basic text for our Society and has helped such large numbers of alcoholic men and women to recovery, there exists a sentiment against any radical changes being made in it. Therefore the first portion of this volume, describing the A.A. recovery program, has been left largely untouched.

But the personal history section has been considerably revised and enlarged in order to present a more accurate representation of our membership as it is today. When the book was first printed, we had scarcely 100 members all told, and every one of them was an almost hopeless case of alcoholism. This has changed. A.A. now helps alcoholics in all stages of the disease. It reaches into every level of life and into nearly all occupations. Our membership now includes many young people. Women, who were at first very reluctant to approach A.A., have come forward in large numbers. Therefore the range of the story section has been broadened so that every alcoholic reader may find a reflection of him or herself in it.

As a souvenir of our past, the original Foreword has

been preserved and is followed by a second one describing Alcoholics Anonymous of 1955.

Following the Forewords, there appears a section called "The Doctor's Opinion." This also has been kept intact, just as it was originally written in 1939 by the late Dr. William D. Silkworth, our Society's great medical benefactor. Besides Dr. Silkworth's original statement, there have been added, in the Appendices, a number of the medical and religious endorsements which have come to us in recent years.

On the last pages of this second edition will be found the Twelve Traditions of Alcoholics Anonymous, the principles upon which our A.A. groups function, together with directions for getting in touch with A.A.

FOREWORD TO FIRST EDITION

This is the Foreword as it appeared in the first printing of the first edition in 1939

WE, OF Alcoholics Anonymous, are more than one hundred men and women who have recovered from a seemingly hopeless state of mind and body. To show other alcoholics *precisely how we have recovered* is the main purpose of this book. For them, we hope these pages will prove so convincing that no further authentication will be necessary. We think this account of our experiences will help everyone to better understand the alcoholic. Many do not comprehend that the alcoholic is a very sick person. And besides, we are sure that our way of living has its advantages for all.

It is important that we remain anonymous because we are too few, at present to handle the overwhelming number of personal appeals which may result from this publication. Being mostly business or professional folk, we could not well carry on our occupations in such an event. We would like it understood that our alcoholic work is an avocation.

When writing or speaking publicly about alcoholism, we urge each of our Fellowship to omit his personal name, designating himself instead as "a member of Alcoholics Anonymous."

Very earnestly we ask the press also, to observe this request, for otherwise we shall be greatly handicapped.

We are not an organization in the conventional

sense of the word. There are no fees or dues whatsoever. The only requirement for membership is an honest desire to stop drinking. We are not allied with any particular faith, sect or denomination, nor do we oppose anyone. We simply wish to be helpful to those who are afflicted.

We shall be interested to hear from those who are getting results from this book, particularly from those who have commenced work with other alcoholics. We should like to be helpful to such cases.

Inquiry by scientific, medical, and religious societies will be welcomed.

ALCOHOLICS ANONYMOUS.

FOREWORD TO SECOND EDITION

SINCE the original Foreword to this book was written in 1939, a wholesale miracle has taken place. Our earliest printing voiced the hope "that every alcoholic who journeys will find the Fellowship of Alcoholics Anonymous at his destination. Already," continues the early text, "twos and threes and fives of us have sprung up in other communities."

Sixteen years have elapsed between our first printing of this book and the presentation in 1955 of our second edition. In that brief space, Alcoholics Anonymous has mushroomed into nearly 6,000 groups whose membership is far above 150,000 recovered alcoholics.* Groups are to be found in each of the United States and all of the provinces of Canada. A.A. has flourishing communities in the British Isles, the Scandinavian countries, South Africa, South America, Mexico, Alaska, Australia and Hawaii. All told, promising beginnings have been made in some 50 foreign countries and U.S. possessions. Some are just now taking shape in Asia. Many of our friends encourage us by saying that this is but a beginning, only the augury of a much larger future ahead.

The spark that was to flare into the first A.A. group was struck at Akron, Ohio, in June 1935, during a talk between a New York stockbroker and an Akron physician. Six months earlier, the broker had been relieved of his drink obsession by a sudden spiritual

* As of 1966, there are over 12,000 groups in over 90 countries with an estimated membership of more than 350,000.

experience, following a meeting with an alcoholic friend who had been in contact with the Oxford Groups of that day. He had also been greatly helped by the late Dr. William D. Silkworth, a New York specialist in alcoholism who is now accounted no less than a medical saint by A.A. members, and whose story of the early days of our Society appears in the next pages. From this doctor, the broker had learned the grave nature of alcoholism. Though he could not accept all the tenets of the Oxford Groups, he was convinced of the need for moral inventory, confession of personality defects, restitution to those harmed, helpfulness to others, and the necessity of belief in and dependence upon God.

Prior to his journey to Akron, the broker had worked hard with many alcoholics on the theory that only an alcoholic could help an alcoholic, but he had succeeded only in keeping sober himself. The broker had gone to Akron on a business venture which had collapsed, leaving him greatly in fear that he might start drinking again. He suddenly realized that in order to save himself he must carry his message to another alcoholic. That alcoholic turned out to be the Akron physician.

This physician had repeatedly tried spiritual means to resolve his alcoholic dilemma but had failed. But when the broker gave him Dr. Silkworth's description of alcoholism and its hopelessness, the physician began to pursue the spiritual remedy for his malady with a willingness he had never before been able to muster. He sobered, never to drink again up to the moment of his death in 1950. This seemed to prove that one alcoholic could affect another as no nonalcoholic could. It also indicated that strenuous work, one alcoholic with another, was vital to permanent recovery.

Hence the two men set to work almost frantically upon alcoholics arriving in the ward of the Akron City Hospital. Their very first case, a desperate one, recovered immediately and became A.A. number three. He never had another drink. This work at Akron continued through the summer of 1935. There were many failures, but there was an occasional heartening success. When the broker returned to New York in the fall of 1935, the first A.A. group had actually been formed, though no one realized it at the time.

A second small group promptly took shape at New York, to be followed in 1937 with the start of a third at Cleveland. Besides these, there were scattered alcoholics who had picked up the basic ideas in Akron or New York who were trying to form groups in other cities. By late 1937, the number of members having substantial sobriety time behind them was sufficient to convince the membership that a new light had entered the dark world of the alcoholic.

It was now time, the struggling groups thought, to place their message and unique experience before the world. This determination bore fruit in the spring of 1939 by the publication of this volume. The membership had then reached about 100 men and women. The fledgling society, which had been nameless, now began to be called Alcoholics Anonymous, from the title of its own book. The flying-blind period ended and A.A. entered a new phase of its pioneering time.

With the appearance of the new book a great deal began to happen. Dr. Harry Emerson Fosdick, the noted clergyman reviewed it with approval. In the fall of 1939 Fulton Oursler, then editor of "Liberty," printed a piece in his magazine, called "Alcoholics and God." This brought a rush of 800 frantic inquiries into the little New York office which meanwhile had been established. Each inquiry was painstakingly answered; pamphlets and books were sent out. Businessmen, traveling out of existing groups, were referred to these prospective newcomers. New groups started up and it was found, to the astonishment of everyone, that A.A.'s message could be transmitted in the mail as well as by word of mouth. By the end of 1939 it was estimated that 800 alcoholics were on their way to recovery.

In the spring of 1940, John D. Rockefeller, Jr. gave a dinner for many of his friends to which he invited A.A. members to tell their stories. News of this got on the world wires; inquiries poured in again and many people went to the bookstores to get the book, "Alcoholics Anonymous." By March 1941 the membership had shot up to 2,000. Then Jack Alexander wrote a feature article in the "Saturday Evening Post" and placed such a compelling picture of A.A. before the general public that alcoholics in need of help really deluged us. By the close of 1941, A.A. numbered 8,000 members. The mushrooming process was in full swing. A.A. had become a national institution.

Our Society then entered a fearsome and exciting adolescent period. The test that it faced was this: Could these large numbers of erstwhile erratic alcoholics successfully meet and work together? Would there be quarrels over membership, leadership and money? Would there be strivings for power and prestige? Would there be schisms which would split A.A. apart? Soon A.A. was beset by these very problems on every side and in every group. But out of this frightening and at first disrupting experience the conviction grew that A.A.'s had to hang together or die separately. We had to unify our Fellowship or pass off the scene.

As we discovered the principles by which the individual alcoholic could live, so we had to evolve principles by which the A.A. groups and A.A. as a whole could survive and function effectively. It was thought that no alcoholic man or woman could be excluded from our Society; that our leaders might serve but never govern; that each group was to be autonomous and there was to be no professional class of therapy. There were to be no fees or dues; our expenses were to be met by our own voluntary contributions. There was to be the least possible organization, even in our service centers. Our public relations were to be based upon attraction rather than promotion. It was decided that all members ought to be anonymous at the level of press, radio, TV and films. And in no circumstances should we give endorsements, make alliances, or enter public controversies.

This was the substance of A.A.'s Twelve Traditions, which are stated in full on page 564 of this book. Though none of these principles had the force of rules or laws, they had become so widely accepted by 1950 that they were confirmed by our first International Conference held at Cleveland. Today the remarkable unity of A.A. is one of the greatest assets that our Society has.

While the internal difficulties of our adolescent

period were being ironed out, public acceptance of A.A. grew by leaps and bounds. For this there were two principal reasons: the large numbers of recoveries, and reunited homes. These made their impressions everywhere. Of alcoholics who came to A.A. and really tried, 50% got sober at once and remained that way; 25% sobered up after some relapses, and among the remainder, those who stayed on with A.A. showed improvement. Other thousands came to a few A.A. meetings and at first decided they didn't want the program. But great numbers of these—about two out of three—began to return as time passed.

Another reason for the wide acceptance of A.A. was the ministration of friends—friends in medicine, religion, and the press, together with innumerable others who became our able and persistent advocates. Without such support, A.A. could have made only the slowest progress. Some of the recommendations of A.A.'s early medical and religious friends will be found further on in this book.

Alcoholics Anonymous is not a religious organization. Neither does A.A. take any particular medical point of view, though we cooperate widely with the men of medicine as well as with the men of religion.

Alcohol being no respecter of persons, we are an accurate cross section of America and, in distant lands, the same democratic evening up process is now going on. By personal religious affiliation, we include Catholics, Protestants, Jews, Hindus, and a sprinkling of Moslems and Buddhists. More than fifteen percent of us are women.

At present, our membership is increasing at the rate of about seven percent a year. So far, upon the total problem of several million actual and potential alcoholics in the world, we have made only a scratch. In all probability, we shall never be able to touch more than a fair fraction of the alcohol problem in all its ramifications. Upon therapy for the alcoholic himself, we surely have no monopoly. Yet it is our great hope that all those who have as yet found no answer may begin to find one in the pages of this book and will presently join us on the high road to a new freedom.

THE DOCTOR'S OPINION

WE OF Alcoholics Anonymous believe that the reader will be interested in the medical estimate of the plan of recovery described in this book. Convincing testimony must surely come from medical men who have had experience with the sufferings of our members and have witnessed our return to health. A well-known doctor, chief physician at a nationally prominent hospital specializing in alcoholic and drug addiction, gave Alcoholics Anonymous this letter:

To Whom It May Concern:

I have specialized in the treatment of alcoholism for many years.

In late 1934 I attended a patient, who, though he had been a competent businessman of good earning capacity, was an alcoholic of a type I had come to regard as hopeless.

In the course of his third treatment he acquired certain ideas concerning a possible means of recovery. As part of his rehabilitation, he commenced to present his conceptions to other alcoholics, impressing upon them that they must do likewise with still others. This has become the basis of a rapidly growing fellowship of these men and their families. This man and over one hundred others appear to have recovered.

I personally know scores of cases who were of the type with whom other methods had failed completely.

These facts appear to be of extreme medical importance; because of the extraordinary possibilities of rapid growth inherent in this group they may mark a new epoch in the annals of alcoholism. These men may well have a remedy for thousands of such situations.

You may rely absolutely on anything they say about themselves.

Very truly yours,
William D. Silkworth, M.D.

The physician who, at our request, gave us this letter, has been kind enough to enlarge upon his views in another statement which follows. In this statement he confirms what we who have suffered alcoholic torture must believe—that the body of the alcoholic is quite as abnormal as his mind. It did not satisfy us to be told that we could not control our drinking just because we were maladjusted to life, that we were in full flight from reality, or were outright mental defectives. These things were true to some extent, in fact, to a considerable extent with some of us. But we are sure that our bodies were sickened as well. In our belief, any picture of the alcoholic which leaves out this physical factor is incomplete.

The doctor's theory that we have an allergy to alcohol interests us. As laymen, our opinion as to its soundness may, of course, mean little. But as ex-problem drinkers, we can say that his explanation makes good sense. It explains many things for which we cannot otherwise account.

Though we work out our solution on the spiritual as well as an altruistic plane, we favor hospitalization for the alcoholic who is very jittery or befogged. More often than not, it is imperative that a man's brain be cleared before he is approached, as he has then a better chance of understanding and accepting what we have to offer.

The doctor writes:

The subject presented in this book seems to me to be of paramount importance to those afflicted with alcoholic addiction.

I say this after many years' experience as Medical Director of one of the oldest hospitals in the country treating alcoholic and drug addiction.

There was, therefore, a sense of real satisfaction when I was asked to contribute a few words on a subject which is covered in such masterly detail in these pages.

We doctors have realized for a long time that some form of moral psychology was of urgent importance to alcoholics, but its application presented difficulties beyond our conception. What with our ultra-modern standards, our scientific approach to everything, we are perhaps not well equipped to apply the powers of good that lie outside our synthetic knowledge.

Many years ago one of the leading contributors to this book came under our care in this hospital and while here he acquired some ideas which he put into practical application at once.

Later, he requested the privilege of being allowed to tell his story to other patients here and with some misgiving, we consented. The cases we have followed through have been most interesting; in fact, many of them are amazing. The unselfishness of these men as we have come to know them, the entire absence of profit motive, and their community spirit, is indeed inspiring to one who has labored long and wearily in this alcoholic field. They believe in themselves, and still more in the Power which pulls chronic alcoholics back from the gates of death.

Of course an alcoholic ought to be freed from his physical craving for liquor, and this often requires a definite hospital procedure, before psychological measures can be of maximum benefit.

We believe, and so suggested a few years ago, that the action of alcohol on these chronic alcoholics is a manifestation of an allergy; that the phenomenon of craving is limited to this class and never occurs in the average temperate drinker. These allergic types can never safely use alcohol in any form at all; and once having formed the habit and found they cannot break it, once having lost their self-confidence, their reliance upon things human, their problems pile up on them and become astonishingly difficult to solve.

Frothy emotional appeal seldom suffices. The message which can interest and hold these alcoholic people must have depth and weight. In nearly all cases, their ideals must be grounded in a power greater than themselves, if they are to re-create their lives.

If any feel that as psychiatrists directing a hospital for alcoholics we appear somewhat sentimental, let them stand with us a while on the firing line, see the tragedies, the despairing wives, the little children; let the solving of these problems become a part of their daily work, and even of their sleeping moments, and the most cynical will not wonder that we have accepted and encouraged this movement. We feel, after many years of experience, that we have found nothing which has contributed more to the rehabilitation of these men than the altruistic movement now growing up among them.

Men and women drink essentially because they like the effect produced by alcohol. The sensation is so elusive that, while they admit it is injurious, they cannot after a time differentiate the true from the false. To them, their alcoholic life seems the only normal one. They are restless, irritable and discontented, unless they can again experience the sense of ease and comfort which comes at once by taking a few drinks—drinks which they see others taking with impunity. After they have succumbed to the desire again, as so many do, and the phenomenon of craving develops, they pass through the well-known stages of a spree, emerging remorseful, with a firm resolution not to drink again. This is repeated over and over, and unless this person can experience an entire psychic change there is very little hope of his recovery.

On the other hand—and strange as this may seem to those who do not understand—once a psychic change has occurred, the very same person who seemed doomed, who had so many problems he despaired of ever solving them, suddenly finds himself easily able to control his desire for alcohol, the only effort necessary being that required to follow a few simple rules.

Men have cried out to me in sincere and despairing appeal: "Doctor, I cannot go on like this! I have everything to live for! I must stop, but I cannot! You must help me!"

Faced with this problem, if a doctor is honest with himself, he must sometimes feel his own inadequacy. Although he gives all that is in him, it often is not enough. One feels that something more than human power is needed to produce the essential psychic change. Though the aggregate of recoveries resulting from psychiatric effort is considerable, we physicians must admit we have made little impression upon the problem as a whole. Many types do not respond to the ordinary psychological approach.

I do not hold with those who believe that alcoholism is entirely a problem of mental control. I have had many men who had, for example, worked a period of months on some problem or business deal which was to be settled on a certain date, favorably to them. They took a drink a day or so prior to the date, and then the phenomenon of craving at once became paramount to all other interests so that the important appointment was not met. These men were not drinking to escape; they were drinking to overcome a craving beyond their mental control.

There are many situations which arise out of the phenomenon of craving which cause men to make the supreme sacrifice rather than continue to fight.

The classification of alcoholics seems most difficult, and in much detail is outside the scope of this book. There are, of course, the psychopaths who are emotionally unstable. We are all familiar with this type. They are always "going on the wagon for keeps." They are over-remorseful and make many resolutions, but never a decision.

There is the type of man who is unwilling to admit that he cannot take a drink. He plans various ways of drinking. He changes his brand or his environment. There is the type who always believes that after being entirely free from alcohol for a period of time he can take a drink without danger. There is the manic-depressive type, who is, perhaps, the least understood by his friends, and about whom a whole chapter could be written.

Then there are types entirely normal in every respect except in the effect alcohol has upon them. They are often able, intelligent, friendly people.

All these, and many others, have one symptom in common: they cannot start drinking without developing the phenomenon of craving. This phenomenon, as we have suggested, may be the manifestation of an allergy which differentiates these people, and sets them apart as a distinct entity. It has never been, by any treatment with which we are familiar, permanently eradicated. The only relief we have to suggest is entire abstinence.

This immediately precipitates us into a seething caldron of debate. Much has been written pro and con, but among physicians, the general opinion seems to be that most chronic alcoholics are doomed.

What is the solution? Perhaps I can best answer this by relating one of my experiences.

About one year prior to this experience a man was brought in to be treated for chronic alcoholism. He had but partially recovered from a gastric hemorrhage and seemed to be a case of pathological mental deterioration. He had lost everything worthwhile in life and was only living, one might say, to drink. He frankly admitted and believed that for him there was no hope. Following the elimination of alcohol, there was found to be no permanent brain injury. He accepted the plan outlined in this book. One year later he called to see me, and I experienced a very strange sensation. I knew the man by name, and partly recognized his features, but there all resemblance ended. From a trembling, despairing, nervous wreck, had emerged a man brimming over with self-reliance and contentment. I talked with him for some time, but was not able to bring myself to feel that I had known him before. To me he was a stranger, and so he left me. A long time has passed with no return to alcohol.

When I need a mental uplift, I often think of another case brought in by a physician prominent in New York. The patient had made his own diagnosis, and deciding his situation hopeless, had hidden in a deserted barn determined to die. He was rescued by a searching party, and, in desperate condition, brought to me. Following his physical rehabilitation, he had a talk with me in which he frankly stated he thought the treatment a waste of effort, unless I could assure him, which no one ever had, that in the future he would have the "will power" to resist the impulse to drink.

His alcoholic problem was so complex, and his depression so great, that we felt his only hope would be through what we then called "moral psychology," and we doubted if even that would have any effect.

However, he did become "sold" on the ideas contained in this book. He has not had a drink for great many years. I see him now and then and he is as fine a specimen of manhood as one could wish to meet.

I earnestly advise every alcoholic to read this book through, and though perhaps he came to scoff, he may remain to pray.

William D. Silkworth, MD.

Chapter 1
BILL'S STORY

WAR FEVER ran high in the New England town to which we new, young officers from Plattsburg were assigned, and we were flattered when the first citizens took us to their homes, making us feel heroic. Here was love, applause, war; moments sublime with intervals hilarious. I was part of life at last, and in the midst of the excitement I discovered liquor. I forgot the strong warnings and the prejudices of my people concerning drink. In time we sailed for "Over There." I was very lonely and again turned to alcohol.

We landed in England. I visited Winchester Cathedral. Much moved, I wandered outside. My attention was caught by a doggerel on an old tombstone:

> "Here lies a Hampshire Grenadier
> Who caught his death
> Drinking cold small beer.
> A good soldier is ne'er forgot
> Whether he dieth by musket
> Or by pot."

Ominous warning—which I failed to heed.

Twenty-two, and a veteran of foreign wars, I went home at last. I fancied myself a leader, for had not the men of my battery given me a special token of appreciation? My talent for leadership, I imagined, would place me at the head of vast enterprises which I would manage with the utmost assurance.

I took a night law course, and obtained employment as investigator for a surety company. The drive for success was on. I'd prove to the world I was important. My work took me about Wall Street and little by little I became interested in the market.   Many people lost money—but some became very rich. Why not I?   I studied economics and business as well as law. Potential alcoholic that I was, I nearly failed my law course. At one of the finals I was too drunk to think or write. Though my drinking was not yet continuous, it disturbed my wife. We had long talks when I would still her forebodings by telling her that men of genius conceived their best projects when drunk; that the most majestic constructions of philosophic thought were so derived.

By the time I had completed the course, I knew the law was not for me. The inviting maelstrom of Wall Street had me in its grip. Business and financial leaders were my heroes.   Out of this alloy of drink and speculation, I commenced to forge the weapon that one day would turn in its flight like a boomerang and all but cut me to ribbons. Living modestly, my wife and I saved $1,000. It went into certain securities, then cheap and rather unpopular. I rightly imagined that they would some day have a great rise. I failed to persuade my broker friends to send me out looking over factories and managements, but my wife and I decided to go anyway. I had developed a theory that most people lost money in stocks through ignorance of markets.   I discovered many more reasons later on.

We gave up our positions and off we roared on a motorcycle, the sidecar stuffed with tent, blankets, a change of clothes, and three huge volumes of a financial reference service. Our friends thought a lunacy commission should be appointed. Perhaps they were right. I had had some success at speculation, so we had a little money, but we once worked on a farm for a month to avoid drawing on our small capital. That was the last honest manual labor on my part for many a day. We covered the whole eastern United States in a year. At the end of it, my reports to Wall Street procured me a position there and the use of a large expense account. The exercise of an option brought in more money, leaving us with a profit of several thousand dollars for that year.

For the next few years fortune threw money and applause my way. I had arrived. My judgment and ideas were followed by many to the tune of paper millions. The great boom of the late twenties was seething and swelling. Drink was taking an important and exhilarating part in my life. There was loud talk in the jazz places uptown. Everyone spent in thousands and chattered in millions. Scoffers could scoff and be damned. I made a host of fair-weather friends.

My drinking assumed more serious proportions, continuing all day and almost every night. The remonstrances of my friends terminated in a row and I became a lone wolf. There were many unhappy scenes in our sumptuous apartment. There had been no real infidelity, for loyalty to my wife, helped at times by extreme drunkenness, kept me out of those scrapes.

In 1929 I contracted golf fever. We went at once to the country, my wife to applaud while I started out to overtake Walter Hagen. Liquor caught up with me much faster than I came up behind Walter. I began to be jittery in the morning. Golf permitted drinking everyday and every night. It was fun to carom around the exclusive course which had inspired such awe in me as a lad. I acquired the impeccable coat of tan one sees upon the well-to-do. The local banker watched me whirl fat checks in and out of his till with amused skepticism.

Abruptly in October 1929 hell broke loose on the New York stock exchange. After one of those days of inferno, I wobbled from a hotel bar to a brokerage office. It was eight o'clock—five hours after the market closed. The ticker still clattered. I was staring at an inch of the tape which bore the inscription XYZ-32. It had been 52 that morning. I was finished and so were many friends. The papers reported men jumping to death from the towers of High Finance. That disgusted me. I would not jump. I went back to the bar. My friends had dropped several million since ten o'clock—so what? Tomorrow was another day. As I drank, the old fierce determination to win came back.

Next morning I telephoned a friend in Montreal. He had plenty of money left and thought I had better go to Canada. By the following spring we were living in our accustomed style. I felt like Napoleon returning from Elba. No St. Helena for me! But drinking caught up with me again and my generous friend had to let me go. This time we stayed broke.

We went to live with my wife's parents. I found a job; then lost it as the result of a brawl with a taxi driver. Mercifully, no one could guess that I was to have no real employment for five years, or hardly draw a sober breath. My wife began to work in a department store, coming home exhausted to find me drunk.

I became an unwelcome hanger-on at brokerage places.

Liquor ceased to be a luxury; it became a necessity. "Bathtub" gin, two bottles a day, and often three, got to be routine. Sometimes a small deal would net a few hundred dollars, and I would pay my bills at the bars and delicatessens. This went on endlessly, and I began to waken very early in the morning shaking violently. A tumbler full of gin followed by half a dozen bottles of beer would be required if I were to eat any breakfast. Nevertheless, I still thought I could control the situation, and there were periods of sobriety which renewed my wife's hope.

Gradually things got worse. The house was taken over by the mortgage holder, my mother-in-law died, my wife and father-in-law became ill.

Then I got a promising business opportunity. Stocks were at the low point of 1932, and I had somehow formed a group to buy. I was to share generously in the profits. Then I went on a prodigious bender, and that chance vanished.

I woke up. This had to be stopped. I saw I could not take so much as one drink. I was through forever. Before then, I had written lots of sweet promises, but my wife happily observed that this time I meant business. And so I did.

Shortly afterward I came home drunk. There had been no fight. Where had been my high resolve? I simply didn't know. It hadn't even come to mind. Someone had pushed a drink my way, and I had taken it. Was I crazy? I began to wonder, for such an appalling lack of perspective seemed near being just that.

Renewing my resolve, I tried again. Some time

passed and confidence began to be replaced by cocksureness. I could laugh at the gin mills. Now I had what it takes! One day I walked into a cafe to telephone. In no time I was beating on the bar asking myself how it happened. As the whisky rose to my head I told myself I would manage better next time, but I might as well get good and drunk then. And I did.

The remorse, horror and hopelessness of the next morning are unforgettable. The courage to do battle was not there. My brain raced uncontrollably and there was a terrible sense of impending calamity. I hardly dared cross the street, lest I collapse and be run down by an early morning truck, for it was scarcely daylight. An all night place supplied me with a dozen glasses of ale. My writhing nerves were stilled at last. A morning paper told me the market had gone to hell again. Well, so had I. The market would recover, but I wouldn't. That was a hard thought. Should I kill myself? No—not now. Then a mental fog settled down. Gin would fix that. So two bottles, and— oblivion.

The mind and body are marvelous mechanisms, for mine endured this agony two more years. Sometimes I stole from my wife's slender purse when the morning terror and madness were on me. Again I swayed dizzily before an open window, or the medicine cabinet where there was poison, cursing myself for a weakling. There were flights from city to country and back, as my wife and I sought escape. Then came the night when the physical and mental torture was so hellish I feared I would burst through my window, sash and all. Somehow I managed to drag my mattress to a lower floor, lest I suddenly leap. A doctor came with a heavy sedative. Next day found me drinking both gin and sedative. This combination soon landed me on the rocks. People feared for my sanity. So did I. I could eat little or nothing when drinking, and I was forty pounds under weight.

My brother-in-law is a physician, and through his kindness and that of my mother I was placed in a nationally-known hospital for the mental and physical rehabilitation of alcoholics. Under the so-called belladonna treatment my brain cleared. Hydrotherapy and mild exercise helped much. Best of all, I met a kind doctor who explained that though certainly selfish and foolish, I had been seriously ill, bodily and mentally.

It relieved me somewhat to learn that in alcoholics the will is amazingly weakened when it comes to combating liquor, though it often remains strong in other respects. My incredible behavior in the face of a desperate desire to stop was explained. Understanding myself now, I fared forth in high hope. For three or four months the goose hung high. I went to town regularly and even made a little money. Surely this was the answer—self–knowledge.

But it was not, for the frightful day came when I drank once more. The curve of my declining moral and bodily health fell off like a ski-jump. After a time I returned to the hospital. This was the finish, the curtain, it seemed to me. My weary and despairing wife was informed that it would all end with heart failure during delirium tremens, or I would develop a wet brain, perhaps within a year. She would soon have to give me over to the undertaker or the asylum.

They did not need to tell me. I knew, and almost welcomed the idea. It was a devastating blow to my pride. I, who had thought so well of myself and my abilities, of my capacity to surmount obstacles, was cornered at last. Now I was to plunge into the dark, joining that endless procession of sots who had gone on before. I thought of my poor wife. There had been much happiness after all. What would I not give to make amends. But that was over now.

No words can tell of the loneliness and despair I found in that bitter morass of self-pity. Quicksand stretched around me in all directions. I had met my match. I had been overwhelmed. Alcohol was my master.

Trembling, I stepped from the hospital a broken man. Fear sobered me for a bit. Then came the insidious insanity of that first drink, and on Armistice Day 1934, I was off again. Everyone became resigned to the certainty that I would have to be shut up somewhere, or would stumble along to a miserable end. How dark it is before the dawn! In reality that was the beginning of my last debauch. I was soon to be catapulted into what I like to call the fourth dimension of existence. I was to know happiness, peace, and usefulness, in a way of life that is incredibly more wonderful as time passes.

Near the end of that bleak November, I sat drinking in my kitchen. With a certain satisfaction I reflected there was enough gin concealed about the house to carry me through that night and the next day. My wife was at work. I wondered whether I dared hide a full bottle of gin near the head of our bed. I would need it before daylight.

My musing was interrupted by the telephone. The cheery voice of an old school friend asked if he might come over. *He was sober.* It was years since I could remember his coming to New York in that condition. I was amazed. Rumor had it that he had been committed for alcoholic insanity. I wondered how he had escaped. Of course he would have dinner, and then I could drink openly with him. Unmindful of his welfare, I thought only of recapturing the spirit of other days. There was that time we had chartered an airplane to complete a jag! His coming was an oasis in this dreary desert of futility. The very thing—an oasis! Drinkers are like that.

The door opened and he stood there, fresh-skinned and glowing. There was something about his eyes. He was inexplicably different. What had happened?

I pushed a drink across the table. He refused it. Disappointed but curious, I wondered what had got into the fellow. He wasn't himself.

"Come, what's all this about?" I queried.

He looked straight at me. Simply, but smilingly, he said, "I've got religion."

I was aghast. So that was it—last summer an alcoholic crackpot; now, I suspected, a little cracked about religion. He had that starry-eyed look. Yes, the old boy was on fire all right. But bless his heart, let him rant! Besides, my gin would last longer than his preaching.

But he did no ranting. In a matter of fact way he told how two men had appeared in court, persuading the judge to suspend his commitment. They had told of a simple religious idea and a practical program of action. That was two months ago and the result was self-evident. It worked!

He had come to pass his experience along to me—if

I cared to have it. I was shocked, but interested. Certainly I was interested. I had to be, for I was hopeless.

He talked for hours. Childhood memories rose before me. I could almost hear the sound of the preacher's voice as I sat, on still Sundays, way over there on the hillside; there was that proffered temperance pledge I never signed; my grandfather's good natured contempt of some church folk and their doings; his insistence that the spheres really had their music; but his denial of the preacher's right to tell him how he must listen; his fearlessness as he spoke of these things just before he died; these recollections welled up from the past. They made me swallow hard.

That war-time day in old Winchester Cathedral came back again.

I had always believed in a Power greater than myself. I had often pondered these things. I was not an atheist. Few people really are, for that means blind faith in the strange proposition that this universe originated in a cipher and aimlessly rushes nowhere. My intellectual heroes, the chemists, the astronomers, even the evolutionists, suggested vast laws and forces at work. Despite contrary indications, I had little doubt that a mighty purpose and rhythm underlay all. How could there be so much of precise and immutable law, and no intelligence? I simply had to believe in a Spirit of the Universe, who knew neither time nor limitation. But that was as far as I had gone.

With ministers, and the world's religions, I parted right there. When they talked of a God personal to me, who was love, superhuman strength and direction, I became irritated and my mind snapped shut against such a theory.

To Christ I conceded the certainty of a great man, not too closely followed by those who claimed Him. His moral teaching—most excellent. For myself, I had adopted those parts which seemed convenient and not too difficult; the rest I disregarded.

The wars which had been fought, the burnings and chicanery that religious dispute had facilitated, made me sick. I honestly doubted whether, on balance, the religions of mankind had done any good. Judging from what I had seen in Europe and since, the power of God in human affairs was negligible, the Brotherhood of Man a grim jest. If there was a Devil, he seemed the Boss Universal, and he certainly had me.

But my friend sat before me, and he made the pointblank declaration that God had done for him what he could not do for himself. His human will had failed. Doctors had pronounced him incurable. Society was about to lock him up. Like myself, he had admitted complete defeat. Then he had, in effect, been raised from the dead, suddenly taken from the scrap heap to a level of life better than the best he had ever known!

Had this power originated in him? Obviously it had not. There had been no more power in him than there was in me at that minute; and this was none at all.

That floored me. It began to look as though religious people were right after all. Here was something at work in a human heart which had done the impossible. My ideas about miracles were drastically revised right then. Never mind the musty past; here sat a miracle directly across the kitchen table. He shouted great tidings.

I saw that my friend was much more than inwardly

reorganized. He was on a different footing. His roots grasped a new soil.

Despite the living example of my friend there remained in me the vestiges of my old prejudice. The word God still aroused a certain antipathy. When the thought was expressed that there might be a God personal to me this feeling was intensified. I didn't like the idea. I could go for such conceptions as Creative Intelligence, Universal Mind or Spirit of Nature but I resisted the thought of a Czar of the Heavens, however loving His sway might be. I have since talked with scores of men who felt the same way.

My friend suggested what then seemed a novel idea. He said, *"Why don't you choose your own conception of God?"*

That statement hit me hard. It melted the icy intellectual mountain in whose shadow I had lived and shivered many years. I stood in the sunlight at last.

It was only a matter of being willing to believe in a Power greater that myself. Nothing more was required of me to make my beginning. I saw that growth could start from that point. Upon a foundation of complete willingness I might build what I saw in my friend. Would I have it? Of course I would!

Thus was I convinced that God is concerned with us humans when we want Him enough. At long last I saw, I felt, I believed. Scales of pride and prejudice fell from my eyes. A new world came into view.

The real significance of my experience in the Cathedral burst upon me. For a brief moment, I had needed and wanted God. There had been a humble willingness to have Him with me—and He came. But soon the sense of His presence had been blotted out by worldly clamors, mostly those within myself. And so it had been ever since. How blind I had been.

At the hospital I was separated from alcohol for the last time. Treatment seemed wise, for I showed signs of delirium tremens.

There I humbly offered myself to God, as I then understood Him, to do with me as He would. I placed myself unreservedly under His care and direction. I admitted for the first time that of myself I was nothing; that without Him I was lost. I ruthlessly faced my sins and became willing to have my new-found Friend take them away, root and branch. I have not had a drink since.

My schoolmate visited me, and I fully acquainted him with my problems and deficiencies. We made a list of people I had hurt or toward whom I felt resentment. I expressed my entire willingness to approach these individuals, admitting my wrong. Never was I to be critical of them. I was to right all such matters to the utmost of my ability.

I was to test my thinking by the new God-consciousness within. Common sense would thus become uncommon sense. I was to sit quietly when in doubt, asking only for direction and strength to meet my problems as He would have me. Never was I to pray for myself, except as my requests bore on my usefulness to others. Then only might I expect to receive. But that would be in great measure.

My friend promised when these things were done I would enter upon a new relationship with my Creator; that I would have the elements of a way of living which answered all my problems. Belief in the power of God, plus enough willingness, honesty and humility to establish and maintain the new order of things, were the essential requirements.

Simple, but not easy; a price had to be paid. It meant destruction of self-centeredness. I must turn in all things to the Father of Light who presides over us all.

These were revolutionary and drastic proposals, but the moment I fully accepted them, the effect was electric. There was a sense of victory, followed by such a peace and serenity as I had never known. There was utter confidence. I felt lifted up, as though the great clean wind of a mountain top blew through and through. God comes to most men gradually, but His impact on me was sudden and profound.

For a moment I was alarmed, and called my friend, the doctor, to ask if I were still sane. He listened in wonder as I talked.

Finally he shook his head saying, "Something has happened to you I don't understand. But you had better hang on to it. Anything is better than the way you were." The good doctor now sees many men who have such experiences. He knows that they are real.

While I lay in the hospital the thought came that there were thousands of hopeless alcoholics who might be glad to have what had been so freely given me. Perhaps I could help some of them. They in turn might work with others.

My friend had emphasized the absolute necessity of demonstrating these principles in all my affairs. Particularly was it imperative to work with others as he had worked with me. Faith without works was dead, he said. And how appallingly true for the alcoholic! For if an alcoholic failed to perfect and enlarge his spiritual life through work and self-sacrifice for others, he could not survive the certain trials and low spots ahead. If he did not work, he would surely drink again, and if he drank, he would surely die. Then faith would be dead indeed. With us it is just like that.

My wife and I abandoned ourselves with enthusiasm to the idea of helping other alcoholics to a solution of their problems. It was fortunate, for my old business associates remained skeptical for a year and a half, during which I found little work. I was not too well at the time, and was plagued by waves of self-pity and resentment. This sometimes nearly drove me back to drink, but I soon found that when all other measures failed, work with another alcoholic would save the day. Many times I have gone to my old hospital in despair. On talking to a man there, I would be amazingly lifted up and set on my feet. It is a design for living that works in rough going.

We commenced to make many fast friends and a fellowship has grown up among us of which it is a wonderful thing to feel a part. The joy of living we really have, even under pressure and difficulty. I have seen hundreds of families set their feet in the path that really goes somewhere; have seen the most impossible domestic situations righted; feuds and bitterness of all sorts wiped out. I have seen men come out of asylums and resume a vital place in the lives of their families and communities. Business and professional men have regained their standing. There is scarcely any form of trouble and misery which has not been overcome among us. In one western city and its environs there are one thousand of us and our families. We meet frequently so that newcomers may find the fellowship

15

they seek. At these informal gatherings one may often see from 50 to 200 persons. We are growing in numbers and power.*

An alcoholic in his cups is an unlovely creature. Our struggles with them are variously strenuous, comic, and tragic. One poor chap committed suicide in my home. He could not, or would not, see our way of life.

There is, however, a vast amount of fun about it all. I suppose some would be shocked at our seeming worldliness and levity. But just underneath there is deadly earnestness. Faith has to work twenty-four hours a day in and through us, or we perish.

Most of us feel we need look no further for Utopia. We have it with us right here and now. Each day my friend's simple talk in our kitchen multiplies itself in a widening circle of peace on earth and good will to men.

* A.A. is now composed of some 12,000 groups (1966).

Chapter 2

THERE IS A SOLUTION

W E, OF **ALCOHOLICS ANONYMOUS,** know thousands of men and women who were once just as hopeless as Bill. Nearly all have recovered. They have solved the drink problem.

We are average Americans. All sections of this country and many of its occupations are represented, as well as many political, economic, social, and religious backgrounds. We are people who normally would not mix. But there exists among us a fellowship, a friendliness, and an understanding which is indescribably wonderful. We are like the passengers of a great liner the moment after rescue from shipwreck when camaraderie, joyousness and democracy pervade the vessel from steerage to Captain's table. Unlike the feelings of the ship's passengers, however, our joy in escape from disaster does not subside as we go our individual ways. The feeling of having shared in a common peril is one element in the powerful cement which binds us. But that in itself would never have held us together as we are now joined.

The tremendous fact for every one of us is that we have discovered a common solution. We have a way out on which we can absolutely agree, and upon which we can join in brotherly and harmonious action. This is the great news this book carries to those who suffer from alcoholism.

An illness of this sort—and we have come to believe it an illness—involves those about us in a way no other human sickness can. If a person has cancer all are sorry for him and no one is angry or hurt. But not so with the alcoholic illness, for with it there goes annihilation of all the things worth while in life. It engulfs all whose lives touch the sufferer's. It brings misunderstanding, fierce resentment, financial insecurity, disgusted friends and employers, warped lives of blameless children, sad wives and parents—anyone can increase the list.

We hope this volume will inform and comfort those who are, or who may be affected. There are many.

Highly competent psychiatrists who have dealt with us have found it sometimes impossible to persuade an alcoholic to discuss his situation without reserve. Strangely enough, wives, parents and intimate friends usually find us even more unapproachable than do the psychiatrist and the doctor.

But the ex-problem drinker who has found this solution, who is properly armed with facts about himself, can generally win the entire confidence of another alcoholic in a few hours. Until such an understanding is reached, little or nothing can be accomplished.

That the man who is making the approach has had the same difficulty, that he obviously knows what he is talking about, that his whole deportment shouts at the new prospect that he is a man with a real answer, that he has no attitude of Holier Than Thou, nothing whatever except the sincere desire to be helpful; that there are no fees to pay, no axes to grind, no people to please, no lectures to be endured—these are the conditions we have found most effective. After such an approach many take up their beds and walk again.

None of us makes a sole vocation of this work, nor do we think its effectiveness would be increased if we did. We feel that elimination of our drinking is but a beginning. A much more important demonstration of our principles lies before us in our respective homes, occupations and affairs. All of us spend much of our spare time in the sort of effort which we are going to describe. A few are fortunate enough to be so situated that they can give nearly all their time to the work.

If we keep on the way we are going there is little doubt that much good will result, but the surface of the problem would hardly be scratched. Those of us who live in large cities are overcome by the reflection that close by hundreds are dropping into oblivion every day. Many could recover if they had the opportunity we have enjoyed. How then shall we present that which has been so freely given us?

We have concluded to publish an anonymous volume setting forth the problem as we see it. We shall bring to the task our combined experience and knowledge. This should suggest a useful program for anyone concerned with a drinking problem.

Of necessity there will have to be discussion of matters medical, psychiatric, social, and religious. We are aware that these matters are, from their very nature, controversial. Nothing would please us so much as to write a book which would contain no basis for contention or argument. We shall do our utmost to achieve that ideal. Most of us sense that real tolerance of other people's shortcomings and viewpoints and a respect for their opinions are attitudes which make us more useful to others. Our very lives, as ex-problem drinkers, depend upon our constant thought of others and how we may help meet their needs.

You may already have asked yourself why it is that all of us became so very ill from drinking. Doubtless you are curious to discover how and why, in the face of expert opinion to the contrary, we have recovered from a hopeless condition of mind and body. If you are an alcoholic who wants to get over it, you may already be asking—"What do I have to do?"

It is the purpose of this book to answer such questions specifically. We shall tell you what we have done. Before going into a detailed discussion, it may be well to summarize some points as we see them.

How many times people have said to us: "I can take it or leave it alone. Why can't he?" "Why don't you drink like a gentleman or quit?" "That fellow can't handle his liquor." "Why don't you try beer and wine?" "Lay off the hard stuff." "His will power must be weak." "He could stop if he wanted to." "She's such a sweet girl, I should think he'd stop for her sake." "The doctor told him that if he ever drank again it would kill him, but there he is all lit up again."

Now these are commonplace observations on drinkers which we hear all the time. Back of them is a world if ignorance and misunderstanding. We see that these expressions refer to people whose reactions are very different from ours.

Moderate drinkers have little trouble in giving up liquor entirely if they have good reason for it. They can take it or leave it alone.

Then we have a certain type of hard drinker. He may have the habit badly enough to gradually impair him physically and mentally. It may cause him to die a few years before his time. If a sufficiently strong reason—ill health, falling in love, change of environment or the warning of a doctor—becomes operative, this man can also stop or moderate, although he may find it difficult and troublesome and may even need medical attention.

But what about the real alcoholic? He may start off as a moderate drinker; he may or may not become a continuous hard drinker; but at some stage of his drinking career he begins to lose all control of his liquor consumption, once he starts to drink.

Here is the fellow who has been puzzling you, especially in his lack of control. He does absurd, incredible, tragic things while drinking. He is a real Dr. Jekyll and Mr. Hyde. He is seldom mildly intoxicated. He is always more or less insanely drunk. His disposition while drinking resembles his normal nature but little. He may be one of the finest fellows in the world. Yet let him drink for a day, and he frequently becomes disgustingly, and even dangerously, anti-social. He has a positive genius for getting tight at exactly the wrong moment, particularly when some important decision must be made or engagement kept. He is often perfectly sensible and well balanced concerning everything except liquor, but in that respect he is incredibly dishonest and selfish. He often possesses special abilities, skills, and aptitudes, and has a promising career ahead of him. He uses his gifts to build up a bright outlook for his family and himself, and then pulls the structure down on his head by a senseless series of sprees. He is the fellow who goes to bed so intoxicated he ought to sleep the clock around. Yet early next morning he searches madly for the bottle he misplaced the night before. If he can afford it, he may have liquor concealed all over his house to be certain no one gets his entire supply away from him to throw down the wastepipe. As matters grow worse, he begins to use a combination of high-powered sedative and liquor to quiet his nerves so he can go to work. Then comes the day when he simply cannot make it and gets drunk all over again. Perhaps he goes to a doctor who gives him morphine or some sedative with which to taper off. Then he begins to appear at hospitals and sanitariums.

This is by no means a comprehensive picture of the true alcoholic, as our behavior patterns vary. But this description should identify him roughly.

Why does he behave like this? If hundreds of experiences have shown him that one drink means another debacle with all its attendant suffering and humiliation, why is it he takes that one drink? Why can't he stay on the water wagon? What has become of the common sense and will power that he still sometimes displays with respect to other matters?

Perhaps there never will be a full answer to these questions. Opinions vary considerably as to why the alcoholic reacts differently from normal people. We are not sure why, once a certain point is reached, little can be done for him. We cannot answer the riddle.

We know that while the alcoholic keeps away from drink, as he may do for months or years, he reacts much like other men. We are equally positive that once he takes any alcohol whatever into his system, something happens, both in the bodily and mental sense, which makes it virtually impossible for him to stop. The experience of any alcoholic will abundantly confirm this.

These observations would be academic and pointless if our friend never took the first drink, thereby setting the terrible cycle in motion. Therefore, the main problem of the alcoholic centers in his mind, rather than in his body. If you ask him why he started on that last bender, the chances are he will offer you any one of a hundred alibis. Sometimes these excuses have a certain plausibility, but none of them really makes sense in the light of the havoc an alcoholic's drinking bout creates. They sound like the philosophy of the man who, having a headache, beats himself on the head with a hammer so that he can't feel the ache. If you draw this fallacious reasoning to the attention of an alcoholic, he will laugh it off, or become irritated and refuse to talk.

Once in a while he may tell the truth. And the truth, strange to say, is usually that he has no more idea why he took that first drink that you have. Some drinkers have excuses with which they are satisfied part of the time. But in their hearts they really do not know why they do it. Once this malady has a real hold, they are a baffled lot. There is the obsession that somehow, someday, they will beat the game. But they often suspect they are down for the count.

How true this is, few realize. In a vague way their families and friends sense that these drinkers are abnormal, but everybody hopefully awaits the day when the sufferer will rouse himself from his lethargy and assert his power of will.

The tragic truth is that if the man be a real alcoholic, the happy day may not arrive. He has lost

23

control. At a certain point in the drinking of every alcoholic, he passes into a state where the most powerful desire to stop drinking is of absolutely no avail. This tragic situation has already arrived in practically every case long before it is suspected.

The fact is that most alcoholics, for reasons yet obscure, have lost the power of choice in drink. Our so-called will power becomes practically nonexistent. We are unable, at certain times, to bring into our consciousness with sufficient force the memory of the suffering and humiliation of even a week or a month ago. We are without defense against the first drink.

The almost certain consequences that follow taking even a glass of beer do not crowd into the mind to deter us. If these thoughts occur, they are hazy and readily supplanted with the old threadbare idea that this time we shall handle ourselves like other people. There is a complete failure of the kind of defense that keeps one from putting his hand on a hot stove.

The alcoholic may say to himself in the most casual way, "It won't burn me this time, so here's how!" Or perhaps he doesn't think at all. How often have some of us begun to drink in this nonchalant way, and after the third or fourth, pounded on the bar and said to ourselves, "For God's sake, how did I ever get started again?" Only to have that thought supplanted by "Well, I'll stop with the sixth drink." Or "What's the use anyhow?"

When this sort of thinking is fully established in an individual with alcoholic tendencies, he has probably placed himself beyond human aid, and unless locked up, may die or go permanently insane. These stark and ugly facts have been confirmed by legions of alcoholics throughout history. But for the grace of God, there would have been thousands more convincing demonstrations. So many want to stop but cannot.

There is a solution. Almost none of us liked the self-searching, the leveling of our pride, the confession of shortcomings which the process requires for its successful consummation. But we saw that it really worked in others, and we had come to believe in the hopelessness and futility of life as we had been living it. When, therefore, we were approached by those in whom the problem had been solved, there was nothing left for us but to pick up the simple kit of spiritual tools laid at our feet. We have found much of heaven and we have been rocketed into a fourth dimension of existence of which we had not even dreamed.

The great fact is just this, and nothing less: That we have had deep and effective spiritual experiences* which have revolutionized our whole attitude toward life, toward our fellows and toward God's universe. The central fact of our lives today is the absolute certainty that our Creator has entered into our hearts and lives in a way which is indeed miraculous. He has commenced to accomplish those things for us which we could never do by ourselves.

If you are as seriously alcoholic as we were, we believe there is no middle-of-the-road solution. We were in a position where life was becoming impossible, and if we had passed into the region from which there is no return through human aid, we had but two alternatives: One was to go on to the bitter end, blotting out the consciousness of our intolerable situation as best we could; and the other, to accept spiritual help. This

*Fully explained–Appendix II.

we did because we honestly wanted to, and were willing to make the effort.

A certain American business man had ability, good sense, and high character. For years he had floundered from one sanitarium to another. He had consulted the best known American psychiatrists. Then he had gone to Europe, placing himself in the care of a celebrated physician (the psychiatrist, Dr. Jung) who prescribed for him. Though experience had made him skeptical, he finished his treatment with unusual confidence. His physical and mental condition were unusually good. Above all, he believed he had acquired such a profound knowledge of the inner workings of his mind and its hidden springs that relapse was unthinkable. Nevertheless, he was drunk in a short time. More baffling still, he could give himself no satisfactory explanation for his fall.

So he returned to this doctor, whom he admired, and asked him point-blank why he could not recover. He wished above all things to regain self-control. He seemed quite rational and well-balanced with respect to other problems. Yet he had no control whatever over alcohol. Why was this?

He begged the doctor to tell him the whole truth, and he got it. In the doctor's judgment he was utterly hopeless; he could never regain his position in society and he would have to place himself under lock and key or hire a bodyguard if he expected to live long. That was a great physician's opinion.

But this man still lives, and is a free man. He does not need a bodyguard nor is he confined. He can go anywhere on this earth where other free men may go without disaster, provided he remains willing to maintain a certain simple attitude.

Some of our alcoholic readers may think they can do without spiritual help. Let us tell you the rest of the conversation our friend had with his doctor.

The doctor said, "You have the mind of a chronic alcoholic. I have never seen one single case recover, where that state of mind existed to the extent that it does in you." Our friend felt as though the gates of hell had closed on him with a clang.

He said to the doctor, "Is there no exception?"

"Yes," replied the doctor, "there is. Exceptions to cases such as yours have been occurring since early times. Here and there, once in a while, alcoholics have had what are called vital spiritual experiences. To me these occurrences are phenomena, They appear to be in the nature of huge emotional displacements and rearrangements. Ideas, emotions, and attitudes which were once the guiding forces of the lives of these men are suddenly cast to one side, and a completely new set of conceptions and motives begin to dominate them. In fact, I have been trying to produce some such emotional rearrangement within you. With many individuals the methods which I employed are successful, but I have never been successful with an alcoholic of your description."*

Upon hearing this, our friend was somewhat relieved, for he reflected that, after all, he was a good church member. This hope, however, was destroyed by the doctor's telling him that while his religious convictions were very good, in his case they did not spell the necessary vital spiritual experience.

* For amplification–see Appendix II.

Here was the terrible dilemma in which our friend found himself when he had the extraordinary experience, which as we have already told you, made him a free man.

We, in our turn, sought the same escape with all the desperation of drowning men. What seemed at first a flimsy reed, has proved to be the loving and powerful hand of God. A new life has been given us or, if you prefer, "a design for living" that really works.

The distinguished American psychologist, William James, in his book, "Varieties of Religious Experience," indicates a multitude of ways in which men have discovered God. We have no desire to convince anyone that there is only one way by which faith can be acquired. If what we have learned and felt and seen means anything at all, it means that all of us, whatever our race, creed, or color are the children of a living Creator with whom we may form a relationship upon simple and understandable terms as soon as we are willing and honest enough to try. Those having religious affiliations will find here nothing disturbing to their beliefs or ceremonies. There is no friction among us over such matters.

We think it no concern of ours what religious bodies our members identify themselves with as individuals. This should be an entirely personal affair which each one decides for himself in the light of past associations, or his present choice. Not all of us join religious bodies, but most of us favor such memberships.

In the following chapter, there appears an explanation of alcoholism, as we understand it, then a chapter addressed to the agnostic. Many who once were in this class are now among our members. Surprisingly enough, we find such convictions no great obstacle to a spiritual experience.

Further on, clear-cut directions are given showing how we recovered. These are followed by three dozen personal experiences.

Each individual, in the personal stories, describes in his own language and from his own point of view the way he established his relationship with God. These give a fair cross section of our membership and a clearcut idea of what has actually happened in their lives.

We hope no one will consider these self-revealing accounts in bad taste. Our hope is that many alcoholic men and women, desperately in need, will see these pages, and we believe that it is only by fully disclosing ourselves and our problems that they will be persuaded to say, "Yes, I am one of them too; I must have this thing."

Chapter 3

MORE ABOUT ALCOHOLISM

M OST OF US have been unwilling to admit we were real alcoholics. No person likes to think he is bodily and mentally different from his fellows. Therefore, it is not surprising that our drinking careers have been characterized by countless vain attempts to prove we could drink like other people. The idea that somehow, someday he will control and enjoy his drinking is the great obsession of every abnormal drinker. The persistence of this illusion is astonishing. Many pursue it into the gates of insanity or death.

We learned that we had to fully concede to our innermost selves that we were alcoholics. This is the first step in recovery. The delusion that we are like other people, or presently may be, has to be smashed.

We alcoholics are men and women who have lost the ability to control our drinking. We know that no real alcoholic *ever* recovers control. All of us felt at times that we were regaining control, but such intervals—usually brief—were inevitably followed by still less control, which let in time to pitiful and incomprehensible demoralization. We are convinced to a man that alcoholics of our type are in the grip of a progressive illness. Over any considerable period we get worse, never better.

We are like men who have lost their legs; they never grow new ones. Neither does there appear to be any kind of treatment which will make alcoholics of our kind like other men. We have tried every imaginable remedy. In some instances there has been brief recovery, followed always by a still worse relapse. Physicians who are familiar with alcoholism agree there is no such thing as making a normal drinker out of an alcoholic. Science may one day accomplish this, but it hasn't done so yet.

Despite all we can say, many who are real alcoholics are not going to believe they are in that class. By every form of self-deception and experimentation, they will try to prove themselves exceptions to the rule, therefore nonalcoholic. If anyone who is showing inability to control his drinking can do the right-about-face and drink like a gentleman, our hats are off to him. Heaven knows, we have tried hard enough and long enough to drink like other people!

Here are some of the methods we have tried: Drinking beer only, limiting the number of drinks, never drinking alone, never drinking in the morning, drinking only at home, never having it in the house, never drinking during business hours, drinking only at parties, switching from scotch to brandy, drinking only natural wines, agreeing to resign if ever drunk on the job, taking a trip, not taking a trip, swearing off forever (with and without a solemn oath), taking more physical exercise, reading inspirational books, going to health farms and sanitariums, accepting voluntary commitment to asylums—we could increase the list ad infinitum.

We do not like to pronounce any individual as alcoholic, but you can quickly diagnose yourself. Step over to the nearest barroom and try some control-led drinking. Try to drink and stop abruptly. Try it more than once. It will not take long for you to decide, if you are honest with yourself about it. It may be worth a bad case of jitters if you get a full knowledge of your condition.

Though there is no way of proving it, we believe that early in our drinking careers most of us could have stopped drinking. But the difficulty is that few alcoholics have enough desire to stop while there is yet time. We have heard of a few instances where people, who showed definite signs of alcoholism, were able to stop for a long period because of an overpowering desire to do so. Here is one.

A man of thirty was doing a great deal of spree drinking. He was very nervous in the morning after these bouts and quieted himself with more liquor. He was ambitious to succeed in business, but saw that he would get nowhere if he drank at all. Once he started, he had no control whatever. He made up his mind that until he had been successful in business and had retired, he would not touch another drop. An exceptional man, he remained bone dry for twenty-five years and retired at the age of fifty-five, after a successful and happy business career. Then he fell victim to a belief which practically every alcoholic has—that his long period of sobriety and self-discipline had qualified him to drink as other men. Out came his carpet slippers and a bottle. In two months he was in a hospital, puzzled and humiliated. He tried to regulate his drinking for a while, making several trips to the hospital meantime. Then, gathering all his forces, he attempted to stop altogether and found he could not. Every means of solving his problem which money could buy was at his disposal. Every attempt failed. Though a robust man at retirement, he went to pieces quickly and was dead within four years.

This case contains a powerful lesson. Most of us have believed that if we remained sober for a long stretch, we could thereafter drink normally. But here is a man who at fifty-five years found he was just where he had left off at thirty. We have seen the truth demonstrated again and again: "Once an alcoholic, always an alcoholic." Commencing to drink after a period of sobriety, we are in a short time as bad as ever. If we are planning to stop drinking, there must be no reservation of any kind, nor any lurking notion that someday we will be immune to alcohol.

Young people may be encouraged by this man's experience to think that they can stop, as he did, on their own will power. We doubt if many of them can do it, because none will really want to stop, and hardly one of them, because of the peculiar mental twist already acquired, will find he can win out. Several of our crowd, men of thirty or less, had been drinking only a few years, but they found themselves as helpless as those who had been drinking twenty years.

To be gravely affected, one does not necessarily have to drink a long time nor take the quantities some of us have. This is particularly true of women. Potential female alcoholics often turn into the real thing and are gone beyond recall in a few years. Certain drinkers, who would be greatly insulted if called alcoholics, are astonished at their inability to stop. We, who are familiar with the symptoms, see large numbers of potential alcoholics among young people everywhere. But try and get them to see it!*

As we look back, we feel we had gone on drinking many years beyond the point where we could quit on our will power. If anyone questions whether he has entered this dangerous area, let him try leaving liquor alone for one year. If he is a real alcoholic and very far advanced, there is scant chance of success. In the early days of our drinking we occasionally remained sober for a year or more, becoming serious drinkers again later. Though you may be able to stop for a considerable period, you may yet be a potential alcoholic. We think few, to whom this book will appeal, can stay dry anything like a year. Some will be drunk the day after making their resolutions; most of them within a few weeks.

For those who are unable to drink moderately the question is how to stop altogether. We are assuming, of course, that the reader desires to stop. Whether such a person can quit upon a nonspiritual basis depends upon the extent to which he has already lost the power to choose whether he will drink or not. Many of us felt that we had plenty of character. There was a tremendous urge to cease forever. Yet we found it impossible. This is the baffling feature of alcoholism as we know it—this utter inability to leave it alone, no matter how great the necessity or the wish.

How then shall we help our readers determine, to their own satisfaction, whether they are one of us? The experiment of quitting for a period of time will be helpful, but we think we can render an even greater service to alcoholic sufferers and perhaps to the medi-

* True when this book was first published. Today A.A. has many young members.

cal fraternity. So we shall describe some of the mental states that precede a relapse into drinking, for obviously this is the crux of the problem.

What sort of thinking dominates an alcoholic who repeats time after time the desperate experiment of the first drink? Friends who have reasoned with him after a spree which has brought him to the point of divorce or bankruptcy are mystified when he walks directly into a saloon. Why does he? Of what is he thinking?

Our first example is a friend we shall call Jim. This man has a charming wife and family. He inherited a lucrative automobile agency. He had a commendable World War record. He is a good salesman. Everybody likes him. He is an intelligent man, normal so far as we can see, except for a nervous disposition. He did no drinking until he was thirty-five. In a few years he became so violent when intoxicated that he had to be committed. On leaving the asylum he came into contact with us.

We told him what we knew of alcoholism and the answer we had found. He made a beginning. His family was re-assembled, and he began to work as a salesman for the business he had lost through drinking. All went well for a time, but he failed to enlarge his spiritual life. To his consternation, he found himself drunk half a dozen times in rapid succession. On each of these occasions we worked with him, reviewing carefully what had happened. He agreed he was a real alcoholic and in a serious condition. He knew he faced another trip to the asylum if he kept on. Moreover, he would lose his family for whom he had a deep affection.

Yet he got drunk again. We asked him to tell us exactly how it happened. This is his story: "I came to work on Tuesday morning. I remember I felt irritated that I had to be a salesman for a concern I once owned. I had a few words with the boss, but nothing serious. Then I decided to drive into the country and see one of my prospects for a car. On the way I felt hungry so I stopped at a roadside place where they have a bar. I had no intention of drinking. I just thought I would get a sandwich. I also had the notion that I might find a customer for a car at this place, which was familiar for I had been going to it for years. I had eaten there many times during the months I was sober. I sat down at a table and ordered a sandwich and a glass of milk. Still no thought of drinking. I ordered another sandwich and decided to have another glass of milk.

"*Suddenly the thought crossed my mind that if I were to put an ounce of whiskey in my milk it couldn't hurt me on a full stomach. I ordered a whiskey and poured it into the milk. I vaguely sensed I was not being any too smart, but felt reassured as I was taking the whiskey on a full stomach.* The experiment went so well that I ordered another whiskey and poured it into more milk. That didn't seem to bother me so I tried another."

Thus started one more journey to the asylum for Jim. Here was the threat of commitment, the loss of family and position, to say nothing of that intense mental and physical suffering which drinking always caused him. *He had much knowledge about himself as an alcoholic. Yet all reasons for not drinking were easily pushed aside in favor of the foolish idea that he could take whiskey if only he mixed it with milk!*

Whatever the precise definition of the word may be, we call this plain insanity. How can such a lack of proportion, of the ability to think straight, be called anything else?

You may think this an extreme case. To us it is not far-fetched, for this kind of thinking has been characteristic of every single one of us. We have sometimes reflected more than Jim did upon the consequences. But there was always the curious mental phenomenon that parallel with our sound reasoning there inevitably ran some insanely trivial excuse for taking the first drink. Our sound reasoning failed to hold us in check. The insane idea won out. Next day we would ask ourselves, in all earnestness and sincerity, how it could have happened.

In some circumstances we have gone out deliberately to get drunk, feeling ourselves justified by nervousness, anger, worry, depression, jealousy or the like. But even in this type of beginning we are obliged to admit that our justification for a spree was insanely insufficient in the light of what always happened. We now see that when we began to drink deliberately, instead of casually, there was little serious or effective thought during the period of premeditation of what the terrific consequences might be.

Our behavior is as absurd and incomprehensible with respect to the first drink as that of an individual with a passion, say, for jay-walking. He gets a thrill out of skipping in front of fast-moving vehicles. He enjoys himself for a few years in spite of friendly warnings. Up to this point you would label him as a foolish chap having queer ideas of fun. Luck then deserts him and he is slightly injured several times in succession. You would expect him, if he were normal, to cut it out. Presently he is hit again and this time has a fractured skull. Within a week after leaving the hospital a fast-moving trolley car breaks his arm. He tells you he has decided to stop jay-walking for good, but in a few weeks he breaks both legs.

On through the years this conduct continues, accompanied by his continual promises to be careful or to keep off the streets altogether. Finally, he can no longer work, his wife gets a divorce and he is held up to ridicule. He tries every known means to get the jay-walking idea out of his head. He shuts himself up in an asylum, hoping to mend his ways. But the day he comes out he races in front of a fire engine, which breaks his back. Such a man would be crazy, wouldn't he?

You may think our illustration is too ridiculous. But is it? We, who have been through the wringer, have to admit if we substituted alcoholism for jay-walking, the illustration would fit us exactly. However intelligent we may have been in other respects, where alcohol has been involved, we have been strangely insane. It' s strong language—but isn't it true?

Some of you are thinking: "Yes, what you tell us is true, but it doesn't fully apply. We admit we have some of these symptoms, but we have not gone to the extremes you fellows did, nor are we likely to, for we understand ourselves so well after what you have told us that such things cannot happen again. We have not lost everything in life through drinking and we certainly do not intend to. Thanks for the information."

That may be true of certain nonalcoholic people who, though drinking foolishly and heavily at the present time, are able to stop or moderate, because their brains and bodies have not been damaged as ours were. But the actual or potential alcoholic, with hardly an exception, will be *absolutely unable to stop drinking on the basis of self-knowledge.* This is a point we wish to emphasize and re-emphasize, to smash home upon our alcoholic readers as it has been revealed to us out of bitter experience. Let us take another illustration.

Fred is partner in a well known accounting firm. His income is good, he has a fine home, is happily married and the father of promising children of college age. He has so attractive a personality that he makes friends with everyone. If ever there was a successful business man, it is Fred. To all appearance he is a stable, well balanced individual. Yet, he is alcoholic. We first saw Fred about a year ago in a hospital where he had gone to recover from a bad case of jitters. It was his first experience of this kind, and he was much ashamed of it. Far from admitting he was an alcoholic, he told himself he came to the hospital to rest his nerves. The doctor intimated strongly that he might be worse than he realized. For a few days he was depressed about his condition. He made up his mind to quit drinking altogether. It never occurred to him that perhaps he could not do so, in spite of his character and standing. Fred would not believe himself an alcoholic, much less accept a spiritual remedy for his problem. We told him what we knew about alcoholism. He was interested and conceded that he had some of the symptoms, but he was a long way from admitting that he could do nothing about it himself. He was positive that this humiliating experience, plus the knowledge he had acquired, would keep him sober the rest of his life. Self-knowledge would fix it.

We heard no more of Fred for a while. One day we were told that he was back in the hospital. This time he was quite shaky. He soon indicated he was anxious to see us. The story he told is most instructive, for here was a chap absolutely convinced he had to stop drinking, who had no excuse for drinking, who exhibited splendid judgment and determination in all his other concerns, yet was flat on his back nevertheless.

Let him tell you about it: "I was much impressed with what you fellows said about alcoholism, and I frankly did not believe it would be possible for me to drink again. I rather appreciated your ideas about the subtle insanity which precedes the first drink, but I was confident it could not happen to me after what I had learned. I reasoned I was not so far advanced as most of you fellows, that I had been usually successful in licking my other personal problems, and that I would therefore be successful where you men failed. I felt I had every right to be self-confident, that it would be only a matter of exercising my will power and keeping on guard.

"In this frame of mind, I went about my business and for a time all was well. I had no trouble refusing drinks, and began to wonder if I had not been making too hard work of a simple matter. One day I went to Washington to present some accounting evidence to a government bureau. I had been out of town before during this particular dry spell, so there was nothing new about that. Physically, I felt fine. Neither did I have any pressing problems or worries. My business came off well, I was pleased and knew my partners would be too. It was the end of a perfect day, not a cloud on the horizon.

"I went to my hotel and leisurely dressed for dinner. *As I crossed the threshold of the dining room, the thought came to mind that it would be nice to have a couple of cocktails with dinner. That was all. Nothing more.* I ordered a cocktail and my meal. Then I ordered another cocktail. After dinner I decided to take a walk. When I returned to the hotel it struck me a highball would be fine before going to bed, so I stepped into the bar and had one. I remember having several more that night and plenty next morning. I have a shadowy recollection of being in an airplane bound for New York, and of finding a friendly taxicab driver at the landing field instead of my wife. The driver escorted me about for several days. I know little of where I went or what I said and did. Then came the hospital with unbearable mental and physical suffering.

"As soon as I regained my ability to think, I went carefully over that evening in Washington. *Not only had I been off guard, I had made no fight whatever against the first drink. This time I had not thought of the consequences at all.* I had commenced to drink as carelessly as though the cocktails were ginger ale. I now remembered what my alcoholic friends had told me, how they prophesied that if I had an alcoholic mind, the time and place would come—I would drink

41

again. They had said that though I did raise a defense, it would one day give way before some trivial reason for having a drink. Well, just that did happen and more, for what I had learned of alcoholism did not occur to me at all. I knew from that moment that I had an alcoholic mind. I saw that will power and self-knowledge would not help in those strange mental blank spots. I had never been able to understand people who said that a problem had them hopelessly defeated. I knew then. It was a crushing blow.

"Two of the members of Alcoholics Anonymous came to see me. They grinned, which I didn't like so much, and then asked me if I thought myself alcoholic and if I were really licked this time. I had to concede both propositions. They piled on me heaps of evidence to the effect that an alcoholic mentality, such as I had exhibited in Washington, was a hopeless condition. They cited cases out of their own experience by the dozen. This process snuffed out the last flicker of conviction that I could do the job myself.

"Then they outlined the spiritual answer and program of action which a hundred of them had followed successfully. Though I had been only a nominal churchman, their proposals were not, intellectually, hard to swallow. But the program of action, though entirely sensible, was pretty drastic. It meant I would have to throw several lifelong conceptions out of the window. That was not easy. But the moment I made up my mind to go through with the process, I had the curious feeling that my alcoholic condition was relieved, as in fact it proved to be.

"Quite as important was the discovery that spiritual principles would solve all my problems. I have since been brought into a way of living infinitely more satisfying and, I hope, more useful than the life I lived before. My old manner of life was by no means a bad one, but I would not exchange its best moments for the worst I have now. I would not go back to it even if I could."

Fred's story speaks for itself. We hope it strikes home to thousands like him. He had felt only the first nip of the wringer. Most alcoholics have to be pretty badly mangled before they really commence to solve their problems.

Many doctors and psychiatrists agree with our conclusions. One of these men, staff member of a world-renowned hospital, recently made this statement to some of us: "What you say about the general hopelessness of the average alcoholic's plight is, in my opinion, correct. As to two of you men, whose stories I have heard, there is no doubt in my mind that you were 100% hopeless, apart from divine help. Had you offered yourselves as patients at this hospital, I would not have taken you, if I had been able to avoid it. People like you are too heart-breaking. Though not a religious person, I have profound respect for the spiritual approach in such cases as yours. For most cases, there is virtually no other solution."

Once more: The alcoholic at certain times has no effective mental defense against the first drink. Except in a few rare cases, neither he nor any other human being can provide such a defense. His defense must come from a Higher Power.

Chapter 4
WE AGNOSTICS

IN THE PRECEDING chapters you have learned something of alcoholism. We hope we have made clear the distinction between the alcoholic and the nonalcoholic. If, when you honestly want to, you find you cannot quit entirely, or if when drinking, you have little control over the amount you take, you are probably alcoholic. If that be the case, you may be suffering from an illness which only a spiritual experience will conquer.

To one who feels he is an atheist or agnostic such an experience seems impossible, but to continue as he is means disaster, especially if he is an alcoholic of the hopeless variety. To be doomed to an alcoholic death or to live on a spiritual basis are not always easy alternatives to face.

But it isn't so difficult. About half our original fellowship were of exactly that type. At first some of us tried to avoid the issue, hoping against hope we were not true alcoholics. But after a while we had to face the fact that we must find a spiritual basis of life—or else. Perhaps it is going to be that way with you. But cheer up, something like half of us thought we were atheists or agnostics. Our experience shows that you need not be disconcerted.

If a mere code of morals or a better philosophy of life were sufficient to overcome alcoholism, many of us would have recovered long ago. But we found that such codes and philosophies did not save us, no matter how much we tried. We could wish to be moral, we could wish to be philosophically comforted, in fact, we could will these things with all our might, but the needed power wasn't there. Our human resources, as marshalled by the will, were not sufficient; they failed utterly.

Lack of power, that was our dilemma. We had to find a power by which we could live, and it had to be a *Power greater than ourselves*. Obviously. But where and how were we to find this Power?

Well, that's exactly what this book is about. Its main object is to enable you to find a Power greater than yourself which will solve your problem. That means we have written a book which we believe to be spiritual as well as moral. And it means, of course, that we are going to talk about God. Here difficulty arises with agnostics. Many times we talk to a new man and watch his hope rise as we discuss his alcoholic problems and explain our fellowship. But his face falls when we speak of spiritual matters, especially when we mention God, for we have re-opened a subject which our man thought he had neatly evaded or entirely ignored.

We know how he feels. We have shared his honest doubt and prejudice. Some of us have been violently anti-religious. To others, the word "God" brought up a particular idea of Him with which someone had tried to impress them during childhood. Perhaps we rejected this particular conception because it seemed inadequate. With that rejection we imagined we had abandoned the God idea entirely. We were bothered with the thought that faith and dependence upon a Power beyond ourselves was somewhat weak, even cowardly. We looked upon this world of warring individuals, warring theological systems, and inexplicable calamity, with deep skepticism. We looked askance at many individuals who claimed to be godly. How could a Supreme Being have anything to do with it all? And who could comprehend a Supreme Being anyhow? Yet, in other moments, we found ourselves thinking, when enchanted by a starlit night, "Who, then, made all this?" There was a feeling of awe and wonder, but it was fleeting and soon lost.

Yes, we of agnostic temperament have had these thoughts and experiences. Let us make haste to reassure you. We found that as soon as we were able to lay aside prejudice and express even a willingness to believe in a Power greater than ourselves, we commenced to get results, even though it was impossible for any of us to fully define or comprehend that Power, which is God.

Much to our relief, we discovered we did not need to consider another's conception of God. Our own conception, however inadequate, was sufficient to make the approach and to effect a contact with Him. As soon as we admitted the possible existence of a Creative Intelligence, a Spirit of the Universe underlying the totality of things, we began to be possessed of a new sense of power and direction, provided we took other simple steps. We found that God does not make too hard terms with those who seek Him. To us, the Realm of Spirit is broad, roomy, all inclusive; never exclusive or forbidding to those who earnestly seek. It is open, we believe, to all men.

When, therefore, we speak to you of God, we mean your own conception of God. This applies, too, to other spiritual expressions which you find in this book. Do not let any prejudice you may have against spiritual terms deter you from honestly asking yourself what they mean to you. At the start, this was all we needed to commence spiritual growth, to effect our first conscious relation with God as we understood Him. Afterward, we found ourselves accepting many things which then seemed entirely out of reach. That was growth, but if we wished to grow we had to begin somewhere. So we used our own conception, however limited it was.

We needed to ask ourselves but one short question. "Do I now believe, or am I even willing to believe, that there is a Power greater than myself?" As soon as a man can say that he does believe, or is willing to believe, we emphatically assure him that he is on his way. It has been repeatedly proven among us that upon this simple cornerstone a wonderfully effective spiritual structure can be built.*

That was great news to us, for we had assumed we could not make use of spiritual principles unless we accepted many things on faith which seemed difficult to believe. When people presented us with spiritual approaches, how frequently did we all say, "I wish I had what that man has. I'm sure it would work if I could only believe as he believes. But I cannot accept as surely true the many articles of faith which are so plain to him." So it was comforting to learn that we could commence at a simpler level.

Besides a seeming inability to accept much on faith,

* Please be sure to read Appendix II on "Spiritual Experience."

we often found ourselves handicapped by obstinacy, sensitiveness, and unreasoning prejudice. Many of us have been so touchy that even casual reference to spiritual things made us bristle with antagonism. This sort of thinking had to be abandoned. Though some of us resisted, we found no great difficulty in casting aside such feelings. Faced with alcoholic destruction, we soon became as open minded on spiritual matters as we had tried to be on other questions. In this respect alcohol was a great persuader. It finally beat us into a state of reasonableness. Sometimes this was a tedious process; we hope no one else will be prejudiced for as long as some of us were.

The reader may still ask why he should believe in a Power greater than himself. We think there are good reasons. Let us have a look at some of them.

The practical individual of today is a stickler for facts and results. Nevertheless, the twentieth century readily accepts theories of all kinds, provided they are firmly grounded in fact. We have numerous theories, for example, about electricity. Everybody believes them without a murmur of doubt. Why this ready acceptance? Simply because it is impossible to explain what we see, feel, direct, and use, without a reasonable assumption as a starting point.

Everybody nowadays, believes in scores of assumptions for which there is good evidence, but no perfect visual proof. And does not science demonstrate that visual proof is the weakest proof? It is being constantly revealed, as mankind studies the material world, that outward appearances are not inward reality at all. To illustrate:

The prosaic steel girder is a mass of electrons whirling around each other at incredible speed. These tiny bodies are governed by precise laws, and these laws hold true throughout the material world. Science tells us so. We have no reason to doubt it. When, however, the perfectly logical assumption is suggested that underneath the material world and life as we see it, there is an All Powerful, Guiding, Creative Intelligence, right there our perverse streak comes to the surface and we laboriously set out to convince ourselves it isn't so. We read wordy books and indulge in windy arguments, thinking we believe this universe needs no God to explain it. Were our contentions true, it would follow that life originated out of nothing, means nothing, and proceeds nowhere.

Instead of regarding ourselves as intelligent agents, spearheads of God's ever advancing Creation, we agnostics and atheists chose to believe that our human intelligence was the last word, the alpha and the omega, the beginning and end of all. Rather vain of us, wasn't it?

We, who have traveled this dubious path, beg you to lay aside prejudice, even against organized religion. We have learned that whatever the human frailties of various faiths may be, those faiths have given purpose and direction to millions. People of faith have a logical idea of what life is all about. Actually, we used to have no reasonable conception whatever. We used to amuse ourselves by cynically dissecting spiritual beliefs and practices when we might have observed that many spiritually-minded persons of all races, colors, and creeds were demonstrating a degree of stability, happiness and usefulness which we should have sought ourselves.

Instead, we looked at the human defects of these people, and sometimes used their shortcomings as a basis of wholesale condemnation. We talked of intolerance, while we were intolerant ourselves. We missed the reality and the beauty of the forest because we were diverted by the ugliness of some of its trees. We never gave the spiritual side of life a fair hearing.

In our personal stories you will find a wide variation in the way each teller approaches and conceives of the Power which is greater than himself. Whether we agree with a particular approach or conception seems to make little difference. Experience has taught us that these are matters about which, for our purpose, we need not be worried. They are questions for each individual to settle for himself.

On one proposition, however, these men and women are strikingly agreed. Every one of them has gained access to, and believes in, a Power greater than himself. This Power has in each case accomplished the miraculous, the humanly impossible. As a celebrated American statesman puts it, "Let's look at the record."

Here are thousands of men and women, worldly indeed. They flatly declare that since they have come to believe in a Power greater than themselves, to take a certain attitude toward that Power, and to do certain simple things, there has been a revolutionary change in their way of living and thinking. In the face of collapse and despair, in the face of the total failure of their human resources, they found that a new power, peace, happiness, and sense of direction flowed into them. This happened soon after they wholeheartedly met a few simple requirements. Once confused and baffled by the seeming futility of existence, they show the underlying reasons why they were making heavy going of life. Leaving aside the drink question, they tell why living was so unsatisfactory. They show how the change came over them. When many hundreds of people are able to say that the consciousness of the Presence of God is today the most important fact of their lives, they present a powerful reason why one should have faith.

This world of ours has made more material progress in the last century than in all the millenniums which went before. Almost everyone knows the reason. Students of ancient history tell us that the intellect of men in those days was equal to the best of today. Yet in ancient times material progress was painfully slow. The spirit of modern scientific inquiry, research and invention was almost unknown. In the realm of the material, men's minds were fettered by superstition, tradition, and all sorts of fixed ideas. Some of the contemporaries of Columbus thought a round earth preposterous. Others came near putting Galileo to death for his astronomical heresies.

We asked ourselves this: Are not some of us just as biased and unreasonable about the realm of the spirit as were the ancients about the realm of the material? Even in the present century, American newspapers were afraid to print an account of the Wright brothers' first successful flight at Kittyhawk. Had not all efforts at flight failed before? Did not Professor Langley's flying machine go to the bottom of the Potomac River? Was it not true that the best mathematical minds had proved man could never fly? Had not people said God had reserved this privilege to the birds? Only thirty years later the conquest of the air was almost an old story and airplane travel was in full swing.

But in most fields our generation has witnessed complete liberation of our thinking. Show any longshoreman a Sunday supplement describing a proposal to explore the moon by means of a rocket and he will say, "I bet they do it—maybe not so long either." Is not our age characterized by the ease with which we discard old ideas for new, by the complete readiness with which we throw away the theory or gadget which does not work for something new which does?

We had to ask ourselves why we shouldn't apply to our human problems this same readiness to change our point of view. We were having trouble with personal relationships, we couldn't control our emotional natures, we were a prey to misery and depression, we couldn't make a living, we had a feeling of uselessness, we were full of fear, we were unhappy, we couldn't seem to be of real help to other people—was not a basic solution of these bedevilments more important than whether we should see newsreels of lunar flight? Of course it was.

When we saw others solve their problems by a simple reliance upon the Spirit of the Universe, we had to stop doubting the power of God. Our ideas did not work. But the God idea did.

The Wright brothers' almost childish faith that they could build a machine which would fly was the mainspring of their accomplishment. Without that, nothing could have happened. We agnostics and atheists were sticking to the idea that self-sufficiency would solve our problems. When others showed us that "God-sufficiency" worked with them, we began to feel like those who had insisted the Wrights would never fly.

Logic is great stuff. We liked it. We still like it. It is not by chance we were given the power to reason, to examine the evidence of our senses, and to draw conclusions. That is one of man's magnificent attributes. We agnostically inclined would not feel satisfied with a proposal which does not lend itself to reasonable approach and interpretation. Hence we are at pains to tell why we think our present faith is reasonable, why we think it more sane and logical to believe than not to believe, whey we say our former thinking was soft and mushy when we threw up our hands in doubt and said, "We don't know."

When we became alcoholics, crushed by a self-imposed crisis we could not postpone or evade, we had to fearlessly face the proposition that either God is everything or else He is nothing. God either is, or He isn't. What was our choice to be?

Arrived at this point, we were squarely confronted with the question of faith. We couldn't duck the issue. Some of us had already walked far over the Bridge of Reason toward the desired shore of faith. The outlines and the promise of the New Land had brought lustre to tired eyes and fresh courage to flagging spirits. Friendly hands had stretched out in welcome. We were grateful that Reason had brought us so far. But somehow, we couldn't quite step ashore. Perhaps we had been leaning too heavily on Reason that last mile and we did not like to lose our support.

That was natural, but let us think a little more closely. Without knowing it, had we not been brought to where we stood by a certain kind of faith? For did we not believe in our own reasoning? Did we not have confidence in our ability to think? What was that but a sort of faith? Yes, we had been faithful, abjectly faithful to the God of Reason. So, in one way or another, we discovered that faith had been involved all the time!

We found, too, that we had been worshippers. What a state of mental goose-flesh that used to bring on! Had we not variously worshiped people, sentiment, things, money, and ourselves? And then, with a better motive, had we not worshipfully beheld the sunset, the sea, or a flower? Who of us had not loved something or somebody? How much did these feelings, these loves, these worships, have to do with pure reason? Little or nothing, we saw at last. Were not these things the tissue out of which our lives were constructed? Did not these feelings, after all, determine the course of our existence? It was impossible to say we had no capacity for faith, or love, or worship. In one form or another we had been living by faith and little else.

Imagine life without faith! Were nothing left but pure reason, it wouldn't be life. But we believed in life—of course we did. We could not prove life in the sense that you can prove a straight line is the shortest distance between two points, yet, there it was. Could we still say the whole thing was nothing but a mass of electrons, created out of nothing, meaning nothing, whirling on to a destiny of nothingness? Of course we couldn't. The electrons themselves seemed more intelligent than that. At least, so the chemist said.

Hence, we saw that reason isn't everything. Neither is reason, as most of us use it, entirely dependable, though it emanate from our best minds. What about people who proved that man could never fly?

Yet we had been seeing another kind of flight, a spiritual liberation from this world, people who rose above their problems. They said God made these things possible, and we only smiled. We had seen spiritual release, but liked to tell ourselves it wasn't true.

Actually we were fooling ourselves, for deep down in every man, woman, and child, is the fundamental idea of God. It may be obscured by calamity, by pomp, by worship of other things, but in some form or other it is there. For faith in a Power greater than ourselves, and miraculous demonstrations of that power in human lives, are facts as old as man himself.

We finally saw that faith in some kind of God was a part of our make-up, just as much as the feeling we have for a friend. Sometimes we had to search fearlessly, but He was there. He was as much a fact as we were. We found the Great Reality deep down within us. In the last analysis it is only there that He may be found. It was so with us.

We can only clear the ground a bit. If our testimony helps sweep away prejudice, enables you to think honestly, encourages you to search diligently within yourself, then, if you wish, you can join us on the Broad Highway. With this attitude you cannot fail. The consciousness of your belief is sure to come to you.

In this book you will read the experience of a man who thought he was an atheist. His story is so interesting that some of it should be told now. His change of heart was dramatic, convincing, and moving.

Our friend was a minister's son. He attended church school, where he became rebellious at what he thought an overdose of religious education. For years thereafter he was dogged by trouble and frustration. Business failure, insanity, fatal illness, suicide—these calamities in his immediate family embittered and depressed him. Post-war disillusionment, ever more serious alcoholism, impending mental and physical collapse, brought him to the point of self-destruction.

One night, when confined in a hospital, he was approached by an alcoholic who had known a spiritual experience. Our friend's gorge rose as he bitterly cried out: "If there is a God, He certainly hasn't done anything for me!" But later, alone in his room, he asked himself this question: "Is it possible that all the religious people I have known are wrong?" While pondering the answer he felt as though he lived in hell. Then, like a thunderbolt, a great thought came. It crowded out all else:

"Who are you to say there is no God?"

This man recounts that he tumbled out of bed to his knees. In a few seconds he was overwhelmed by a conviction of the Presence of God. It poured over and through him with the certainty and majesty of a great tide at flood. The barriers he had built through the years were swept away. He stood in the Presence of Infinite Power and Love. He had stepped from bridge to shore. For the first time, he lived in conscious companionship with his Creator.

Thus was our friend's cornerstone fixed in place. No later vicissitude has shaken it. His alcoholic problem was taken away. That very night, years ago, it disappeared. Save for a few brief moments of temptation the thought of drink has never returned; and at such times a great revulsion has risen up in him. Seemingly he could not drink even if he would. God had restored his sanity.

What is this but a miracle of healing? Yet its elements are simple. Circumstances made him willing to believe. He humbly offered himself to his Maker—then he knew.

Even so had God restored us all to our right minds. To this man, the revelation was sudden. Some of us grow into it more slowly. But He has come to all who have honestly sought Him.

When we drew near to Him He disclosed Himself to us!

Chapter 5

HOW IT WORKS

R ARELY HAVE we seen a person fail who has thoroughly followed our path. Those who do not recover are people who cannot or will not completely give themselves to this simple program, usually men and women who are constitutionally incapable of being honest with themselves. There are such unfortunates. They are not at fault; they seem to have been born that way. They are naturally incapable of grasping and developing a manner of living which demands rigorous honesty. Their chances are less than average. There are those, too, who suffer from grave emotional and mental disorders, but many of them do recover if they have the capacity to be honest.

Our stories disclose in a general way what we used to be like, what happened, and what we are like now. If you have decided you want what we have and are willing to go to any length to get it—then you are ready to take certain steps.

At some of these we balked. We thought we could find an easier, softer way. But we could not. With all the earnestness at our command, we beg of you to be fearless and thorough from the very start. Some of us have tried to hold on to our old ideas and the result was nil until we let go absolutely.

Remember that we deal with alcohol—cunning, baffling, powerful! Without help it is too much for us. But there is One who has all power—that One is God. May you find Him now!

Half measures availed us nothing. We stood at the turning point. We asked His protection and care with complete abandon.

Here are the steps we took, which are suggested as a program of recovery:

1. We admitted we were powerless over alcohol—that our lives had become unmanageable.
2. Came to believe that a Power greater than ourselves could restore us to sanity.
3. Made a decision to turn our will and our lives over to the care of God *as we understood Him.*
4. Made a searching and fearless moral inventory of ourselves.
5. Admitted to God, to ourselves, and to another human being the exact nature of our wrongs.
6. Were entirely ready to have God remove all these defects of character.
7. Humbly asked Him to remove our shortcomings.
8. Made a list of all persons we had harmed, and became willing to make amends to them all.
9. Made direct amends to such people wherever possible, except when to do so would injure them or others.
10. Continued to take personal inventory and when we were wrong promptly admitted it.
11. Sought through prayer and meditation to improve our conscious contact with God *as we understood Him,* praying only for knowledge of His will for us and the power to carry that out.

12.Having had a spiritual awakening as the result of these steps, we tried to carry this message to alcoholics, and to practice these principles in all our affairs.

Many of us exclaimed, "What an order! I can't go through with it." Do not be discouraged. No one among us has been able to maintain anything like perfect adherence to these principles. We are not saints. The point is, that we are willing to grow along spiritual lines. The principles we have set down are guides to progress. We claim spiritual progress rather than spiritual perfection.

Our description of the alcoholic, the chapter to the agnostic, and our personal adventures before and after make clear three pertinent ideas:

(a) That we were alcoholic and could not manage our own lives.

(b) That probably no human power could have relieved our alcoholism.

(c) That God could and would if He we were sought.

Being convinced, *we were at Step Three*, which is that we decided to turn our will and our life over to God as we understood Him. Just what do we mean by that, and just what do we do?

The first requirement is that we be convinced that any life run on self-will can hardly be a success. On that basis we are almost always in collision with something or somebody, even though our motives are good. Most people try to live by self-propulsion. Each person is like an actor who wants to run the whole show; is forever trying to arrange the lights, the ballet, the scenery and the rest of the players in his own way. If his arrangements would only stay put, if only people would do as he wished, the show would be great. Everybody, including himself, would be pleased. Life would be wonderful. In trying to make these arrangements our actor may sometimes be quite virtuous. He may be kind, considerate, patient, generous; even modest and self-sacrificing. On the other hand, he may be mean, egotistical, selfish and dishonest. But, as with most humans, he is more likely to have varied traits.

What usually happens? The show doesn't come off very well. He begins to think life doesn't treat him right. He decides to exert himself more. He becomes, on the next occasion, still more demanding or gracious, as the case may be. Still the play does not suit him. Admitting he may be somewhat at fault, he is sure that other people are more to blame. He becomes angry, indignant, self-pitying. What is his basic trouble? Is he not really a self-seeker even when trying to be kind? Is he not a victim of the delusion that he can wrest satisfaction and happiness out of this world if he only manages well? Is it not evident to all the rest of the players that these are the things he wants? And do not his actions make each of them wish to retaliate, snatching all they can get out of the show? Is he not, even in his best moments, a producer of confusion rather than harmony?

Our actor is self-centered—ego-centric, as people like to call it nowadays. He is like the retired business man who lolls in the Florida sunshine in the winter complaining of the sad state of the nation; the minister who sighs over the sins of the twentieth century; politicians and reformers who are sure all would be Utopia

61

if the rest of the world would only behave; the outlaw safe cracker who thinks society has wronged him; and the alcoholic who has lost all and is locked up. Whatever our protestations, are not most of us concerned with ourselves, our resentments, or our self-pity?

Selfishness—self-centeredness! That, we think, is the root of our troubles. Driven by a hundred forms of fear, self-delusion, self-seeking, and self-pity, we step on the toes of our fellows and they retaliate. Sometimes they hurt us, seemingly without provocation, but we invariably find that at some time in the past we have made decisions based on self which later placed us in a position to be hurt.

So our troubles, we think, are basically of our own making. They arise out of ourselves, and the alcoholic is an extreme example of self-will run riot, though he usually doesn't think so. Above everything, we alcoholics must be rid of this selfishness. We must, or it kills us! God makes that possible. And there often seems no way of entirely getting rid of self without His aid. Many of us had moral and philosophical convictions galore, but we could not live up to them even though we would have liked to. Neither could we reduce our self-centeredness much by wishing or trying on our own power. We had to have God's help.

This is the how and why of it. First of all, we had to quit playing God. It didn't work. Next, we decided that hereafter in this drama of life, God was going to be our Director. He is the Principal; we are His agents. He is the Father, and we are His children. Most good ideas are simple, and this concept was the keystone of the new and triumphant arch through which we passed to freedom.

When we sincerely took such a position, all sorts of remarkable things followed. We had a new Employer. Being all powerful, He provided what we needed, if we kept close to Him and performed His work well. Established on such a footing we became less and less interested in ourselves, our little plans and designs. More and more we became interested in seeing what we could contribute to life. As we felt new power flow in, as we enjoyed peace of mind, as we discovered we could face life successfully, as we became conscious of His presence, we began to lose our fear of today, tomorrow or the hereafter. We were reborn.

We were now at Step Three. Many of us said to our Maker, *as we understood Him:* "God, I offer myself to Thee—to build with me and to do with me as Thou wilt. Relieve me of the bondage of self, that I may better do Thy will. Take away my difficulties, that victory over them may bear witness to those I would help of Thy Power, Thy Love, and Thy Way of life. May I do Thy will always!" We thought well before taking this step making sure we were ready; that we could at last abandon ourselves utterly to Him.

We found it very desirable to take this spiritual step with an understanding person, such as our wife, best friend, or spiritual adviser. But it is better to meet God alone than with one who might misunderstand. The wording was, of course, quite optional so long as we expressed the idea, voicing it without reservation. This was only a beginning, though if honestly and humbly made, an effect, sometimes a very great one, was felt at once.

Next we launched out on a course of vigorous action, the first step of which is a personal housecleaning, which many of us never attempted. Though our decision was a vital and crucial step, it could have little permanent effect unless at once followed by a strenuous effort to face, and to be rid of, the things in ourselves which had been blocking us. Our liquor was but a symptom. So we had to get down to causes and conditions.

Therefore, we started upon a personal inventory. *This was Step Four.* A business which takes no regular inventory usually goes broke. Taking a commercial inventory is a fact-finding and a fact-facing process. It is an effort to discover the truth about the stock-in-trade. One object is to disclose damaged or unsaleable goods, to get rid of them promptly and without regret. If the owner of the business is to be successful, he cannot fool himself about values.

We did exactly the same thing with our lives. We took stock honestly. First, we searched out the flaws in our make-up which caused our failure. Being convinced that self, manifested in various ways, was what had defeated us, we considered its common manifestations.

Resentment is the "number one" offender. It destroys more alcoholics than anything else. From it stem all forms of spiritual disease, for we have been not only mentally and physically ill, we have been spiritually sick. When the spiritual malady is overcome, we straighten out mentally and physically. In dealing with resentments, we set them on paper. We listed people, institutions or principles with whom we were angry. We asked ourselves why we were angry. In most cases it was found that our self-esteem, our pocket-books, our ambitions, our personal relationships, (including sex) were hurt or threatened. So we were sore. We were "burned up."

On our grudge list we set opposite each name our injuries. Was it our self-esteem, our security, our ambitions, our personal, or sex relations, which had been interfered with?

We were usually as definite as this example:

I'm resentful at:	The Cause	Affects My:
Mr. Brown	His attention to my wife.	Sex relations.
		Self-esteem (fear)
	Told my wife of my mistress.	Sex relations.
		Self-esteem (fear)
	Brown may get my job at the office.	Security.
		Self-esteem (fear)
Mrs. Jones	She's a nut—she snubbed me. She committed her husband for drinking. He's my friend. She's a gossip.	Personal relationship.Self-esteem (fear)
My employer	Unreasonable- Unjust- Overbearing- Threatens to fire me for drinking and padding my expense account.	Self-esteem (fear) Security.
My wife	Misunderstands and nags. Likes Brown. Wants house put in her name.	Pride-Personal Sex relations— Security (fear)

We went back through our lives. Nothing counted but thoroughness and honesty. When we were finished we considered it carefully. The first thing apparent was that this world and its people were often quite wrong. To conclude that others were wrong was as far as most of us ever got. The usual outcome was that people continued to wrong us and we stayed sore. Sometimes it was remorse and then we were sore at ourselves. But the more we fought and tried to have our own way, the worse matters got. As in war, the victor only *seemed* to win. Our moments of triumph were short-lived.

It is plain that a life which includes deep resentment leads only to futility and unhappiness. To the precise extent that we permit these, do we squander the hours that might have been worth while. But with the alcoholic, whose hope is the maintenance and growth of a spiritual experience, this business of resentment is infinitely grave. We found that it is fatal. For when harboring such feelings we shut ourselves off from the sunlight of the Spirit. The insanity of alcohol returns and we drink again. And with us, to drink is to die.

If we were to live, we had to be free of anger. The grouch and the brainstorm were not for us. They may be the dubious luxury of normal men, but for alcoholics these things are poison.

We turned back to the list, for it held the key to the future. We were prepared to look for it from an entirely different angle. We began to see that the world and its people really dominated us. In that state, the wrong-doing of others, fancied or real, had power to actually kill. How could we escape? We saw that these resentments must be mastered, but how? We could not wish them away any more than alcohol.

This was our course: We realized that the people who wronged us were perhaps spiritually sick.

Though we did not like their symptoms and the way these disturbed us, they, like ourselves, were sick too. We asked God to help us show them the same tolerance, pity, and patience that we would cheerfully grant a sick friend. When a person offended we said to ourselves. "This is a sick man. How can I be helpful to him? God save me from being angry. Thy will be done."

We avoid retaliation or argument. We wouldn't treat sick people that way. If we do, we destroy our chance of being helpful. We cannot be helpful to all people, but at least God will show us how to take a kindly and tolerant view of each and every one.

Referring to our list again. Putting out of our minds the wrongs others had done, we resolutely looked for our own mistakes. Where had we been selfish, dishonest, self-seeking and frightened? Though a situation had not been entirely our fault, we tried to disregard the other person involved entirely. Where were we to blame? The inventory was ours, not the other man's. When we saw our faults we listed them. We placed them before us in black and white. We admitted our wrongs honestly and were willing to set these matters straight.

Notice that the word "fear" is bracketed alongside the difficulties with Mr. Brown, Mrs. Jones, the employer, and the wife. This short word somehow touches about every aspect of our lives. It was an evil and corroding thread; the fabric of our existence was shot through with it. It set in motion trains of circumstances which brought us misfortune we felt we didn't deserve. But did not we, ourselves, set the ball rolling? Sometimes we think fear ought to be classed with stealing. It seems to cause more trouble.

We reviewed our fears thoroughly. We put them on paper, even though we had no resentment in connection with them. We asked ourselves why we had them. Wasn't it because self-reliance failed us? Self-reliance was good as far as it went, but it didn't go far enough. Some of us once had great self-confidence, but it didn't fully solve the fear problem, or any other. When it made us cocky, it was worse.

Perhaps there is a better way—we think so. For we are now on a different basis; the basis of trusting and relying upon God. We trust infinite God rather than our finite selves. We are in the world to play the role He assigns. Just to the extent that we do as we think He would have us, and humbly rely on Him, does He enable us to match calamity with serenity.

We never apologize to anyone for depending upon our Creator. We can laugh at those who think spirituality the way of weakness. Paradoxically, it is the way of strength. The verdict of the ages is that faith means courage. All men of faith have courage. They trust their God. We never apologize for God. Instead we let Him demonstrate, through us, what He can do. We ask Him to remove our fear and direct our attention to what He would have us be. At once, we commence to outgrow fear.

Now about sex. Many of us needed an overhauling there. But above all, we tried to be sensible on this question. It's so easy to get way off the track. Here we find human opinions running to extremes—absurd extremes, perhaps. One set of voices cry that sex is a lust of our lower nature, a base necessity of procreation. Then we have the voices who cry for sex and more sex; who bewail the institution of marriage; who think that most of the troubles of the race are traceable to sex causes. They think we do not have enough of it, or that it isn't the right kind. They see its significance everywhere. One school would allow man no flavor for his fare and the other would have us all on a straight pepper diet. We want to stay out of this controversy. We do not want to be the arbiter of anyone's sex conduct. We all have sex problems. We'd hardly be human if we didn't. What can we do about them?

We reviewed our own conduct over the years past. Where had we been selfish, dishonest, or inconsiderate? Whom had we hurt? Did we unjustifiably arouse jealousy, suspicion or bitterness? Where were we at fault, what should we have done instead? We got this all down on paper and looked at it.

In this way we tried to shape a sane and sound ideal for our future sex life. We subjected each relation to this test—was it selfish or not? We asked God to mold our ideals and help us to live up to them. We remembered always that our sex powers were God-given and therefore good, neither to be used lightly or selfishly nor to be despised and loathed.

Whatever our ideal turns out to be, we must be willing to grow toward it. We must be willing to make amends where we have done harm, provided that we do not bring about still more harm in so doing. In other words, we treat sex as we would any other problem. In meditation, we ask God what we should do about each specific matter. The right answer will come, if we want it.

God alone can judge our sex situation. Counsel with

persons is often desirable, but we let God be the final judge. We realize that some people are as fanatical about sex as others are loose. We avoid hysterical thinking or advice.

Suppose we fall short of the chosen ideal and stumble? Does this mean we are going to get drunk? Some people tell us so. But this is only a half-truth. It depends on us and on our motives. If we are sorry for what we have done, and have the honest desire to let God take us to better things, we believe we will be forgiven and will have learned our lesson. If we are not sorry, and our conduct continues to harm others, we are quite sure to drink. We are not theorizing. These are facts out of our experience.

To sum up about sex: We earnestly pray for the right ideal, for guidance in each questionable situation, for sanity, and for the strength to do the right thing. If sex is very troublesome, we throw ourselves the harder into helping others. We think of their needs and work for them. This takes us out of ourselves. It quiets the imperious urge, when to yield would mean heartache.

If we have been thorough about our personal inventory, we have written down a lot. We have listed and analyzed our resentments. We have begun to comprehend their futility and their fatality. We have commenced to see their terrible destructiveness. We have begun to learn tolerance, patience and good will toward all men, even our enemies, for we look on them as sick people. We have listed the people we have hurt by our conduct, and are willing to straighten out the past if we can.

In this book you read again and again that faith did

for us what we could not do for ourselves. We hope you are convinced now that God can remove whatever self-will has blocked you off from Him. If you have already made a decision, and an inventory of your grosser handicaps, you have made a good beginning. That being so you have swallowed and digested some big chunks of truth about yourself.

Chapter 6
INTO ACTION

HAVING MADE our personal inventory, what shall we do about it? We have been trying to get a new attitude, a new relationship with our Creator, and to discover the obstacles in our path. We have admitted certain defects; we have ascertained in a rough way what the trouble is; we have put our finger on the weak items in our personal inventory. Now these are about to be cast out. This requires action on our part, which, when completed, will mean that we have admitted to God, to ourselves, and to another human being, the exact nature of our defects. This brings us to *the Fifth Step* in the program of recovery mentioned in the preceding chapter.

This is perhaps difficult—especially discussing our defects with another person. We think we have done well enough in admitting these things to ourselves. There is doubt about that. In actual practice, we usually find a solitary self-appraisal insufficient. Many of us thought it necessary to go much further. We will be more reconciled to discussing ourselves with another person when we see good reasons why we should do so. The best reason first: If we skip this vital step, we may not overcome drinking. Time after time newcomers have tried to keep to themselves certain facts about their lives. Trying to avoid this humbling experience, they have turned to easier methods. Almost invariably they got drunk. Having persevered with the rest of the program, they wondered why they fell. We think the reason is that they never completed their housecleaning. They took inventory all right, but hung on to some of the worst items in stock. They only *thought* they had lost their egoism and fear; they only *thought* they had humbled themselves. But they had not learned enough of humility, fearlessness and honesty, in the sense we find it necessary, until they told someone else *all* their life story.

More than most people, the alcoholic leads a double life. He is very much the actor. To the outer world he presents his stage character. This is the one he likes his fellows to see. He wants to enjoy a certain reputation, but knows in his heart he doesn't deserve it.

The inconsistency is made worse by the things he does on his sprees. Coming to his senses, he is revolted at certain episodes he vaguely remembers. These memories are a nightmare. He trembles to think someone might have observed him. As far as he can, he pushes these memories far inside himself. He hopes they will never see the light of day. He is under constant fear and tension—that makes for more drinking.

Psychologists are inclined to agree with us. We have spent thousands of dollars for examinations. We know but few instances where we have given these doctors a fair break. We have seldom told them the whole truth nor have we followed their advice. Unwilling to be honest with these sympathetic men, we were honest with no one else. Small wonder many in the medical profession have a low opinion of alcoholics and their chance for recovery!

We must be entirely honest with somebody if we

expect to live long or happily in this world. Rightly and naturally, we think well before we choose the person or persons with whom to take this intimate and confidential step. Those of us belonging to a religious denomination which requires confession must, and of course, will want to go to the properly appointed authority whose duty it is to receive it. Though we have no religious connection, we may still do well to talk with someone ordained by an established religion. We often find such a person quick to see and understand our problem. Of course, we sometimes encounter people who do not understand alcoholics.

If we cannot or would rather not do this, we search our acquaintance for a close-mouthed, understanding friend. Perhaps our doctor or psychologist will be the person. It may be one of our own family, but we cannot disclose anything to our wives or our parents which will hurt them and make them unhappy. We have no right to save our own skin at another person's expense. Such parts of our story we tell to someone who will understand, yet be unaffected. The rule is we must be hard on ourselves, but always considerate of others.

Notwithstanding the great necessity for discussing ourselves with someone, it may be one is so situated that there is no suitable person available. If that is so, this step may be postponed, only, however, if we hold ourselves in complete readiness to go through with it at the first opportunity. We say this because we are very anxious that we talk to the right person. It is important that he be able to keep a confidence; that he fully understand and approve what we are driving at;

that he will not try to change our plan. But we must not use this as a mere excuse to postpone.

When we decide who is to hear our story, we waste no time. We have a written inventory and we are prepared for a long talk. We explain to our partner what we are about to do and why we have to do it. He should realize that we are engaged upon a life-and-death errand. Most people approached in this way will be glad to help; they will be honored by our confidence.

We pocket our pride and go to it, illuminating every twist of character, every dark cranny of the past. Once we have taken this step, withholding nothing, we are delighted. We can look the world in the eye. We can be alone at perfect peace and ease. Our fears fall from us. We begin to feel the nearness of our Creator. We may have had certain spiritual beliefs, but now we begin to have a spiritual experience. The feeling that the drink problem has disappeared will often come strongly. We feel we are on the Broad Highway, walking hand in hand with the Spirit of the Universe.

Returning home we find a place where we can be quiet for an hour, carefully reviewing what we have done. We thank God from the bottom of our heart that we know Him better. Taking this book down from our shelf we turn to the page which contains the twelve steps. Carefully reading the first five proposals we ask if we have omitted anything, for we are building an arch through which we shall walk a free man at last. Is our work solid so far? Are the stones properly in place? Have we skimped on the cement put into the foundation? Have we tried to make mortar without sand?

If we can answer to our satisfaction, we then look at *Step Six*. We have emphasized willingness as being indispensable. Are we now ready to let God remove from us all the things which we have admitted are objectionable? Can He now take them all—every one? If we still cling to something we will not let go, we ask God to help us be willing.

When ready, we say something like this: "My Creator, I am now willing that you should have all of me, good and bad. I pray that you now remove from me every single defect of character which stands in the way of my usefulness to you and my fellows. Grant me strength, as I go out from here, to do your bidding. Amen." We have then completed *step seven*.

Now we need more action, without which we find that "Faith without works is dead." Let's look at *Steps Eight and Nine*. We have a list of all persons we have harmed and to whom we are willing to make amends. We made it when we took inventory. We subjected ourselves to a drastic self-appraisal. Now we go out to our fellows and repair the damage done in the past. We attempt to sweep away the debris, which has accumulated out of our effort to live on self-will and run the show ourselves. If we haven't the will to do this, we ask until it comes. Remember it was agreed at the beginning *we would go to any lengths for victory over alcohol.*

Probably there are still some misgivings. As we look over the list of business acquaintances and friends we have hurt, we may feel diffident about going to some of them on a spiritual basis. Let us be reassured. To some people we need not, and probably should not emphasize the spiritual feature on our first approach.

We might prejudice them. At the moment we are trying to put our lives in order. But this is not an end in itself. Our real purpose is to fit ourselves to be of maximum service to God and the people about us. It is seldom wise to approach an individual, who still smarts from our injustice to him, and announce that we have gone religious. In the prize ring, this would be called leading with the chin. Why lay ourselves open to being branded fanatics or religious bores? We may kill a future opportunity to carry a beneficial message. But our man is sure to be impressed with a sincere desire to set right the wrong. He is going to be more interested in a demonstration of good will than in our talk of spiritual discoveries.

We don't use this as an excuse for shying away from the subject of God. When it will serve any good purpose, we are willing to announce our convictions with tact and common sense. The question of how to approach the man we hated will arise. It may be he has done us more harm than we have done him and, though we may have acquired a better attitude toward him, we are still not too keen about admitting our faults. Nevertheless, with a person we dislike, we take the bit in our teeth. It is harder to go to an enemy than to a friend, but we find it much more beneficial to us. We go to him in a helpful and forgiving spirit, confessing our former ill feeling and expressing our regret.

Under no condition do we criticize such a person or argue. Simply we tell him that we will never get over drinking until we have done our utmost to straighten out the past. We are there to sweep off our side of the street, realizing that nothing worth while

77

can be accomplished until we do so, never trying to tell him what he should do. His faults are not discussed. We stick to our own. If our manner is calm, frank, and open, we will be gratified with the result.

In nine cases out of ten the unexpected happens. Sometimes the man we are calling upon admits his own fault, so feuds of years' standing melt away in an hour. Rarely do we fail to make satisfactory progress. Our former enemies sometimes praise what we are doing and wish us well. Occasionally, they will offer assistance. It should not matter, however, if someone does throw us out of his office. We have made our demonstration, done our part. It's water over the dam.

Most alcoholics owe money. We do not dodge our creditors. Telling them what we are trying to do, we make no bones about our drinking; they usually know it anyway, whether we think so or not. Nor are we afraid of disclosing our alcoholism on the theory it may cause financial harm. Approached in this way, the most ruthless creditor will sometimes surprise us. Arranging the best deal we can we let these people know we are sorry. Our drinking has made us slow to pay. We must lose our fear of creditors no matter how far we have to go, for we are liable to drink if we are afraid to face them.

Perhaps we have committed a criminal offense, which might land us in jail if it were known to the authorities. We may be short in our accounts and unable to make good. We have already admitted this in confidence to another person, but we are sure we would be imprisoned or lose our job if it were known. Maybe it's only a petty offense such as padding the expense account. Most of us have done that sort of thing.

Maybe we are divorced, and have remarried but haven't kept up the alimony to number one. She is indignant about it, and has a warrant out for our arrest. That's a common form of trouble too.

Although these reparations take innumerable forms, there are some general principles which we find guiding. Reminding ourselves that we have decided to go to any lengths to find a spiritual experience, we ask that we be given strength and direction to do the right thing, no matter what the personal consequences may be. We may lose our position or reputation or face jail, but we are willing. We have to be. We must not shrink at anything.

Usually, however, other people are involved. Therefore, we are not to be the hasty and foolish martyr who would needlessly sacrifice others to save himself from the alcoholic pit. A man we know had remarried. Because of resentment and drinking, he had not paid alimony to his first wife. She was furious. She went to court and got an order for his arrest. He had commenced our way of life, had secured a position, and was getting his head above water. It would have been impressive heroics if he had walked up to the Judge and said, "Here I am."

We thought he ought to be willing to do that if necessary, but if he were in jail he could provide nothing for either family. We suggested he write his first wife admitting his faults and asking forgiveness. He did, and also sent a small amount of money. He told her what he would try to do in the future. He said he was perfectly willing to go to jail if she insisted. Of course she did not, and the whole situation has long since been adjusted.

Before taking drastic action which might implicate other people we secure their consent. If we have obtained permission, have consulted with others, asked God to help and the drastic step is indicated we must not shrink.

This brings to mind a story about one of our friends. While drinking, he accepted a sum of money from a bitterly-hated business rival, giving him no receipt for it. He subsequently denied having received the money and used the incident as a basis for discrediting the man. He thus used his own wrong-doing as a means of destroying the reputation of another. In fact, his rival was ruined.

He felt that he had done a wrong he could not possibly make right. If he opened that old affair, he was afraid it would destroy the reputation of his partner, disgrace his family and take away his means of livelihood. What right had he to involve those dependent upon him? How could he possibly make a public statement exonerating his rival?

After consulting with his wife and partner he came to the conclusion that it was better to take those risks than to stand before his Creator guilty of such ruinous slander. He saw that he had to place the outcome in God's hands or he would soon start drinking again, and all would be lost anyhow. He attended church for the first time in many years. After the sermon, he quietly got up and made an explanation. His action met widespread approval, and today he is one of the most trusted citizens of his town. This all happened years ago.

The chances are that we have domestic troubles. Perhaps we are mixed up with women in a fashion we wouldn't care to have advertised. We doubt if, in this respect, alcoholics are fundamentally much worse than other people. But drinking does complicate sex relations in the home. After a few years with an alcoholic, a wife gets worn out, resentful and uncommunicative. How could she be anything else? The husband begins to feel lonely, sorry for himself. He commences to look around in the night clubs, or their equivalent, for something besides liquor. Perhaps he is having a secret and exciting affair with "the girl who understands." In fairness we must say that she may understand, but what are we going to do about a thing like that? A man so involved often feels very remorseful at times, especially if he is married to a loyal and courageous girl who has literally gone through hell for him.

Whatever the situation, we usually have to do something about it. If we are sure our wife does not know, should we tell her? Not always, we think. If she knows in a general way that we have been wild, should we tell her in detail? Undoubtedly we should admit our fault. She may insist on knowing all the particulars. She will want to know who the woman is and where she is. We feel we ought to say to her that we have no right to involve another person. We are sorry for what we have done and, God willing, it shall not be repeated. More than that we cannot do; we have no right to go further. Though there may be justifiable exceptions, and though we wish to lay down no rule of any sort, we have often found this the best course to take.

Our design for living is not a one-way street. It is as good for the wife as for the husband. If we can forget, so can she. It is better, however, that one does not needlessly name a person upon whom she can vent jealousy.

Perhaps there are some cases where the utmost frankness is demanded. No outsider can appraise such an intimate situation. It may be that both will decide that the way of good sense and loving kindness is to let by-gones be by-gones. Each might pray about it, having the other one's happiness uppermost in mind. Keep it always in sight that we are dealing with that most terrible human emotion—jealousy. Good generalship may decide that the problem be attacked on the flank rather than risk a face-to-face combat.

If we have no such complication, there is plenty we should do at home. Sometimes we hear an alcoholic say that the only thing he needs to do is to keep sober. Certainly he must keep sober, for there will be no home if he doesn't. But he is yet a long way from making good to the wife or parents whom for years he has so shockingly treated. Passing all under-standing is the patience mothers and wives have had with alcoholics. Had this not been so, many of us would have no homes today, would perhaps be dead.

The alcoholic is like a tornado roaring his way through the lives of others. Hearts are broken. Sweet relationships are dead. Affections have been uprooted. Selfish and inconsiderate habits have kept the home in turmoil. We feel a man is unthinking when he says that sobriety is enough. He is like the farmer who came up out of his cyclone cellar to find his home ruined. To his wife, he remarked, "Don't see anything the matter here, Ma. Ain't it grand the wind stopped blowin'?"

Yes, there is a long period of reconstruction ahead. We must take the lead. A remorseful mumbling that we are sorry won't fill the bill at all. We ought to sit down with the family and frankly analyze the past as we now see it, being very careful not to criticize them. Their defects may be glaring, but the chances are that our own actions are partly responsible. So we clean house with the family, asking each morning in meditation that our Creator show us the way of patience, tolerance, kindliness and love.

The spiritual life is not a theory. *We have to live it.* Unless one's family expresses a desire to live upon spiritual principles we think we ought not to urge them. We should not talk incessantly to them about spiritual matters. They will change in time. Our behavior will convince them more than our words. We must remember that ten or twenty years of drunkenness would make a skeptic out of anyone.

There may be some wrongs we can never fully right. We don't worry about them if we can honestly say to ourselves that we would right them if we could. Some people cannot be seen—we send them an honest letter. And there may be a valid reason for postponement in some cases. But we don't delay if it can be avoided. We should be sensible, tactful, considerate and humble without being servile or scraping. As God's people we stand on our feet; we don't crawl before anyone.

If we are painstaking about this phase of our development, we will be amazed before we are half way through. We are going to know a new freedom and a new happiness. We will not regret the past nor wish to shut to door on it. We will comprehend the word serenity and we will know peace. No matter how far down the scale we have gone, we will see how our experience can benefit others. That feeling of uselessness and self-pity will disappear. We will lose interest in selfish things and gain interest in our fellows. Self-seeking will slip away. Our whole attitude and outlook upon life will change. Fear of people and of economic insecurity will leave us. We will intuitively know how to handle situations which used to baffle us. We will suddenly realize that God is doing for us what we could not do for ourselves.

Are these extravagant promises? We think not. They are being fulfilled among us—sometimes quickly, sometimes slowly. They will always materialize if we work for them.

This thought brings us to *Step Ten*, which suggests we continue to take personal inventory and continue to set right any new mistakes as we go along. We vigorously commenced this way of living as we cleaned up the past. We have entered the world of the Spirit. Our next function is to grow in understanding and effectiveness. This is not an overnight matter. It should continue for our lifetime. Continue to watch for selfishness, dishonesty, resentment, and fear. When these crop up, we ask God at once to remove them. We discuss them with someone immediately and make amends quickly if we have harmed anyone. Then we resolutely turn our thoughts to someone we can help. Love and tolerance of others is our code.

And we have ceased fighting anything or anyone—even alcohol. For by this time sanity will have returned. We will seldom be interested in liquor. If tempted, we recoil from it as from a hot flame. We react sanely and normally, and we will find that this has happened automatically. We will see that our new attitude toward liquor has been given us without any thought or effort on our part. It just comes! That is the miracle of it. We are not fighting it, neither are we avoiding temptation. We feel as though we had been placed in a position of neutrality—safe and protected. We have not even sworn off. Instead, the problem has been removed. It does not exist for us. We are neither cocky nor are we afraid. That is our experience. That is how we react so long as we keep in fit spiritual condition.

It is easy to let up on the spiritual program of action and rest on our laurels. We are headed for trouble if we do, for alcohol is a subtle foe. We are not cured of alcoholism. What we really have is a daily reprieve contingent on the maintenance of our spiritual condition. Every day is a day when we must carry the vision of God's will into all of our activities. "How can I best serve Thee—Thy will (not mine) be done." These are thoughts which must go with us constantly. We can exercise our will power along this line all we wish. It is the proper use of the will.

Much has already been said about receiving strength, inspiration, and direction from Him who has all knowledge and power. If we have carefully followed directions, we have begun to sense the flow of His Spirit into us. To some extent we have become God-conscious. We have begun to develop this vital sixth sense. But we must go further and that means more action.

Step Eleven suggests prayer and meditation. We shouldn't be shy on this matter of prayer. Better men than we are using it constantly. It works, if we have the proper attitude and work at it. It would be easy to be vague about this matter. Yet, we believe we can make some definite and valuable suggestions.

When we retire at night, we constructively review our day. Were we resentful, selfish, dishonest or afraid? Do we owe an apology? Have we kept something to ourselves which should be discussed with another person at once? Were we kind and loving toward all? What could we have done better? Were we thinking of ourselves most of the time? Or were we thinking of what we could do for others, of what we could pack into the stream of life? But we must be careful not to drift into worry, remorse or morbid reflection, for that would diminish our usefulness to others. After making our review we ask God's forgiveness and inquire what corrective measures should be taken.

On awakening let us think about the twenty-four hours ahead. We consider our plans for the day. Before we begin, we ask God to direct our thinking, especially asking that it be divorced from self-pity, dishonest or self-seeking motives. Under these conditions we can employ our mental faculties with assurance, for after all God gave us brains to use. Our thought-life will be placed on a much higher plane when our thinking is cleared of wrong motives.

In thinking about our day we may face indecision. We may not be able to determine which course to take. Here we ask God for inspiration, an intuitive thought or a decision. We relax and take it easy. We don't struggle. We are often surprised how the right answers come after we have tried this for a while.

What used to be the hunch or the occasional inspiration gradually becomes a working part of the mind. Being still inexperienced and having just made conscious contact with God, it is not probable that we are going to be inspired at all times. We might pay for this presumption in all sorts of absurd actions and ideas. Nevertheless, we find that our thinking will, as time passes, be more and more on the plane of inspiration. We come to rely upon it.

We usually conclude the period of meditation with a prayer that we be shown all through the day what our next step is to be, that we be given whatever we need to take care of such problems. We ask especially for freedom from self-will, and are careful to make no request for ourselves only. We may ask for ourselves, however, if others will be helped. We are careful never to pray for our own selfish ends. Many of us have wasted a lot of time doing that and it doesn't work. You can easily see why.

If circumstances warrant, we ask our wives or friends to join us in morning meditation. If we belong to a religious denomination which requires a definite morning devotion, we attend to that also. If not members of religious bodies, we sometimes select and memorize a few set prayers which emphasize the principles we have been discussing. There are many helpful books also. Suggestions about these may be obtained from one's priest, minister, or rabbi. Be quick to see where religious people are right. Make use of what they offer.

As we go through the day we pause, when agitated or doubtful, and ask for the right thought or action. We constantly remind ourselves we are no longer running the show, humbly saying to ourselves many times each day "Thy will be done." We are then in much less danger of excitement, fear, anger, worry, self-pity, or foolish decisions. We become much more efficient. We do not tire so easily, for we are not burning up energy foolishly as we did when we were trying to arrange life to suit ourselves.

It works—it really does.

We alcoholics are undisciplined. So we let God discipline us in the simple way we have just outlined.

But this is not all. There is action and more action. "Faith without works is dead." The next chapter is entirely devoted to *Step Twelve*.

Chapter 7

WORKING WITH OTHERS

PRACTICAL EXPERIENCE shows that nothing will so much insure immunity from drinking as intensive work with other alcoholics. It works when other activities fail. This is our *twelfth suggestion:* Carry this message to other alcoholics! You can help when no one else can. You can secure their confidence when others fail. Remember they are very ill.

Life will take on new meaning. To watch people recover, to see them help others, to watch loneliness vanish, to see a fellowship grow up about you, to have a host of friends—this is an experience you must not miss. We know you will not want to miss it. Frequent contact with newcomers and with each other is the bright spot of our lives.

Perhaps you are not acquainted with any drinkers who want to recover. You can easily find some by asking a few doctors, ministers, priests or hospitals. They will be only too glad to assist you. Don't start out as an evangelist or reformer. Unfortunately a lot of prejudice exists. You will be handicapped if you arouse it. Ministers and doctors are competent and you can learn much from them if you wish, but it happens that because of your own drinking experience you can be uniquely useful to other alcoholics. So cooperate; never criticize. To be helpful is our only aim.

When you discover a prospect for Alcoholics Anonymous, find out all you can about him. If he does not want to stop drinking, don't waste time trying to persuade him. You may spoil a later opportunity. This advice is given for his family also. They should be patient, realizing they are dealing with a sick person.

If there is any indication that he wants to stop, have a good talk with the person most interested in him—usually his wife. Get an idea of his behavior, his problems, his background, the seriousness of his condition, and his religious leanings. You need this information to put yourself in his place, to see how you would like him to approach you if the tables were turned.

Sometimes it is wise to wait till he goes on a binge. The family may object to this, but unless he is in a dangerous physical condition, it is better to risk it. Don't deal with him when he is very drunk, unless he is ugly and the family needs your help. Wait for the end of the spree, or at least for a lucid interval. Then let his family or a friend ask him if he wants to quit for good and if he would go to any extreme to do so. If he says yes, then his attention should be drawn to you as a person who has recovered. You should be described to him as one of a fellowship who, as part of their own recovery, try to help others and who will be glad to talk to him if he cares to see you.

If he does not want to see you, never force yourself upon him. Neither should the family hysterically plead with him to do anything, nor should they tell him much about you. They should wait for the end of his next drinking bout. You might place this book where he can see it in the interval. Here no specific rule can be given. The family must decide these things. But urge them not to be over-anxious, for that might spoil matters.

Usually the family should not try to tell your story. When possible, avoid meeting a man through his family. Approach through a doctor or an institution is a better bet. If your man needs hospitalization, he should have it, but not forcibly unless he is violent. Let the doctor, if he will, tell him he has something in the way of a solution.

When your man is better, the doctor might suggest a visit from you. Though you have talked with the family, leave them out of the first discussion. Under these conditions your prospect will see he is under no pressure. He will feel he can deal with you without being nagged by his family. Call on him while he is still jittery. He may be more receptive when depressed.

See you're man alone, if possible. At first engage in general conversation. After a while, turn the talk to some phase of drinking. Tell him enough about your drinking habits, symptoms, and experiences to encourage him to speak of himself. If he wishes to talk, let him do so. You will thus get a better idea of how you ought to proceed. If he is not communicative, give him a sketch of your drinking career up to the time you quit. But say nothing, for the moment, of how that was accomplished. If he is in a serious mood dwell on the troubles liquor has caused you, being careful not to moralize or lecture. If his mood is light, tell him humorous stories of your escapades. Get him to tell some of his.

When he sees you know all about the drinking game, commence to describe yourself as an alcoholic.

91

Tell him how baffled you were, how you finally learned that you were sick. Give him an account of the struggles you made to stop. Show him the mental twist which leads to the first drink of a spree. We suggest you do this as we have done it in chapter on alcoholism. If he is alcoholic, he will understand you at once. He will match your mental inconsistencies with some of his own.

If you are satisfied that he is a real alcoholic, begin to dwell on the hopeless feature of the malady. Show him, from your own experience, how the queer mental condition surrounding that first drink prevents normal functioning of the will power. Don't, at this stage, refer to this book, unless he has seen it and wishes to discuss it. And be careful not to brand him as an alcoholic. Let him draw his own conclusion. If he sticks to the idea that he can still control his drinking, tell him that possibly he can—if he is not too alcoholic. But insist that if he is severely afflicted, there may be little chance he can recover by himself.

Continue to speak of alcoholism as an illness, a fatal malady. Talk about the conditions of body and mind which accompany it. Keep his attention focussed mainly on your personal experience. Explain that many are doomed who never realize their predicament. Doctors are rightly loath to tell alcoholic patients the whole story unless it will serve some good purpose. But you may talk to him about the hopelessness of alcoholism because you offer a solution. You will soon have your friend admitting he has many, if not all, of the traits of the alcoholic. If his own doctor is willing to tell him that he is alcoholic, so much the better. Even though your protegé may not have entirely admitted his condition, he has become very curious to know how you got well. Let him ask you that question, if he will. *Tell him exactly what happened to you.* Stress the spiritual feature freely. If the man be agnostic or atheist, make it emphatic that *he does not have to agree with your conception of God.* He can choose any conception he likes, provided it makes sense to him. *The main thing is that he be willing to believe in a Power greater than himself and that he live by spiritual principles.*

When dealing with such a person, you had better use everyday language to describe spiritual principles. There is no use arousing any prejudice he may have against certain theological terms and conceptions about which he may already be confused. Don't raise such issues, no matter what your own convictions are.

Your prospect may belong to a religious denomination. His religious education and training may be far superior to yours. In that case he is going to wonder how you can add anything to what he already knows. But he will be curious to learn why his own convictions have not worked and why yours seem to work so well. He may be an example of the truth that faith alone is insufficient. To be vital, faith must be accompanied by self sacrifice and unselfish, constructive action. Let him see that you are not there to instruct him in religion. Admit that he probably knows more about it than you do, but call to his attention the fact that however deep his faith and knowledge, he could not have applied it or he would not drink. Perhaps your story will help him see where he has failed to practice the very precepts he knows so well. We represent no particular faith or denomination. We are dealing only with general principles common to most denominations.

Outline the program of action, explaining how you made a self-appraisal, how you straightened out your past and why you are now endeavoring to be helpful to him. It is important for him to realize that your attempt to pass this on to him plays a vital part in your own recovery. Actually, he may be helping you more than you are helping him. Make it plain he is under no obligation to you, that you hope only that he will try to help other alcoholics when he escapes his own difficulties. Suggest how important it is that he place the welfare of other people ahead of his own. Make it clear that he is not under pressure, that he needn't see you again if he doesn't want to. You should not be offended if he wants to call it off, for he has helped you more than you have helped him. If your talk has been sane, quiet and full of human understanding, you have perhaps made a friend. Maybe you have disturbed him about the question of alcoholism. This is all to the good. The more hopeless he feels, the better. He will be more likely to follow your suggestions.

Your candidate may give reasons why he need not follow all of the program. He may rebel at the thought of a drastic housecleaning which requires discussion with other people. Do not contradict such views. Tell him you once felt as he does, but you doubt whether you would have much progress had you not taken action. On your first visit tell him about the Fellowship of Alcoholics Anonymous. If he shows interest, lend him your copy of this book.

Unless your friend wants to talk further about himself, do not wear out your welcome. Give him a chance to think it over. If you do stay, let him steer the conversation in any direction he likes. Sometimes a new man is anxious to proceed at once, and you may be tempted to let him do so. This is sometimes a mistake. If he has trouble later, he is likely to say you rushed him. You will be most successful with alcoholics if you do not exhibit any passion for crusade or reform. Never talk down to an alcoholic from any moral or spiritual hilltop; simply lay out the kit of spiritual tools for his inspection. Show him how they worked with you. Offer him friendship and fellowship. Tell him that if he wants to get well you will do anything to help.

If he is not interested in your solution, if he expects you to act only as a banker for his financial difficulties or a nurse for his sprees, you may have to drop him until he changes his mind. This he may do after he gets hurt some more.

If he is sincerely interested and wants to see you again, ask him to read this book in the interval. After doing that, he must decide for himself whether he wants to go on. He should not be pushed or prodded by you, his wife, or his friends. If he is to find God, the desire must come from within.

If he thinks he can do the job in some other way, or prefers some other spiritual approach, encourage him to follow his own conscience. We have no monopoly on God; we merely have an approach that worked with us. But point out that we alcoholics have much in common and that you would like, in any case, to be friendly. Let it go at that.

Do not be discouraged if your prospect does not respond at once. Search out another alcoholic and try again. You are sure to find someone desperate enough to accept with eagerness what you offer. We find it a waste of time to keep chasing a man who cannot or will not work with you. If you leave such a person alone, he may soon become convinced that he cannot recover by himself. To spend too much time on any one situation is to deny some other alcoholic an opportunity to live and be happy. One of our Fellowship failed entirely with his first half dozen prospects. He often says that if he had continued to work on them, he might have deprived many others, who have since recovered, of their chance.

Suppose now you are making your second visit to a man. He has read this volume and says he is prepared to go through with the Twelve Steps of the program of recovery. Having had the experience yourself, you can give him much practical advice. Let him know you are available if he wishes to make a decision and tell his story, but do not insist upon it if he prefers to consult someone else.

He may be broke and homeless. If he is, you might try to help him about getting a job, or give him a little financial assistance. But you should not deprive your family or creditors of money they should have. Perhaps you will want to take the man into your home for a few days. But be sure you use discretion. Be certain he will be welcomed by your family, and that he is not trying to impose upon you for money, connections or shelter. Permit that and you only harm him. You will be making it possible for him to be insincere.

You may be aiding in his destruction rather than his recovery.

Never avoid these responsibilities, but be sure you are doing the right thing if you assume them. Helping others is the foundation stone of your recovery. A kindly act once in a while isn't enough. You have to act the Good Samaritan every day, if need be. It may mean the loss of many nights' sleep, great interference with your pleasures, interruptions to your business. It may mean sharing your money and your home, counseling frantic wives and relatives, innumerable trips to police courts, sanitariums, hospitals, jails and asylums. Your telephone may jangle at any time of the day or night. Your wife may sometimes say she is neglected. A drunk may smash the furniture in your home, or burn a mattress. You may have to fight with him if he is violent. Sometimes you will have to call a doctor and administer sedatives under his direction. Another time you may have to send for the police or an ambulance. Occasionally you will have to meet such conditions.

We seldom allow an alcoholic to live in our homes for long at a time. It is not good for him, and it sometimes creates serious complications in a family.

Though an alcoholic does not respond, there is no reason why you should neglect his family. You should continue to be friendly to them. The family should be offered your way of life. Should they accept and practice spiritual principles, there is a much better chance that the head of the family will recover. And even though he continues to drink, the family will find life more bearable.

For the type of alcoholic who is able and willing to

get well, little charity, in the ordinary sense of the word, is needed or wanted. The men who cry for money and shelter before conquering alcohol, are on the wrong track. Yet we do go to great extremes to provide each other with these very things, when such action is warranted. This may seem inconsistent, but we think it is not.

It is not the matter of giving that is in question, but when and how to give. That often makes the difference between failure and success. The minute we put our work on a service plane, the alcoholic commences to rely upon our assistance rather than upon God. He clamors for this or that, claiming he cannot master alcohol until his material needs are cared for. Nonsense. Some of us have taken very hard knocks to learn this truth: Job or no job—wife or no wife—we simply do not stop drinking so long as we place dependence upon other people ahead of dependence on God.

Burn the idea into the consciousness of every man that he can get well regardless of anyone. The only condition is that he trusts in God and clean house.

Now, the domestic problem: There may be divorce, separation, or just strained relations. When your prospect has made such reparation as he can to his family, and has thoroughly explained to them the new principles by which he is living, he should proceed to put those principles into action at home. That is, if he is lucky enough to have a home. Though his family be at fault in many respects, he should not be concerned about that. He should concentrate on his own spiritual demonstration. Argument and faultfinding are to be avoided like the plague. In many homes this is a difficult thing to do, but it must be done if any results are to be expected. If persisted in for a few months, the effect on a man's family is sure to be great. The most incompatible people discover they have a basis upon which they can meet. Little by little the family may see their own defects and admit them. These can then be discussed in an atmosphere of helpfulness and friendliness.

After they have seen tangible results, the family will perhaps want to go along. These things will come to pass naturally and in good time provided, however, the alcoholic continues to demonstrate that he can be sober, considerate, and helpful, regardless of what anyone says or does. Of course, we all fall much below this standard many times. But we must try to repair the damage immediately lest we pay the penalty by a spree.

If there be divorce or separation, there should be no undue haste for the couple to get together. The man should be sure of his recovery. The wife should fully understand his new way of life. If their old relationship is to be resumed it must be on a better basis, since the former did not work. This means a new attitude and spirit all around. Sometimes it is to the best interests of all concerned that a couple remain apart. Obviously, no rule can be laid down. Let the alcoholic continue his program day by day. When the time for living together has come, it will be apparent to both parties

Let no alcoholic say he cannot recover unless he has his family back. This just isn't so. In some cases the wife will never come back for one reason or another. Remind the prospect that his recovery is not dependent upon people. It is dependent upon his relationship with God. We have seen men get well whose families have not returned at all. We have seen others slip when the family came back too soon.

Both you and the new man must walk day by day in the path of spiritual progress. If you persist, remarkable things will happen. When we look back, we realize that the things which came to us when we put ourselves in God's hands were better than anything we could have planned. Follow the dictates of a Higher Power and you will presently live in a new and wonderful world, no matter what your present circumstances!

When working with a man and his family, you should take care not to participate in their quarrels. You may spoil your chance of being helpful if you do. But urge upon a man's family that he has been a very sick person and should be treated accordingly. You should warn against arousing resentment or jealousy. You should point out that his defects of character are not going to disappear over night. Show them that he has entered upon a period of growth. Ask them to remember, when they are impatient, the blessed fact of his sobriety.

If you have been successful in solving your own domestic problems, tell the newcomer's family how that was accomplished. In this way you can set them on the right track without becoming critical of them. The story of how you and your wife settled your difficulties is worth any amount of criticism.

Assuming we are spiritually fit, we can do all sorts of things alcoholics are not supposed to do. People have said we must not go where liquor is served; we must not have it in our homes; we must shun friends who drink; we must avoid moving pictures which show drinking scenes; we must not go into bars; our friends must hide their bottles if we go to their houses; we mustn't think or be reminded about alcohol at all. Our experience shows that this is not necessarily so.

We meet these conditions every day. An alcoholic who cannot meet them, still has an alcoholic mind; there is something the matter with his spiritual status. His only chance for sobriety would be some place like the Greenland Ice Cap, and even there an Eskimo might turn up with a bottle of scotch and ruin everything! Ask any woman who has sent her husband to distant places on the theory he would escape the alcohol problem.

In our belief any scheme of combating alcoholism which proposes to shield the sick man from temptation is doomed to failure. If the alcoholic tries to shield himself he may succeed for a time, but he usually winds up with a bigger explosion than ever. We have tried these methods. These attempts to do the impossible have always failed.

So our rule is not to avoid a place where there is drinking, *if we have a legitimate reason for being there.* That includes bars, nightclubs, dances, receptions, weddings, and even plain ordinary whoopee parties. To a person who has had experience with an alcoholic, this may seem like tempting Providence, but it isn't.

You will note that we made an important qualification. Therefore, ask yourself on each occasion, "Have I any good social, business, or personal reason for going to this place? Or am I expecting to steal a little vicarious pleasure from the atmosphere of such places? If you answer these questions satisfactorily, you need have no apprehension. Go or stay away, whichever seems best. But be sure you are on solid spiritual ground before you start and that your motive in going is thoroughly good. Do not think of what you will get out of the occasion. Think of what you can bring to it. But if you are shaky, you had better work with another alcoholic instead!

Why sit with a long face in places where there is drinking, sighing about the good old days. If it is a happy occasion, try to increase the pleasure of those there; if a business occasion, go and attend to your business enthusiastically. If you are with a person who wants to eat in a bar, by all means go along. Let your friends know they are not to change their habits on your account. At a proper time and place explain to all your friends why alcohol disagrees with you. If you do this thoroughly, few people will ask you to drink. While you were drinking, you were withdrawing from life little by little. Now you are getting back into the social life of this world. Don't start to withdraw again just because your friends drink liquor.

Your job now is to be at the place where you may be of maximum helpfulness to others, so never hesitate to go anywhere if you can be helpful. You should not hesitate to visit the most sordid spot on earth on such an errand. Keep on the firing line of life with these motives and God will keep you unharmed.

Many of us keep liquor in our homes. We often need it to carry green recruits through a severe hangover. Some of us still serve it to our friends provided they are not alcoholic. But some of us think we should not serve liquor to anyone. We never argue this question. We feel that each family, in the light of their own circumstances, ought to decide for themselves.

We are careful never to show intolerance or hatred of drinking as an institution. Experience shows that such an attitude is not helpful to anyone. Every new alcoholic looks for this spirit among us and is immensely relieved when he finds we are not witch-burners. A spirit of intolerance might repel alcoholics whose lives could have been saved, had it not been for such stupidity. We would not even do the cause of temperate drinking any good, for not one drinker in a thousand likes to be told anything about alcohol by one who hates it.

Some day we hope that Alcoholics Anonymous will help the public to a better realization of the gravity of the alcoholic problem, but we shall be of little use if our attitude is one of bitterness or hostility. Drinkers will not stand for it.

After all, our problems were of our own making. Bottles were only a symbol. Besides, we have stopped fighting anybody or anything. We have to!

Chapter 8
TO WIVES

WITH FEW EXCEPTIONS, our book thus far has spoken of men. But what we have said applies quite as much to women. Our activities in behalf of women who drink are on the increase. There is every evidence that women regain their health as readily as men if they try our suggestions.

But for every man who drinks others are involved— the wife who trembles in fear of the next debauch; the mother and father who see their son wasting away.

Among us are wives, relatives and friends whose problem has been solved, as well as some who have not yet found a happy solution. We want the wives of Alcoholics Anonymous to address the wives of men who drink too much. What they say will apply to nearly everyone bound by ties of blood or affection to an alcoholic.

As wives of Alcoholics Anonymous, we would like you to feel that we understand as perhaps few can. We want to analyze mistakes we have made. We want to leave you with the feeling that no situation is too difficult and no unhappiness too great to be overcome.

We have traveled a rocky road, there is no mistake about that. We have had long rendezvous with hurt pride, frustration, self-pity, misunderstanding and fear. These are not pleasant companions. We have been driven to maudlin sympathy, to bitter resentment. Some of us veered from extreme to extreme, ever hoping that one day our loved ones would be themselves once more.

Our loyalty and the desire that our husbands hold up their heads and be like other men have begotten all sorts of predicaments. We have been unselfish and self-sacrificing. We have told innumerable lies to protect our pride and our husbands' reputations. We have prayed, we have begged, we have been patient. We have struck out viciously. We have run away. We have been hysterical. We have been terror stricken. We have sought sympathy. We have had retaliatory love affairs with other men.

Our homes have been battle-grounds many an evening. In the morning we have kissed and made up. Our friends have counseled chucking the men and we have done so with finality, only to be back in a little while hoping, always hoping. Our men have sworn great solemn oaths that they were through drinking forever. We have believed them when no one else could or would. Then, in days, weeks, or months, a fresh outburst.

We seldom had friends at our homes, never knowing how or when the men of the house would appear. We could make few social engagements. We came to live almost alone. When we were invited out, our husbands sneaked so many drinks that they spoiled the occasion. If, on the other hand, they took nothing, their self-pity made them killjoys.

There were never financial security. Positions were always in jeopardy or gone. An armored car could not have brought the pay envelopes home. The checking account melted like snow in June.

Sometimes there were other women. How heartbreaking was this discovery; how cruel to be told they understood our men as we did not!

The bill collectors, the sheriffs, the angry taxi drivers, the policemen, the bums, the pals, and even the ladies they sometimes brought home—our husbands thought we were so inhospitable. "Joykiller, nag, wet blanket"—that's what they said. Next day they would be themselves again and we would forgive and try to forget.

We have tried to hold the love of our children for their father. We have told small tots that father was sick, which was much nearer the truth than we realized. They struck the children, kicked out door panels, smashed treasure crockery, and ripped the keys out of pianos. In the midst of such pandemonium they may have rushed out threatening to live with the other woman forever. In desperation, we have even got tight ourselves—the drunk to end all drunks. The unexpected result was that our husbands seemed to like it.

Perhaps at this point we got a divorce and took the children home to father and mother. Then we were severely criticized by our husband's parents for desertion. Usually we did not leave. We stayed on and on. We finally sought employment ourselves as destitution faced us and our families.

We began to ask medical advice as the sprees got closer together. The alarming physical and mental symptoms, the deepening pall of remorse, depression and inferiority that settled down on our loved ones—

these things terrified and distracted us. As animals on a treadmill, we have patiently and wearily climbed, falling back in exhaustion after each futile effort to reach solid ground. Most of us have entered the final stage with its commitment to health resorts, sanitariums, hospitals, and jails. Sometimes there were screaming delirium and insanity. Death was often near.

Under these conditions we naturally made mistakes. Some of them rose out of ignorance of alcoholism. Sometimes we sensed dimly that we were dealing with sick men. Had we fully understood the nature of the alcoholic illness, we might have behaved differently.

How could men who loved their wives and children be so unthinking, so callous, so cruel? There could be no love in such persons, we thought. And just as we were being convinced of their heart-lessness, they would surprise us with fresh resolves and new attentions. For a while they would be their old sweet selves, only to dash the new structure of affection to pieces once more. Asked why they commenced to drink again, they would reply with some silly excuse, or none. It was so baffling, so heartbreaking. Could we have been so mistaken in the men we married? When drinking, they were strangers. Sometimes they were so inaccessible that it seemed as though a great wall had been built around them.

And even if they did not love their families, how could they be so blind about themselves? What had become of their judgment, their common sense, their will power? Why could they not see that drink meant ruin to them? Why was it, when these dangers were pointed out that they agreed, and then got drunk again immediately?

These are some of the questions which race through the mind of every woman who has an alcoholic husband. We hope this book has answered some of them. Perhaps your husband has been living in that strange world of alcoholism where everything is distorted and exaggerated. You can see that he really does love you with his better self. Of course, there is such a thing as incompatibility, but in nearly every instance the alcoholic only seems to be unloving and inconsiderate; it is usually because he is warped and sickened that he says and does these appalling things. Today most of our men are better husbands and fathers than ever before.

Try not to condemn your alcoholic husband no matter what he says or does. He is just another very sick, unreasonable person. Treat him, when you can, as though he had pneumonia. When he angers you, remember that he is very ill.

There is an important exception to the foregoing. We realize some men are thoroughly bad-intentioned, that no amount of patience will make any difference. An alcoholic of this temperament may be quick to use this chapter as a club over your head. Don't let him get away with it. If you are positive he is one of this type you may feel you had better leave. Is it right to let him ruin your life and the lives of your children? Especially when he has before him a way to stop his drinking and abuse if he really wants to pay the price.

The problem with which you struggle usually falls within one of four categories:

One: Your husband may be only a heavy drinker.

His drinking may be constant or it may be heavy only on certain occasions. Perhaps he spends too much money for liquor. It may be slowing him up mentally and physically, but he does not see it. Sometimes he is a source of embarrassment to you and his friends. He is positive he can handle his liquor, that it does him no harm, that drinking is necessary in his business. He would probably be insulted if he were called an alcoholic. This world is full of people like him. Some will moderate or stop altogether, and some will not. Of those who keep on, a good number will become true alcoholics after a while.

Two: Your husband is showing lack of control, for he is unable to stay on the water wagon even when he wants to. He often gets entirely out of hand when drinking. He admits this is true, but is positive that he will do better. He has begun to try, with or without your cooperation, various means of moderating or staying dry. Maybe he is beginning to lose his friends. His business may suffer somewhat. He is worried at times, and is becoming aware that he cannot drink like other people. He sometimes drinks in the morning and through the day also, to hold his nervousness in check. He is remorseful after serious drinking bouts and tells you he wants to stop. But when he gets over the spree, he begins to think once more how he can drink moderately next time. We think this person is in danger. These are the earmarks of a real alcoholic. Perhaps he can still tend to business fairly well. He has by no means ruined everything. As we say among ourselves, *"He wants to want to stop."*

Three: This husband has gone much further than husband number two. Though once like number two he became worse. His friends have slipped away, his home is a near-wreck and he cannot hold a position. Maybe the doctor has been called in, and the weary round of sanitariums and hospitals has begun. He admits he cannot drink like other people, but does not see why. He clings to the notion that he will yet find a way to do so. He may have come to the point where he desperately wants to stop but cannot. His case presents additional questions, which we shall try to answer for you. You can be quite hopeful of a situation like this.

Four: You may have a husband of whom you completely despair. He has been placed in one institution after another. He is violent, or appears definitely insane when drunk. Sometimes he drinks on the way home from the hospital. Perhaps he has had delirium tremens. Doctors may shake their heads and advise you to have him committed. Maybe you have already been obliged to put him away. This picture may not be as dark as it looks. Many of our husbands were just as far gone. Yet they got well.

Let's now go back to husband number one. Oddly enough, he is often difficult to deal with. He enjoys drinking. It stirs his imagination. His friends feel closer over a highball. Perhaps you enjoy drinking with him yourself when he doesn't go too far. You have passed happy evenings together chatting and drinking before your fire. Perhaps you both like parties which would be dull without liquor. We have enjoyed such evenings ourselves; we had a good time. We know all about liquor as a social lubricant. Some, but not all of us, think it has its advantages when reasonably used.

The first principle of success is that you should never be angry. Even though your husband becomes unbearable and you have to leave him temporarily, you should, if you can, go without rancor. Patience and good temper are most necessary.

Our next thought is that you should never tell him what he must do about his drinking. If he gets the idea that you are a nag or a killjoy, your chance of accomplishing anything useful may be zero. He will use that as an excuse to drink more. He will tell you he is misunderstood. This may lead to lonely evenings for you. He may seek someone else to console him—not always another man.

Be determined that your husband's drinking is not going to spoil your relations with your children or your friends. They need your companionship and your help. It is possible to have a full and useful life, though your husband continues to drink. We know women who are unafraid, even happy under these conditions. Do not set your heart on reforming your husband. You may be unable to do so, no matter how hard you try.

We know these suggestions are sometimes difficult to follow, but you will save many heartbreak if you can succeed in observing them. Your husband may come to appreciate your reasonableness and patience. This may lay the groundwork for a friendly talk about his alcoholic problem. Try to have him bring up the subject himself. Be sure you are not critical during such a discussion. Attempt instead, to put yourself in his place. Let him see that you want to be helpful rather than critical.

When a discussion does arise, you might suggest he

read this book or at least the chapter on alcoholism. Tell him you have been worried, though perhaps needlessly. You think he ought to know the subject better, as everyone should have a clear understanding of the risk he takes if he drinks too much. Show him you have confidence in his power to stop or moderate. Say you do not want to be a wet blanket; that you only want him to take care of his health. Thus you may succeed in interesting him in alcoholism.

He probably has several alcoholics among his own acquaintances. You might suggest that you both take an interest in them. Drinkers like to help other drinkers. Your husband may be willing to talk to one of them.

If this kind of approach does not catch your husband's interest, it may best to drop the subject, but after a friendly talk your husband will usually revive the topic himself. This may take patient waiting, but it will be worth it. Meanwhile you might try to help the wife of another serious drinker. If you act upon these principles, your husband may stop or moderate.

Suppose, however, that your husband fits the description of number two. The same principles which apply to husband number one should be practiced. But after his next binge, ask him if he would really like to get over drinking for good. Do not ask that he do it for you or anyone else. Just would he *like* to?

The chances are he would. Show him your copy of this book and tell him what you have found out about alcoholism. Show him that as alcoholics, the writers of the book understand. Tell him some of the interesting stories you have read. If you think he will be shy of a spiritual remedy, ask him to look at the chapter on alcoholism. Then perhaps he will be interested enough to continue.

If he is enthusiastic your cooperation will mean a great deal. If he is lukewarm or thinks he is not an alcoholic, we suggest you leave him alone. Avoid urging him to follow our program. The seed has been planted in his mind. He knows that thousands of men, much like himself, have recovered. But don't remind him of this after he has been drinking, for he may be angry. Sooner or later, you are likely to find him reading the book once more. Wait until repeated stumbling convinces him he must act, for the more you hurry him the longer his recovery may be delayed.

If you have a number three husband, you may be in luck. Being certain he wants to stop, you can go to him with this volume as joyfully as though you had struck oil. He may not share your enthusiasm, but he is practically sure to read the book and he may go for the program at once. If he does not, you will probably not have long to wait. Again, you should not crowd him. Let him decide for himself. Cheerfully see him through more sprees. Talk about his condition or this book only when he raises the issue. In some cases it may be better to let someone outside the family present the book. They can urge action without arousing hostility. If your husband is otherwise a normal individual, your chances are good at this stage.

You would suppose that men in the fourth classification would be quite hopeless, but that is not so. Many of Alcoholics Anonymous were like that. Everybody had given them up. Defeat seemed certain. Yet often such men had spectacular and powerful recoveries.

There are exceptions. Some men have been so impaired by alcohol that they cannot stop. Sometimes there are cases where alcoholism is complicated by other disorders. A good doctor or psychiatrist can tell you whether these complications are serious. In any event, try to have your husband read this book. His reaction may be one of enthusiasm. If he is already committed to an institution, but can convince you and your doctor that he means business, give him a chance to try our method, unless the doctor thinks his mental condition too abnormal or dangerous. We make this recommendation with some confidence. For years we have been working with alcoholics committed to institutions. Since this book was first published, A.A. has released thousand of alcoholics from asylums and hospitals of every kind. The majority have never returned. The power of God goes deep!

You may have the reverse situation on your hands. Perhaps you have a husband who is at large, but who should be committed. Some men cannot or will not get over alcoholism. When they become too dangerous, we think the kind thing is to lock them up, but of course a good doctor should always be consulted. The wives and children of such men suffer horribly, but not more than the men themselves.

But sometimes you must start life anew. We know women who have done it. If such women adopt a spiritual way of life their road will be smoother.

If you husband is a drinker, you probably worry over what other people are thinking and you hate to meet your friends. You draw more and more into yourself and you think everyone is talking about conditions at your home. You avoid the subject of drinking, even with your own parents. You do not know what to tell the children. When your husband is bad, you become a trembling recluse, wishing the telephone had never been invented.

We find that most of this embarrassment is unnecessary. While you need not discuss your husband at length, you can quietly let your friends know the nature of his illness. But you must be on guard not to embarrass or harm your husband.

When you have carefully explained to such people that he is a sick person, you will have created a new atmosphere. Barriers which have sprung up between you and your friends will disappear with the growth of sympathetic understanding. You will no longer be self-conscious or feel that you must apologize as though your husband were a weak character. He may be anything but that. Your new courage, good nature and lack of self-consciousness will do wonders for you socially.

The same principle applies in dealing with the children. Unless they actually need protection from their father, it is best not to take sides in any argument he has with them while drinking. Use your energies to promote a better understanding all around. Then the terrible tension which grips the home of every problem drinker will be lessened.

Frequently, you have felt obliged to tell your husband's employer and his friends that he was sick, when as a matter of fact he was tight. Avoid answering these inquiries as much as you can. Whenever possible, let your husband explain. Your desire to protect him should not cause you to lie to people when they have a right to know where he is and what he is doing. Discuss this with him when he is sober and in good spirits. Ask him what you should do if he places you in such a position again. But be careful not to be resentful about the last time he did so.

There is another paralyzing fear. You may be afraid your husband will lose his position; you are thinking of the disgrace and hard times which will befall you and the children. This experience may come to you. Or you may already have had it several times. Should it happen again, regard it in a different light. Maybe it will prove a blessing! It may convince your husband he wants to stop drinking forever. And now you know that he can stop if he will! Time after time, this apparent calamity has been a boon to us, for it opened up a path which led to the discovery of God.

We have elsewhere remarked how much better life is when lived on a spiritual plane. If God can solve the age-old riddle of alcoholism, He can solve your problems too. We wives found that, like everybody else, we were afflicted with pride, self-pity, vanity and all the things which go to make up the self-centered person; and we were not above selfishness or dishonesty. As our husbands began to apply spiritual principles in their lives, we began to see the desirability of doing so too.

At first, some of us did not believe we needed this help. We thought, on the whole, we were pretty good women, capable of being nicer if our husbands stopped drinking. But it was a silly idea that we were too good to need God. Now we try to put spiritual principles to work in every department of our lives. When we do that, we find it solves our problems too; the ensuing lack of fear, worry and hurt feelings is a wonderful thing. We urge you to try our program, for nothing will be so helpful to your husband as the radically changed attitude toward him which God will show you how to have. Go along with your husband if you possibly can.

If you and your husband find a solution for the pressing problem of drink you are, of course, going to be very happy. But all problems will not be solved at once. Seed has started to sprout in a new soil, but growth has only begun. In spite of your new-found happiness, there will be ups and downs. Many of the old problems will still be with you. This is as it should be.

The faith and sincerity of both you and your husband will be put to the test. These work-outs should be regarded as part of your education, for thus you will be learning to live. You will make mistakes, but if you are in earnest they will not drag you down. Instead, you will capitalize them. A better way of life will emerge when they are overcome.

Some of the snags you will encounter are irritation, hurt feelings and resentments. Your husband will sometimes be unreasonable and you will want to criticize. Starting from a speck on the domestic horizon, great thunderclouds of dispute may gather. These family dissensions are very dangerous, especially to your husband. Often you must carry the burden of avoiding them or keeping them under control. Never forget that resentment is a deadly hazard to an alcoholic. We do not mean that you have to agree with your husband whenever there is an honest difference of opinion. Just be careful not to disagree in a resentful or critical spirit.

You and your husband will find that you can dispose of serious problems easier than you can the trivial ones. Next time you and he have a heated discussion, no matter what the subject, it should be the privilege of either to smile or say; "This is getting serious. I'm sorry I got disturbed. Let's talk about it later." If your husband is trying to live on a spiritual basis, he will also be doing everything in his power to avoid disagreement or contention.

Your husband knows he owes you more than sobriety. He wants to make good. Yet you must not expect too much. His ways of thinking and doing are the habits of years. Patience, tolerance, understanding and love are the watchwords. Show him these things in yourself and they will be reflected back to you from him. Live and let live is the rule. If you both show a willingness to remedy your own defects, there will be little need to criticize each other.

We women carry with us a picture of the ideal man, the sort of chap we would like our husbands to be. It is the most natural thing in the world, once his liquor problem is solved, to feel that he will now measure up to that cherished vision. The chances are he will not for, like yourself, he is just beginning his development. Be patient.

Another feeling we are very likely to entertain is one of resentment that love and loyalty could not cure our husbands of alcoholism. We do not like the thought that the contents of a book or the work of another alcoholic has accomplished in a few weeks that for which we struggled for years. At such moments we forget that alcoholism is an illness over which we could not possibly have had any power. Your husband will be the first to say it was your devotion and care which brought him to the point where he could have a spiritual experience. Without you he would have gone to pieces long ago. When resentful thoughts come, try to pause and count your blessings. After all, your family is reunited, alcohol is no longer a problem and you and your husband are working together toward an undreamed-of future.

Still another difficulty is that you may become jealous of the attention he bestows on other people, especially alcoholics. You have been starving for his companionship, yet he spends long hours helping other men and their families. You feel he should now be yours. The fact is that he should work with other people to maintain his own sobriety. Sometimes he will be so interested that he becomes really neglectful. Your house is filled with strangers. You may not like some of them. He gets stirred up about their troubles, but not at all about yours. It will do little good if you point that out and urge more attention for yourself. We find it a real mistake to dampen his enthusiasm for alcoholic work. You should join in his efforts as much as you possibly can. We suggest that you direct some of your thought to the wives of his new alcoholic friends. They need the counsel and love of a woman who has gone through what you have.

It is probably true that you and your husband have been living too much alone, for drinking many times isolates the wife of an alcoholic. Therefore, you probably need fresh interests and a great cause to live for as much as your husband. If you cooperate, rather than complain, you will find that his excess enthusiasm will tone down. Both of you will awaken to a new sense of responsibility for others. You, as well as your husband, ought to think of what you can put into life instead of how much you can take out. Inevitably your lives will be fuller for doing so. You will lose the old life to find one much better.

Perhaps your husband will make a fair start on the new basis, but just as things are going beautifully he dismays you by coming home drunk. If you are satisfied he really wants to get over drinking, you need not be alarmed. Though it is infinitely better that he have no relapse at all, as has been true with many of our men, it is by no means a bad thing in some cases. Your husband will see at once that he must redouble his spiritual activities if he expects to survive. You need not remind him of his spiritual deficiency—he will know of it. Cheer him up and ask him how you can be still more helpful.

The slightest sign of fear or intolerance may lessen your husband's chance of recovery. In a weak moment he may take your dislike of his high-stepping friends as one of those insanely trivial excuses to drink.

We never, never try to arrange a man's life so as to shield him from temptation. The slightest disposition on your part to guide his appointments or his affairs so he will not be tempted will be noticed. Make him feel absolutely free to come and go as he likes. This is important. If he gets drunk, don't blame yourself. God has either removed your husband's liquor problem or He has not. If not, it had better be found out right away. Then you and your husband can get right down to fundamentals. If a repetition is to be prevented, place the problem, along with everything else, in God's hands.

We realize that we have been giving you much direction and advice. We may have seemed to lecture. If that is so we are sorry, for we ourselves, don't always care for people who lecture us. But what we have related is based upon experience, some of it painful. We had to learn these things the hard way. That is why we are anxious that you understand, and that you avoid these unnecessary difficulties.

So to you out there—who may soon be with us—we say "Good luck and God bless you!"

Chapter 9

THE FAMILY AFTERWARD

O UR WOMEN FOLK have suggested certain attitudes a wife may take with the husband who is recovering. Perhaps they created the impression that he is to be wrapped in cotton wool and placed on a pedestal. Successful readjustment means the opposite. All members of the family should meet upon the common ground of tolerance, understanding and love. This involves a process of deflation. The alcoholic, his wife, his children, his "in-laws," each one is likely to have fixed ideas about the family's attitude towards himself or herself. Each is interested in having his or her wishes respected. We find the more one member of the family demands that the others concede to him, the more resentful they become. This makes for discord and unhappiness.

And why? Is it not because each wants to play the lead? Is not each trying to arrange the family show to his liking? Is he not unconsciously trying to see what he can take from the family life rather than give?

Cessation of drinking is but the first step away from a highly strained, abnormal condition. A doctor said to us, "Years of living with an alcoholic is almost sure to make any wife or child neurotic. The entire family is, to some extent, ill." Let families realize, as they start their journey, that all will not be fair weather. Each in his turn may be footsore and may straggle.

There will be alluring shortcuts and by-paths down which they may wander and lose their way.

Suppose we tell you some of the obstacles a family will meet; suppose we suggest how they may be avoided—even converted to good use for others. The family of an alcoholic longs for the return of happiness and security. They remember when father was romantic, thoughtful and successful. Today's life is measured against that of other years and, when it falls short, the family may be unhappy.

Family confidence in dad is rising high. The good old days will soon be back, they think. Sometimes they demand that dad bring them back instantly! God, they believe, almost owes this recompense on a long overdue account. But the head of the house has spent years in pulling down the structures of business, romance, friendship, health—these things are now ruined or damaged. It will take time to clear away the wreck. Though old buildings will eventually be replaced by finer ones, the new structures will take years to complete.

Father knows he is to blame; it may take him many seasons of hard work to be restored financially, but he shouldn't be reproached. Perhaps he will never have much money again. But the wise family will admire him for what he is trying to be, rather than for what he is trying to get.

Now and then the family will be plagued by spectres from the past, for the drinking career of almost every alcoholic has been marked by escapades, funny, humiliating, shameful or tragic. The first impulse will be to bury these skeletons in a dark closet and padlock the door. The family may be possessed by the idea

123

that future happiness can be based only upon for-getfulness of the past. We think that such a view is self-centered and in direct conflict with the new way of living.

Henry Ford once made a wise remark to the effect that experience is the thing of supreme value in life. That is true only if one is willing to turn the past to good account. We grow by our willingness to face and rectify errors and convert them into assets. The alcoholic's past thus becomes the principal asset of the family and frequently it is almost the only one!

This painful past may be of infinite value to other families still struggling with their problem. We think each family which has been relieved owes something to those who have not, and when the occasion requires, each member of it should be only too willing to bring former mistakes, no matter how grievous, out of their hiding places. Showing others who suffer how we were given help is the very thing which makes life seem so worth while to us now. Cling to the thought that, in God's hands, the dark past is the greatest possession you have—the key to life and happiness for others. With it you can avert death and misery for them.

It is possible to dig up past misdeeds so they become a blight, a veritable plague. For example, we know of situations in which the alcoholic or his wife have had love affairs. In the first flush of spiritual experience they forgave each other and drew closer together. The miracle of reconciliation was at hand. Then, under one provocation or another, the aggrieved one would unearth the old affair and angrily cast its ashes about. A few of us have had these growing pains and they hurt a great deal. Husbands and wives have sometimes been obliged to separate for a time until new perspective, new victory over hurt pride could be rewon. In most cases, the alcoholic survived this ordeal without relapse, but not always. So we think that unless some good and useful purpose is to be served, past occurrences should not be discussed.

We families of Alcoholics Anonymous keep few skeletons in the closet. Everyone knows about the others' alcoholic troubles. This is a condition which, in ordinary life, would produce untold grief; there might be scandalous gossip, laughter at the expense of other people, and a tendency to take advantage of intimate information. Among us, these are rare occurrences. We do talk about each other a great deal, but we almost invariably temper such talk by a spirit of love and tolerance.

Another principle we observe carefully is that we do not relate intimate experiences of another person unless we are sure he would approve. We find it better, when possible, to stick to our own stories. A man may criticize or laugh at himself and it will affect others favorably, but criticism or ridicule coming from another often produces the contrary effect. Members of a family should watch such matters carefully, for one careless, inconsiderate remark has been known to raise the very devil. We alcoholics are sensitive people. It takes some of us a long time to outgrow that serious handicap.

Many alcoholics are enthusiasts. They run to extremes. At the beginning of recovery a man will take, as a rule, one of two directions. He may either plunge into a frantic attempt to get on his feet in business, or he may be so enthralled by his new life that he talks or thinks of little else. In either case certain family problems will arise. With these we have had experience galore.

We think it dangerous if he rushes headlong at his economic problem. The family will be affected also, pleasantly at first, as they feel their money troubles are about to be solved, then not so pleasantly as they find themselves neglected. Dad may be tired at night and preoccupied by day. He may take small interest in the children and may show irritation when reproved for his delinquencies. If not irritable, he may seem dull and boring, not gay and affectionate as the family would like him to be. Mother may complain of inattention. They are all disappointed, and often let him feel it. Beginning with such complaints, a barrier arises. He is straining every nerve to make up for lost time. He is striving to recover fortune and reputation and feels he is doing very well.

Sometimes mother and children don't think so. Having been neglected and misused in the past, they think father owes them more than they are getting. They want him to make a fuss over them. They expect him to give them the nice times they used to have before he drank so much, and to show his contrition for what they suffered. But dad doesn't give freely of himself. Resentment grows. He becomes still less communicative. Sometimes he explodes over a trifle. The family is mystified. They criticize, pointing out how he is falling down on his spiritual program.

This sort of thing can be avoided. Both father and the family are mistaken, though each side may have some justification. It is of little use to argue and only makes the impasse worse. The family must realize that dad, though marvelously improved, is still convalescing. They should be thankful he is sober and able to be of this world once more. Let them praise his progress. Let them remember that his drinking wrought all kinds of damage that may take long to repair. If they sense these things, they will not take so seriously his periods of crankiness, depression, or apathy, which will disappear when there is tolerance, love, and spiritual understanding.

The head of the house ought to remember that he is mainly to blame for what befell his home. He can scarcely square the account in his lifetime. But he must see the danger of over-concentration on financial success. Although financial recovery is on the way for many of us, we found we could not place money first. For us, material well-being always followed spiritual progress; it never preceded.

Since the home has suffered more than anything else, it is well that a man exert himself there. He is not likely to get far in any direction if he fails to show unselfishness and love under his own roof. We know there are difficult wives and families, but the man who is getting over alcoholism must remember he did much to make them so.

As each member of a resentful family begins to see his shortcomings and admits them to the others, he lays a basis for helpful discussion. These family talks will be constructive if they can be carried on without heated argument, self-pity, self-justification or resentful criticism. Little by little, mother and children will see they ask too much, and father will see he gives too little. Giving, rather than getting, will become the guiding principle.

Assume on the other hand that father has, at the outset, a stirring spiritual experience. Overnight, as it were, he is a different man. He becomes a religious enthusiast. He is unable to focus on anything else. As soon as his sobriety begins to be taken as a matter of course, the family may look at their strange new dad with apprehension, then with irritation. There is talk about spiritual matters morning, noon and night. He may demand that the family find God in a hurry, or exhibit amazing indifference to them and say he is above worldly considerations. He may tell mother, who has been religious all her life, that she doesn't know what it's all about, and that she had better get his brand of spirituality while there is yet time

When father takes this tack, the family may react unfavorably. They may be jealous of a God who has stolen dad's affections. While grateful that he drinks no more, they may not like the idea that God has accomplished the miracle where they failed. They often forget father was beyond human aid. They may not see why their love and devotion did not straighten him out. Dad is not so spiritual after all, they say. If he means to right his past wrongs, why all this concern for everyone in the world but his family? What about his talk that God will take care of them? They suspect father is a bit balmy!

He is not so unbalanced as they might think. Many of us have experienced dad's elation. We have indulged in spiritual intoxication. Like a gaunt prospector, belt drawn in over the last ounce of food, our pick struck gold. Joy at our release from a lifetime of frustration knew no bounds. Father feels he has struck something better than gold. For a time he may try to hug the new treasure to himself. He may not see at once that he has barely scratched a limitless lode which will pay dividends only if he mines it for the rest of his life and insists on giving away the entire product.

If the family cooperates, dad will soon see that he is suffering from a distortion of values. He will perceive that his spiritual growth is lopsided, that for an average man like himself, a spiritual life which does not include his family obligations may not be so perfect after all. If the family will appreciate that dad's current behavior is but a phase of his development, all will be well. In the midst of an understanding and sympathetic family, these vagaries of dad's spiritual infancy will quickly disappear.

The opposite may happen should the family condemn and criticize. Dad may feel that for years his drinking has placed him on the wrong side of every argument, but that now he has become a superior person with God on his side. If the family persists in criticism, this fallacy may take a still greater hold on father. Instead of treating the family as he should, he may retreat further into himself and feel he has spiritual justification for so doing.

Though the family does not fully agree with dad's spiritual activities, they should let him have his head. Even if he displays a certain amount of neglect and irresponsibility towards the family, it is well to let him go as far as he likes in helping other alcoholics. During those first days of convalescence, this will do more to insure his sobriety than anything else. Though

129

some of his manifestations are alarming and disagreeable, we think dad will be on a firmer
foundation than the man who is placing business or
professional success ahead of spiritual development.
He will be less likely to drink again, and anything is
preferable to that.

Those of us who have spent much time in the
world of spiritual make-believe have eventually seen
the childishness of it. This dream world has been
replaced by a great sense of purpose, accompanied
by a growing consciousness of the power of God in
our lives. We have come to believe He would like us
to keep our heads in the clouds with Him, but that
our feet ought to be firmly planted on earth. That is
where our fellow travelers are, and that is where our
work must be done. These are the realities for us.
We have found nothing incompatible between a
powerful spiritual experience and a life of sane and
happy usefulness.

One more suggestion: Whether the family has
spiritual convictions or not, they may do well to
examine the principles by which the alcoholic
member is trying to live. They can hardly fail to
approve these simple principles, though the head of
the house still fails somewhat in practicing them.
Nothing will help the man who is off on a spiritual
tangent so much as the wife who adopts a sane
spiritual program, making a better practical use of it.

There will be other profound changes in the
household. Liquor incapacitated father for so
many years that mother became head of the
house. She met these responsibilities gallantly.
By force of circumstances, she was often
obliged to treat father as a sick or wayward child. Even when he wanted to assert himself

he could not, for his drinking placed him constantly in the wrong. Mother made all the plans and gave the directions. When sober, father usually obeyed. Thus mother, through no fault of her own, became accustomed to wearing the family trousers. Father, coming suddenly to life again, often begins to assert himself. This means trouble, unless the family watches for these tendencies in each other and comes to a friendly agreement about them.

Drinking isolates most homes from the outside world. Father may have laid aside for years all normal activities--clubs, civic duties, sports. When he renews interest in such things, a feeling of jealousy may arise. The family may feel they hold a mortgage on dad, so big that no equity should be left for outsiders. Instead of developing new channels of activity for themselves, mother and children demand that he stay home and make up the deficiency.

At the very beginning, the couple ought to frankly face the fact that each will have to yield here and there if the family is going to play an effective part in the new life. Father will necessarily spend much time with other alcoholics, but this activity should be balanced. New acquaintances who know nothing of alcoholism might be made and thoughtful consideration given their needs. The problems of the community might engage attention. Though the family has no religious connections, they may wish to make contact with or take membership in a religious body.

Alcoholics who have derided religious people will be helped by such contacts. Being possessed of a spiritual experience, the alcoholic will find he has much in common with these people, though he may

131

differ with them on many matters. If he does not argue about religion, he will make new friends and is sure to find new avenues of usefulness and pleasure. He and his family can be a bright spot in such congregations. He may bring new hope and new courage to many a priest, minister, or rabbi, who gives his all to minister to our troubled world. We intend the foregoing as a helpful suggestion only. So far as we are concerned, there is nothing obligatory about it. As non-denominational people, we cannot make up others' minds for them. Each individual should consult his own conscience.

We have been speaking to you of serious, sometimes tragic things. We have been dealing with alcohol in its worst aspect. But we aren't a glum lot. If newcomers could see no joy or fun in our existence, they wouldn't want it. We absolutely insist on enjoying life. We try not to indulge in cynicism over the state of the nations, nor do we carry the world's troubles on our shoulders. When we see a man sinking into the mire that is alcoholism, we give him first aid and place what we have at his disposal. For his sake, we do recount and almost relive the horrors of our past. But those of us who have tried to shoulder the entire burden and trouble of others find we are soon overcome by them.

So we think cheerfulness and laughter make for usefulness. Outsiders are sometimes shocked when we burst into merriment over a seemingly tragic experience out of the past. But why shouldn't we laugh? We have recovered, and have been given the power to help others.

Everybody knows that those in bad health, and those who seldom play, do not laugh much. So let each family play together or separately, as much as their circumstances warrant. We are sure God wants us to be happy, joyous, and free. We cannot subscribe to the belief that this life is a vale of tears, though it once was just that for many of us. But it is clear that we made our own misery. God didn't do it. Avoid then, the deliberate manufacture of misery, but if trouble comes, cheerfully capitalize it as an opportunity to demonstrate His omnipotence.

Now about health: A body badly burned by alcohol does not often recover overnight nor do twisted thinking and depression vanish in a twinkling. We are convinced that a spiritual mode of living is a most powerful health restorative. We, who have recovered from serious drinking, are miracles of mental health. But we have seen remarkable transformations in our bodies. Hardly one of our crowd now shows any mark of dissipation.

But this does not mean that we disregard human health measures. God has abundantly supplied this world with fine doctors, psychologists, and practitioners of various kinds. Do not hesitate to take your health problems to such persons. Most of them give freely of themselves, that their fellows may enjoy sound minds and bodies. Try to remember that though God has wrought miracles among us, we should never belittle a good doctor or psychiatrist. Their services are often indispensable in treating a newcomer and in following his case afterward.

One of the many doctors who had the opportunity of reading this book in manuscript form told us that the use of sweets was often helpful, of course, depending upon a doctor's advice. He thought all alcoholics

133

should constantly have chocolate available for its quick energy value at times of fatigue. He added that occasionally in the night a vague craving arose which would be satisfied by candy. Many of us have noticed a tendency to eat sweets and have found this practice beneficial.

A word about sex relations. Alcohol is so sexually stimulating to some men that they have over-indulged. Couples are occasionally dismayed to find that when drinking is stopped the man tends to be impotent. Unless the reason is understood, there may be an emotional upset. Some of us had this experience, only to enjoy, in a few months, a finer intimacy than ever. There should be no hesitancy in consulting a doctor or psychologist if the condition persists. We do not know of many cases where this difficulty lasted long.

The alcoholic may find it hard to re-establish friendly relations with his children. Their young minds were impressionable while he was drinking. Without saying so, they may cordially hate him for what he has done to them and to their mother. The children are sometimes dominated by a pathetic hardness and cynicism. They cannot seem to forgive and forget. This may hang on for months, long after their mother has accepted dad's new way of living and thinking.

In time they will see that he is a new man and in their own way they will let him know it. When this happens, they can be invited to join in morning meditation and then they can take part in the daily discussion without rancor or bias. From that point on, progress will be rapid. Marvelous results often follow such a reunion.

Whether the family goes on a spiritual basis or not, the alcoholic member has to if he would recover. The others must be convinced of his new status beyond the shadow of a doubt. Seeing is believing to most families who have lived with a drinker.

Here is a case in point: One of our friends is a heavy smoker and coffee drinker. There was no doubt he over-indulged. Seeing this, and meaning to be helpful, his wife commenced to admonish him about it. He admitted he was overdoing these things, but frankly said that he was not ready to stop. His wife is one of those persons who really feels there is something rather sinful about these commodities, so she nagged and her intolerance finally threw him into a fit of anger. He got drunk.

Of course our friend was wrong—dead wrong. He had to painfully admit that and mend his spiritual fences. Though he is now a most effective member of Alcoholics Anonymous, he still smokes and drinks coffee, but neither his wife nor anyone else stands in judgment. She sees she was wrong to make a burning issue out of such a matter when his more serious ailments were being rapidly cured.

We have three little mottoes which are apropos. Here they are:

> *First Things First*
> *Live and Let Live*
> *Easy Does It.*

Chapter 10
TO EMPLOYERS

A MONG MANY employers nowadays, we think of one member who has spent much of his life in the world of big business. He has hired and fired hundreds of men. He knows the alcoholic as the employer sees him. His present views ought to prove exceptionally useful to businessmen everywhere.

But let him tell you:

I was at one time assistant manager of a corporation department employing sixty-six hundred men. One day my secretary came in saying that Mr. B—insisted on speaking with me. I told her to say that I was not interested. I had warned him several times that he had but one more chance. Not long afterward he had called me from Hartford on two successive days, so drunk he could hardly speak. I told him he was through—finally and forever.

My secretary returned to say that it was not Mr. B—on the phone; it was Mr. B–'s brother, and he wished to give me a message. I still expected a plea for clemency, but these words came through the receiver: "I just wanted to tell you Paul jumped from a hotel window in Hartford last Saturday. He left us a note saying you were the best boss he ever had, and that you were not to blame in any way."

Another time, as I opened a letter which lay on my

136

desk, a newspaper clipping fell out. It was the obituary of one of the best salesmen I ever had. After two weeks of drinking, he had placed his toe on the trigger of a loaded shotgun—the barrel was in his mouth. I had discharged him for drinking six weeks before.

Still another experience: A woman's voice came faintly over long distance from Virginia. She wanted to know if her husband's company insurance was still in force. Four days before he had hanged himself in his woodshed. I had been obliged to discharge him for drinking, though he was brilliant, alert, and one of the best organizers I have ever known.

Here were three exceptional men lost to this world because I did not understand alcoholism as I do now. What irony—I became an alcoholic myself! And but for the intervention of an understanding person, I might have followed in their footsteps. My downfall cost the business community unknown thousands of dollars, for it takes real money to train a man for an executive position. This kind of waste goes on unabated. We think the business fabric is shot through with a situation which might be helped by better understanding all around.

Nearly every modern employer feels a moral responsibility for the well-being of his help, and he tries to meet these responsibilities. That he has not always done so for the alcoholic is easily understood. To him the alcoholic has often seemed a fool of the first magnitude. Because of the employee's special ability, or of his own strong personal attachment to him, the employer has sometimes kept such a man at work long beyond a reasonable period. Some employers have tried every known remedy. In only a few instances

137

has there been a lack of patience and tolerance. And we, who have imposed on the best of employers, can scarcely blame them if they have been short with us.

Here, for instance, is a typical example: An officer of one of the largest banking institutions in America knows I no longer drink. One day he told me about an executive of the same bank who, from his description, was undoubtedly alcoholic. This seemed to me like an opportunity to be helpful, so I spent two hours talking about alcoholism, the malady, and described the symptoms and results as well as I could. His comment was, "Very interesting. But I'm sure this man is done drinking. He has just returned from a three months' leave of absence, has taken a cure, looks fine, and to clinch the matter, the board of directors told him this was his last chance."

The only answer I could make was that if the man followed the usual pattern, he would go on a bigger bust than ever. I felt this was inevitable and wondered if the bank was doing the man an injustice. Why not bring him into contact with some of our alcoholic crowd? He might have a chance. I pointed out that I had had nothing to drink whatever for three years, and this is the face of difficulties that would have made nine out of ten men drink their heads off. Why not at least afford him an opportunity to hear my story? "Oh no," said my friend, "this chap is either through with liquor, or he is minus a job. If he has your will power and guts, he will make the grade."

I wanted to throw up my hands in discouragement, for I saw that I had failed to help my banker friend understand. He simply could not believe that his brother-executive suffered from a serious illness. There was nothing to do but wait.

Presently the man did slip and was fired. Following his discharge, we contacted him. Without much ado, he accepted the principles and procedure that had helped us. He is undoubtedly on the road to recovery. To me, this incident illustrates lack of understanding as to what really ails the alcoholic, and lack of knowledge as to what part employers might profitably take in salvaging their sick employees.

If you desire to help it might be well to disregard your own drinking, or lack of it. Whether you are a hard drinker, a moderate drinker or a teetotaler, you may have some pretty strong opinions, perhaps prejudices. Those who drink moderately may be more annoyed with an alcoholic than a total abstainer would be. Drinking occasionally, and understanding your own reactions, it is possible for you to become quite sure of many things which, so far as the alcoholic is concerned, are not always so. As a moderate drinker, you can take your liquor or leave it alone. Whenever you want to, you control your drinking. Of an evening, you can go on a mild bender, get up in the morning, shake your head and go to business. To you, liquor is no real problem. You cannot see why it should be to anyone else, save the spineless and stupid.

When dealing with an alcoholic, there may be a natural annoyance that a man could be so weak, stupid and irresponsible. Even when you understand the malady better, you may feel this feeling rising.

A look at the alcoholic in your organization is many times illuminating. Is he not usually brilliant, fast-thinking, imaginative and likeable? When sober, does he not work hard and have a knack of getting things done? If he had these qualities and did not drink would he be worth retaining? Should he have the same consideration as other ailing employees? Is he worth salvaging? If your decision is yes, whether the reason be humanitarian or business or both, then the following suggestions may be helpful.

Can you discard the feeling that you are dealing only with habit, with stubbornness, or a weak will? If this presents difficulty, re-reading chapters two and three, where the alcoholic sickness is discussed at length might be worth while. You, as a businessman, want to know the necessities before considering the result. If you concede that your employee is ill, can he be forgiven for what he has done in the past? Can his past absurdities be forgotten? Can it be appreciated that he has been a victim of crooked thinking, directly caused by the action of alcohol on his brain?

I well remember the shock I received when a prominent doctor in Chicago told me of cases where pressure of the spinal fluid actually ruptured the brain. No wonder an alcoholic is strangely irrational. Who wouldn't be, with such a fevered brain? Normal drinkers are not so affected, nor can they understand the aberrations of the alcoholic.

Your man has probably been trying to conceal a number of scrapes, perhaps pretty messy ones. They may be disgusting. You may be at a loss to understand how such a seemingly above-board chap could be so involved. But these scrapes can generally be charged, no matter how bad, to the abnormal action of alcohol on his mind. When drinking, or getting over a bout, an alcoholic, sometimes the model of honesty when normal, will do incredible things. Afterward, his revulsion will be terrible. Nearly always, these antics indicate nothing more than temporary conditions.

This is not to say that all alcoholics are honest and upright when not drinking. Of course that isn't so, and such people often may impose on you. Seeing your attempt to understand and help, some men will try to take advantage of your kindness. If you are sure your man does not want to stop, he may as well be discharged, the sooner the better. You are not doing him a favor by keeping him on. Firing such an individual may prove a blessing to him. It may be just the jolt he needs. I know, in my own particular case, that nothing my company could have done would have stopped me for, so long as I was able to hold my position, I could not possibly realize how serious my situation was. Had they fired me first, and had they then taken steps to see that I was presented with the solution contained in this book, I might have returned to them six months later, a well man.

But there are many men who want to stop, and with them you can go far. Your understanding treatment of their cases will pay dividends.

Perhaps you have such a man in mind. He wants to quit drinking and you want to help him, even if it be only a matter of good business. You now know more about alcoholism. You can see that he is mentally and physically sick. You are willing to overlook his past performances. Suppose an approach is made something like this:

State that you know about his drinking, and that it must stop. You might say you appreciate his abilities, would like to keep him, but cannot if he continues to drink. A firm attitude at this point has helped many of us.

Next he can be assured that you do not intend to lecture, moralize, or condemn; that if this was done formerly, it was because of misunderstanding. If possible express a lack of hard feeling toward him. At this point, it might be well to explain alcoholism, the illness. Say that you believe he is a gravely-ill person, with this qualification—being perhaps fatally ill, does he want to get well? You ask, because many alcoholics, being warped and drugged, do not want to quit. But does he? Will he take every necessary step, submit to anything to get well, to stop drinking forever?

If he says yes, does he really mean it, or down inside does he think he is fooling you, and that after rest and treatment he will be able to get away with a few drinks now and then? We believe a man should be thoroughly probed on these points. Be satisfied he is not deceiving himself or you.

Whether you mention this book is a matter for your discretion. If he temporizes and still thinks he can ever drink again, even beer, he might as well be discharged after the next bender which, if an alcoholic, he is almost certain to have. He should understand that emphatically. Either you are dealing with a man who can and will get well or you are not. If not, why waste time with him? This may seem severe, but it is usually the best course.

After satisfying yourself that your man wants to recover and that he will go to any extreme to do so, you may suggest a definite course of action. For most alcoholics who are drinking, or who are just getting over a spree, a certain amount of physical treatment is desirable, even imperative. The matter of physical treatment should, of course, be referred to your own doctor. Whatever the method, its object is to thoroughly clear mind and body of the effects of alcohol. In competent hands, this seldom takes long nor is it very expensive. Your man will fare better if placed in such physical condition that he can think straight and no longer craves liquor. If you propose such a procedure to him, it may be necessary to advance the cost of treatment, but we believe it should be made plain that any expense will later be deducted from his pay. It is better for him to feel fully responsible.

If your man accepts your offer, it should be pointed out that physical treatment is but a small part of the picture. Though you are providing him with the best possible medical attention, he should understand that he must undergo a change of heart. To get over drinking will require a transformation of thought and attitude. We all had to place recovery above everything, for without recovery we would have lost both home and business.

Can you have every confidence in his ability to recover? While on the subject of confidence, can you adopt the attitude that so far as you are concerned this will be a strictly personal matter, that his alcoholic derelictions, the treatment about to be undertaken, will never be discussed without his consent? It might be well to have a long chat with him on his return.

To return to the subject matter of this book: It contains full suggestions by which the employee may solve his problem. To you, some of the ideas which it contains are novel. Perhaps you are not quite in sympathy with the approach we suggest. By no means do we offer it as the last word on this subject, but so far as we are concerned, it has worked with us. After all, are you not looking for results rather than methods? Whether your employee likes it or not, he will learn the grim truth about alcoholism. That won't hurt him a bit, even though he does not go for this remedy.

We suggest you draw the book to the attention of the doctor who is to attend your patient during treatment. If the book is read the moment the patient is able, while acutely depressed, realization of his condition may come to him.

We hope the doctor will tell the patient the truth about his condition, whatever that happens to be. When the man is presented with this volume it is best that no one tell him he must abide by its suggestions. The man must decide for himself.

You are betting, of course, that your changed attitude plus the contents of this book will turn the trick. In some cases it will, and in others it may not. But we think that if you persevere, the percentage of successes will gratify you. As our work spreads and our numbers increase, we hope your employees may be put in personal contact with some of us. Meanwhile, we are sure a great deal can be accomplished by the use of the book alone.

On your employee's return, talk with him. Ask him if he thinks he has the answer. If he feels free to discuss his problems with you, if he knows you understand and will not be upset by anything he wishes to say he will probably be off to a fast start.

In this connection, can you remain undisturbed if the man proceeds to tell you shocking things? He may, for example, reveal that he has padded his expense account or that he has planned to take your best customers away from you. In fact, he may say almost anything if he has accepted our solution which, as you know, demands rigorous honesty. Can you charge this off as you would a bad account and start fresh with him? If he owes you money you may wish to make terms.

If he speaks of his home situation, you can undoubtedly make helpful suggestions. Can he talk frankly with you so long as he does not bear business tales or criticize his associates? With this kind of employee such an attitude will command undying loyalty.

The greatest enemies of us alcoholics are resentment, jealousy, envy, frustration, and fear. Wherever men are gathered together in business there will be rivalries and, arising out of these, a certain amount of office politics. Sometimes we alcoholics have an idea that people are trying to pull us down. Often this is not so at all. But sometimes our drinking will be used politically.

One instance comes to mind in which a malicious individual was always making friendly little jokes about an alcoholic's drinking exploits. In this way he was slyly carrying tales. In another case, an alcoholic was sent to a hospital for treatment. Only a few knew of it at first but, within a short time, it was billboarded throughout the entire company. Naturally this sort of thing decreased the man's chance of recovery. The employer can many times protect the victim from this kind of talk. The employer cannot play favorites, but he can always defend a man from needless provocation and unfair criticism.

As a class, alcoholics are energetic people. They work hard and they play hard. Your man should be on his mettle to make good. Being somewhat weakened, and faced with physical and mental readjustment to a life which knows no alcohol, he may overdo. You may have to curb his desire to work sixteen hours a day. You may need to encourage him to play once in a while. He may wish to do a lot for other alcoholics and something of the sort may come up during business hours. A reasonable amount of latitude will be helpful. This work is necessary to maintain his sobriety.

After your man has gone along without drinking for a few months, you may be able to make use of his services with other employees who are giving you the alcoholic run-around—provided, of course, they are willing to have a third party in the picture. An alcoholic who has recovered, but holds a relatively unimportant job, can talk to a man with a better position. Being on a radically different basis of life, he will never take advantage of the situation.

Your man may be trusted. Long experience with alcoholic excuses naturally arouses suspicion. When his wife next calls saying he is sick, you might jump to the conclusion he is drunk. If he is, and is still trying to recover, he will tell you about it even if it means the loss of his job. For he knows he must be honest if he would live at all. He will appreciate knowing you are not bothering your head about him, that you are not suspicious nor are you trying to run his life so he will be shielded from temptation to drink. If he is conscientiously following the program of recovery he can go anywhere your business may call him.

In case he does stumble, even once, you will have to decide whether to let him go. If you are sure he doesn't mean business, there is no doubt you should discharge him. If, on the contrary, you are sure he is doing his utmost, you may wish to give him another chance. But you should feel under no obligation to keep him on, for your obligation has been well discharged already.

There is another thing you might wish to do. If your organization is a large one, your junior executives might be provided with this book. You might let them know you have no quarrel with the alcoholics of your organization. These juniors are often in a difficult position. Men under them are frequently their friends. So, for one reason or another, they cover these men, hoping matters will take a turn for the better. They often jeopardize their own positions by trying to help serious drinkers who should have been fired long ago, or else given an opportunity to get well.

After reading this book, a junior executive can go to such a man and say approximately this, "Look here, Ed. Do you want to stop drinking or not? You put me on the spot every time you get drunk. It isn't fair to me or the firm. I have been learning something about alcoholism. If you are an alcoholic, you are a mighty sick man. You act like one. The firm wants to help you get over it, and if you are interested, there is a way out. If you take it, your past will be forgotten and the fact that you went away for treatment will not be mentioned.   But if you cannot or will not stop drinking, I think you ought to resign."

Your junior executive may not agree with the contents of our book. He need not, and often should not show it to his alcoholic prospect. But at least he will understand the problem and will no longer be misled by ordinary promises. He will be able to take a position with such a man, which is eminently fair and square. He will have no further reason for covering up an alcoholic employee.

It boils right down to this: No man should be fired just because he is alcoholic. If he wants to stop, he should be afforded a real chance. If he cannot or does not want to stop, he should be discharged.   The exceptions are few.

We think this method of approach will accomplish several things. It will permit the rehabilitation of good men. At the same time you will feel no reluctance to rid yourself of those who cannot or will not stop. Alcoholism may be causing your organization considerable damage in its waste of time, men and reputation.   We hope our suggestions will help you plug up this sometimes serious leak. We think we are sensible when we urge that you stop this waste and give your worthwhile man a chance.

The other day an approach was made to the vice president of a large industrial concern. He remarked: "I'm mighty glad you fellows got over your drinking. But the policy of this company is not to interfere with the habits of our employees. If a man drinks so much that his job suffers, we fire him. I don't see how you can be of any help to us for, as you see, we don't have any alcoholic problem." This same company spends millions for research every year. Their cost of production is figured to a fine decimal point. They have recreational facilities. There is company insurance. There is a real interest, both humanitarian and business, in the well-being of employees. But alcoholism—well, they just don't believe they have it.

Perhaps this is a typical attitude. We, who have collectively seen a great deal of business life, at least from the alcoholic angle, had to smile at this gentleman's sincere opinion. He might be shocked if he knew how much alcoholism is costing his organization a year. That company may harbor many actual or potential alcoholics. We believe that managers of large enterprises often have little idea how prevalent this problem is. Even if you feel your organization has no alcoholic problem, it might pay to take another look down the line. You may make some interesting discoveries.

Of course, this chapter refers to alcoholics, sick people, deranged men. What our friend, the vice president, had in mind was the habitual or whoopee drinker. As to them, his policy is undoubtedly sound, but he did not distinguish between such people and the alcoholic.

It is not to be expected that an alcoholic employee will receive a disproportionate amount of time and attention. He should not be made a favorite. The right kind of man, the kind who recovers, will not want this sort of thing. He will not impose. Far from it. He will work like the devil and thank you to his dying day.

Today, I own a little company. There are two

alcoholic employees, who produce as much as five normal salesmen. But why not? They have a new attitude, and they have been saved from a living death. I have enjoyed every moment spent in getting them straightened out.*

• See Appendix VI–We shall be happy to hear from you if we can be of help.

Chapter 11
A VISION FOR YOU

F OR MOST normal folks, drinking means convivi-
ality, companionship and colorful imagination. It
means release from care, boredom and worry. It is
joyous intimacy with friends and a feeling that life is
good. But not so with us in those last days of heavy
drinking. The old pleasures were gone. They were
but memories. Never could we recapture the great
moments of the past. There was an insistent
yearning to enjoy life as we once did and a heart-
breaking obsession that some new miracle of control
would enable us to do it. There was always one more
attempt—and one more failure.

The less people tolerated us, the more we withdrew
from society, from life itself. As we became subjects
of King Alcohol, shivering denizens of his mad realm,
the chilling vapor that is loneliness settled down. It
thickened, ever becoming blacker. Some of us sought
out sordid places, hoping to find understanding companionship and approval. Momentarily we did—then
would come oblivion and the awful awakening to
face the hideous Four Horsemen—Terror, Bewilder-
ment, Frustration, Despair. Unhappy drinkers who
read this page will understand!

Now and then a serious drinker, being dry at the
moment says, "I don't miss it at all. Feel better. Work
better. Having a better time." As ex-problem drink-

ers, we smile at such a sally. We know our friend is like a boy whistling in the dark to keep up his spirits. He fools himself. Inwardly he would give anything to take half a dozen drinks and get away with them. He will presently try the old game again, for he isn't happy about his sobriety. He cannot picture life without alcohol. Some day he will be unable to imagine life either with alcohol or without it. Then he will know loneliness such as few do. He will be at the jumping-off place. He will wish for the end.

We have shown how we got out from under. You say, "Yes, I'm willing. But am I to be consigned to a life where I shall be stupid, boring and glum, like some righteous people I see? I know I must get along without liquor, but how can I? Have you a sufficient substitute?"

Yes, there is a substitute and it is vastly more than that. It is a fellowship in Alcoholics Anonymous. There you will find release from care, boredom and worry. Your imagination will be fired. Life will mean something at last. The most satisfactory years of your existence lie ahead. Thus we find the fellowship, and so will you.

"How is that to come about?" you ask. "Where am I to find these people?"

You are going to meet these new friends in your own community. Near you, alcoholics are dying helplessly like people in a sinking ship. If you live in a large place, there are hundreds. High and low, rich and poor, these are future fellows of Alcoholics Anonymous. Among them you will make lifelong friends. You will be bound to them with new and wonderful ties, for you will escape disaster together and you will commence shoulder to shoulder your common journey. Then you will know what it means to give of yourself that others may survive and rediscover life. You will learn the full meaning of "Love they neighbor as thyself."

It may seem incredible that these men are to become happy, respected, and useful once more. How can they rise out of such misery, bad repute and hopelessness? The practical answer is that since these things have happened among us, they can happen with you. Should you wish them above all else, and be willing to make use of our experience, we are sure they will come. The age of miracles is still with us. Our own recovery proves that!

Our hope is that when this chip of a book is launched on the world tide of alcoholism, defeated drinkers will seize upon it, to follow its suggestions. Many, we are sure, will rise to their feet and march on. They will approach still other sick ones and fellowships of Alcoholics Anonymous may spring up in each city and hamlet, havens for those who must find a way out.

In the chapter "Working With Others" you gathered an idea of how we approach and aid others to health. Suppose now that through you several families have adopted this way of life. You will want to know more of how to proceed from that point. Perhaps the best way of treating you to a glimpse of your future will be to describe the growth of the fellowship among us. Here is a brief account:

Years ago, in 1935, one of our number made a journey to a certain western city. From a business standpoint, his trip came off badly. Had he been successful in his enterprise, he would have been set on his feet financially which, at the time, seemed vitally important. But his venture wound up in a lawsuit and bogged down completely. The proceeding was shot through with much hard feeling and controversy.

Bitterly discouraged, he found himself in a strange place, discredited and almost broke. Still physically weak, and sober but a few months, he saw that his predicament was dangerous. He wanted so much to talk with someone, but whom?

One dismal afternoon he paced a hotel lobby wondering how his bill was to be paid. At one end of the room stood a glass covered directory of local churches. Down the lobby a door opened into an attractive bar. He could see the gay crowd inside. In there he would find companionship and release. Unless he took some drinks, he might not have the courage to scrape an acquaintance and would have a lonely week-end.

Of course he couldn't drink, but why not sit hopefully at a table, a bottle of ginger ale before him? After all, had he not been sober six months now? Perhaps he could handle, say, three drinks—no more! Fear gripped him. He was on thin ice. Again it was the old, insidious insanity—that first drink. With a shiver, he turned away and walked down the lobby to the church directory. Music and gay chatter still floated to him from the bar.

But what about his responsibilities—his family and the men who would die because they would not know how to get well, ah—yes, those other alcoholics? There must be many such in this town. He would phone a clergyman. His sanity returned and he thanked

God. Selecting a church at random from the directory, he stepped into a booth and lifted the receiver.

His call to the clergyman led him presently to a certain resident of the town, who, though formerly able and respected, was then nearing the nadir of alcoholic despair. It was the usual situation; home in jeopardy, wife ill, children distracted, bills in arrears and standing damaged. He had a desperate desire to stop, but saw no way out, for he had earnestly tried many avenues of escape. Painfully aware of being somehow abnormal, the man did not fully realize what it meant to be alcoholic.*

When our friend related his experience, the man agreed that no amount of will power he might muster could stop his drinking for long. A spiritual experience, he conceded, was absolutely necessary, but the price seemed high upon the basis suggested. He told how he lived in constant worry about those who might find out about his alcoholism. He had, of course, the familiar alcoholic obsession that few knew of his drinking. Why, he argued, should he lose the remainder of his business, only to bring still more suffering to his family by foolishly admitting his plight to people from whom he made his livelihood? He would do anything, he said, but that.

Being intrigued, however, he invited our friend to his home. Some time later, and just as he thought he was getting control of his liquor situation, he went on a roaring bender. For him, this was the spree that ended all sprees. He saw that he would have to face

• This refers to Bill's first visit with Dr. Bob. These men later became co-founders of A.A. Bill's story opens the text of this book; Dr. Bob's heads the Story Section.

his problems squarely that God might give him mastery.

One morning he took the bull by the horns and set out to tell those he feared what his trouble had been. He found himself surprisingly well received, and learned that many knew of his drinking. Stepping into his car, he made the rounds of people he had hurt. He trembled as he went about, for this might mean ruin, particularly to a person in his line of business.

At midnight he came home exhausted, but very happy. He has not had a drink since. As we shall see, he now means a great deal to his community, and the major liabilities of thirty years of hard drinking have been repaired in four.

But life was not easy for the two friends. Plenty of difficulties presented themselves. Both saw that they must keep spiritually active. One day they called up the head nurse of a local hospital. They explained their need and inquired if she had a first class alcoholic prospect.

She replied, "Yes, we've got a corker. He's just beaten up a couple of nurses. Goes off his head completely when he's drinking. But he's a grand chap when he's sober, though he's been in here eight times in the last six months. Understand he was once a well-known lawyer in town, but just now we've got him strapped down tight."*

Here was a prospect all right but, by the description, none too promising. The use of spiritual principles in

* This refers to Bill's and Dr. Bob's first visit to A.A. Number Three. See the Pioneer Section. This resulted in A.A.'s first group at Akron, Ohio, in 1935.

such cases were not so well understood as it is now. But one of the friends said, "Put him in a private room. We'll be down."

Two days later, a future fellow of Alcoholics Anonymous stared glassily at the strangers beside his bed. "Who are you fellows, and why this private room? I was always in a ward before."

Said one of the visitors; "We're giving you a treatment for alcoholism."

Hopelessness was written large on the man's face as he replied, "Oh, but that's no use. Nothing would fix me. I'm a goner. The last three times, I got drunk on the way home from here. I'm afraid to go out the door. I can't understand it."

For an hour, the two friends told him about their drinking experiences. Over and over, he would say: "That's me. That's me. I drink like that."

The man in the bed was told of the acute poisoning from which he suffered, how it deteriorates the body of an alcoholic and warps his mind. There was much talk about the mental state preceding the first drink.

"Yes, that's me," said the sick man, "the very image. You fellows know your stuff all right, but I don't see what good it'll do. You fellows are somebody. I was once, but I'm a nobody now. From what you tell me, I know more than ever I can't stop." At this both the visitors burst into a laugh. Said the future Fellow Anonymous: "Damn little to laugh about that I can see."

The two friends spoke of their spiritual experience and told him about the course of action they carried out.

He interrupted: "I used to be strong for the church,

but that won't fix it. I've prayed to God on hangover mornings and sworn that I'd never touch another drop but by nine o'clock I'd be boiled as an owl."

Next day found the prospect more receptive. He had been thinking it over. "Maybe you're right," he said. "God ought to be able to do anything." Then he added, "He sure didn't do much for me when I was trying to fight this booze racket alone."

On the third day the lawyer gave his life to the care and direction of his Creator, and said he was perfectly willing to do anything necessary. His wife came, scarcely daring to be hopeful, though she thought she saw something different about her husband already. He had begun to have a spiritual experience.

That afternoon he put on his clothes and walked from the hospital a free man. He entered a political campaign, making speeches, frequenting men's gathering places of all sorts, often staying up all night. He lost the race by only a narrow margin. But he had found God—and in finding God had found himself.

That was in June 1935. He never drank again. He too, has become a respected and useful member of his community. He has helped other men recover, and is a power in the church from which he was long absent.

So, you see, there were three alcoholics in that town, who now felt they had to give to others what they had found, or be sunk. After several failures to find others, a fourth turned up. He came through an acquaintance that had heard the good news. He proved to be a devil-may-care young fellow whose parents could not make out whether he wanted to stop drinking or not. They were deeply religious people, much shocked by their son's refusal to have anything to do with the church. He suffered horribly from his sprees, but it seemed as if nothing could be done for him. He consented, however, to go to the hospital, where he occupied the very room recently vacated by the lawyer.

He had three visitors. After a bit, he said, "The way you fellows put this spiritual stuff makes sense. I'm ready to do business. I guess the old folks were right after all." So one more was added to the Fellowship.

All this time our friend of the hotel lobby incident remained in that town. He was there three months. He now returned home, leaving behind his first acquaintances, the lawyer and the devil-may-care chap. These men had found something brand new in life. Though they knew they must help other alcoholics if they would remain sober, that motive became secondary. It was transcended by the happiness they found in giving themselves for others. They shared their homes, their slender resources, and gladly devoted their spare hours to fellow-sufferers. They were willing, by day or night, to place a new man in the hospital and visit him afterward. They grew in numbers. They experienced a few distressing failures, but in those cases they made an effort to bring the man's family into a spiritual way of living, thus relieving much worry and suffering.

A year and six months later these three had succeeded with seven more. Seeing much of each other, scarce an evening passed that someone's home did not shelter a little gathering of men and women, happy in their release, and constantly thinking how they might present their discovery to some newcomer. In addition to these casual get-togethers, it became customary to set apart one night a week for a meeting to be attended by anyone or everyone interested in a spiritual way of life. Aside from fellowship and sociability, the prime object was to provide a time and place where new people might bring their problems.

Outsiders became interested. One man and his wife placed their large home at the disposal of this strangely assorted crowd. This couple has since become so fascinated that they have dedicated their home to the work. Many a distracted wife has visited this house to find loving and understanding companionship among women who knew her problem, to hear from the lips of their husbands what had happened to them, to be advised how her own wayward mate might be hospitalized and approached when next he stumbled.

Many a man, yet dazed from his hospital experience, has stepped over the threshold of that home into freedom. Many an alcoholic who entered there came away with an answer. He succumbed to that gay crowd inside, who laughed at their own misfortunes and understood his. Impressed by those who visited him at the hospital, he capitulated entirely when, later, in an upper room of this house, he heard the story of some man whose experience closely tallied with his own. The expression on the faces of the women, that indefinable something in the eyes of the men, the stimulating and electric atmosphere of the place, conspired to let him know that here was haven at last.

The very practical approach to his problems, the absence of intolerance of any kind, the informality, the genuine democracy, the uncanny understanding which these people had were irresistible. He and his wife would leave elated by the thought of what they could now do for some stricken acquaintance and his family. They knew they had a host of new friends; it seemed they had known these strangers always. They had seen miracles, and one was to come to them. They had visioned the Great Reality—their loving and All-Powerful Creator.

Now, this house will hardly accommodate its weekly visitors, for they number sixty or eighty as a rule. Alcoholics are being attracted from far and near. From surrounding towns, families drive long distances to be present. A community thirty miles away has fifteen fellows of Alcoholics Anonymous. Being a large place, we think that some day its Fellowship will number many hundreds.*

But life among Alcoholics Anonymous is more than attending gatherings and visiting hospitals. Cleaning up old scrapes, helping to settle family differences, explaining the disinherited son to his irate parents, lending money and securing jobs for each other, when justified—these are everyday occurrences. No one is too discredited or has sunk too low to be welcomed cordially—if he means business. Social distinctions, petty rivalries and jealousies—these are laughed out of countenance. Being wrecked in the same vessel, being restored and united under one God, with hearts and minds attuned to the welfare of others, the things which matter so much to some people no longer signify much to them. How could they?

Under only slightly different conditions, the same thing is taking place in many eastern cities. In one of

*Written in 1939.

161

these there is a well-known hospital for the treatment of alcoholic and drug addiction. Six years ago one of our number was a patient there. Many of us have felt, for the first time, the Presence and Power of God within its walls. We are greatly indebted to the doctor in attendance there, for he, although it might prejudice his own work, has told us of his belief in ours.

Every few days this doctor suggests our approach to one of his patients. Understanding our work, he can do this with an eye to selecting those who are willing and able to recover on a spiritual basis. Many of us, former patients, go there to help. Then, in this eastern city, there are informal meetings such as we have described to you, where you may now see scores of members. There are the same fast friendships, there is the same helpfulness to one another as you find among our western friends. There is a good bit of travel between East and West and we foresee a great increase in this helpful interchange.

Some day we hope that every alcoholic who journeys will find a Fellowship of Alcoholics Anonymous at his destination. To some extent this is already true. Some of us are salesmen and go about. Little clusters of twos and threes and fives of us have sprung up in other communities, through contact with our two larger centers. Those of us who travel drop in as often as we can. This practice enables us to lend a hand, at the same time avoiding certain alluring distractions of the road, about which any traveling man can inform you.*

Thus we grow. And so can you, though you be but

* Written in 1939. As of 1966, there are some 12,000 groups in over 90 countries with an estimated membership of over 350,000.

one man with this book in your hand. We believe and hope it contains all you will need to begin.

We know what you are thinking. You are saying to yourself: "I'm jittery and alone. I couldn't do that." But you can. You forget that you have just now tapped a source of power much greater than yourself. To duplicate, with such backing, what we have accomplished is only a matter of willingness, patience and labor.

We know of an A.A. member who was living in a large community. He had lived there but a few weeks when he found that the place probably contained more alcoholics per square mile than any city in the country. This was only a few days ago at this writing. (1939) The authorities were much concerned. He got in touch with a prominent psychiatrist who had undertaken certain responsibilities for the mental health of the community. The doctor proved to be able and exceedingly anxious to adopt any workable method of handling the situation. So he inquired, what did our friend have on the ball?

Our friend proceeded to tell him. And with such good effect that the doctor agreed to a test among his patients and certain other alcoholics from a clinic which he attends. Arrangements were also made with the chief psychiatrist of a large public hospital to select still others from the stream of misery which flows through that institution.

So our fellow worker will soon have friends galore. Some of them may sink and perhaps never get up, but if our experience is a criterion, more than half of those approached will become fellows of Alcoholic Anonymous. When a few men in this city have found themselves, and have discovered the joy of helping others to face life again, there will be no stopping until everyone in that town has had his opportunity to recover—if he can and will.

Still you may say: "But I will not have the benefit of contact with you who write this book." We cannot be sure. God will determine that, so you must remember that your real reliance is always upon Him. He will show you how to create the fellowship you crave.*

Our book is meant to be suggestive only. We realize we know only a little. God will constantly disclose more to you and to us. Ask Him in your morning meditation what you can do each day for the man who is still sick. The answers will come, if your own house is in order. But obviously you cannot transmit something you haven't got. See to it that your relationship with Him is right, and great events will come to pass for you and countless others. This is the Great Fact for us.

Abandon yourself to God as you understand God. Admit your faults to Him and to your fellows. Clear away the wreckage of your past. Give freely of what you find and join us. We shall be with you in the Fellowship of the Spirit, and you will surely meet some of us as your trudge the Road of Happy Destiny.

May God bless you and keep you—until then.

*Alcoholics Anonymous will be glad to hear from you. Address P.O. Box 459, Grand Central Post Office, New York, N.Y. 10017

APPENDICES

I

THE A.A. TRADITION

To those now in its fold, Alcoholics Anonymous has made the difference between misery and sobriety, and often the difference between life and death. A.A. can, of course, mean just as much to uncounted alcoholics not yet reached.

Therefore, no society of men and women ever had a more urgent *need* for continuous effectiveness and permanent unity. We alcoholics see that we must work together and hang together, else most of us will finally die alone.

The "12 Traditions" of Alcoholics Anonymous are, we A.A.'s believe, the best answers that our experience has yet given to those ever urgent questions, "How can A.A. best function?" and, "How can A.A. best stay whole and so survive?"

On the next page, A.A.'s "12 Traditions" are seen in their so-called "short form," the form in general use today. This is a condensed version of the original "long form" A.A. Traditions as first printed in 1945. Because the "long form" is more explicit and of possible historic value, it is also reproduced.

THE TWELVE TRADITIONS

One—Our common welfare should come first; personal recovery depends upon A.A. unity.

Two—For our group purpose there is but one ultimate authority—a loving God as He may express Himself in our group conscience. Our leaders are but trusted servants; they do not govern.

Three—The only requirement for A.A. membership is a desire to stop drinking.

Four—Each group should be autonomous except in matters affecting other groups or A.A. as a whole.

Five—Each group has but one primary purpose—to carry its message to the alcoholic who still suffers.

Six—An A.A. group ought never endorse, finance or lend the A.A. name to any related facility or outside enterprise, lest problems of money, property and prestige divert us from our primary purpose.

Seven—Every A.A. group ought to be fully self-supporting, declining outside contributions.

Eight—Alcoholics Anonymous should remain forever non-professional, but our service centers may employ special workers.

Nine—A.A., as such, ought never be organized; but we may create service boards or committees directly responsible to those they serve.

Ten—Alcoholics Anonymous has no opinion on outside issues; hence the A.A. name ought never be drawn into public controversy.

Eleven—Our public relations policy is based on attraction rather than promotion; we need always maintain personal anonymity at the level of press, radio and films.

Twelve—Anonymity is the spiritual foundation of our traditions, ever reminding us to place principles before personalities.

THE TWELVE TRADITIONS
(THE LONG FORM)

Our A.A. experience has taught us that:

1.—Each member of Alcoholics Anonymous is but a small part of a great whole. A.A. must continue to live or most of us will surely die. Hence our common welfare comes first. But individual welfare follows close afterward.

2.—For our group purpose there is but one ultimate authority—a loving God as He may express Himself in our group conscience.

3.—Our membership ought to include all who suffer from alcoholism. Hence we may refuse none who wish to recover. Nor ought A.A. membership ever depend upon money or conformity. Any two or three alcoholics gathered together for sobriety may call themselves an A.A. Group, provided that, as a group, they have no other affiliation.

4.—With respect to its own affairs, each A.A. group should be responsible to no other authority than its own conscience. But when its plans concern the welfare of neighboring groups also, those groups ought to be consulted. And no group, regional committee, or individual should ever take any action that might greatly affect A.A. as a whole without conferring with the Trustees of the General Service Board. On such issues our common welfare is paramount.

5.—Each Alcoholics Anonymous group ought to be a spiritual entity *having but one primary purpose*— that of carrying its message to the alcoholic who still suffers.

6.—Problems of money, property, and authority may easily divert us from our primary spiritual aim. We think, therefore, that any considerable property of genuine use to A.A. should be separately incorporated and managed, thus dividing the material from the spiritual. An A.A. group, as such, should never go into business. Secondary aids to A.A., such as clubs or hospitals which require much property or administration, ought to be incorporated and so set apart that, if necessary, they can be freely discarded by the groups. Hence such facilities ought not to use the A.A. name. Their management should be the sole responsibility of those people who financially support them. For clubs, A.A. managers are usually preferred. But hospitals, as well as other places of recuperation, ought to be well outside A.A.—and medically supervised. While an A.A. group may cooperate with anyone, such cooperation ought never go so far as affiliation or endorsement, actual or implied. An A.A. group can bind itself to no one.

7—The A.A. groups themselves ought to be fully supported by the voluntary contributions of their own members. We think that each group should soon achieve this ideal; that any public solicitation of funds using the name of Alcoholics Anonymous is highly dangerous, whether by groups, clubs, hospitals, or other outside agencies; that acceptance of large gifts from any source, or of contributions carrying any obligation whatever, is unwise. Then too, we view with much concern those A.A. treasuries which continue, beyond prudent reserves, to accumulate funds for no stated A.A. purpose. Experience has often warned us that nothing can so surely destroy our spiritual heritage as futile disputes over property, money, and authority.

8—Alcoholics Anonymous should remain forever non-professional. We define professionalism as the occupation of counseling alcoholics for fees or hire. But we may employ alcoholics where they are going to perform those services for which we might otherwise have to engage non-alcoholics. Such special services may be well recompensed. But our usual A.A. "12th Step" work is never to be paid for.

9—Each A.A. group needs the least possible organization. Rotating leadership is the best. The small group may elect its Secretary, the large group its Rotating Committee, and the groups of a large Metropolitan area their Central or Intergroup Committee, which often employs a full-time Secretary. The trustees of the General Service Board are, in effect, our A.A. General Service Committee. They are the custodians of our A.A. Tradition and the receivers of voluntary A.A. contributions by which we maintain our A.A. General Service Office at New York. They are authorized by the groups to handle our over-all public relations and they guarantee the integrity of our principle newspaper, "The A.A. Grapevine." All such representatives are to be guided in the spirit of service, for true leaders in A.A. are but trusted and experienced servants of the whole. They derive no real authority from their titles; they do not govern. Universal respect is the key to their usefulness.

10—No A.A. group or member should ever, in such a way as to implicate A.A., express any opinion on outside controversial issues—particularly those of politics, alcohol reform, or sectarian religion. The Alcoholics Anonymous groups oppose no one. Concerning such matters they can express no view whatever.

11—Our relations with the general public should be characterized by personal anonymity. We think A.A. ought to avoid sensational advertising. Our names and pictures as A.A. members ought not be broadcast, filmed, or publicly printed. Our public relations should be guided by the principle of attraction rather than promotion. There is never need to praise ourselves. We feel it better to let our friends recommend us.

12—And finally, we of Alcoholics Anonymous believe

that the principle of Anonymity has an immense spiritual significance. It reminds us that we are to place principles before personalities; that we are actually to practice a genuine humility. This to the end that our great blessings may never spoil us; that we shall forever live in thankful contemplation of Him who presides over us all.

II
SPIRITUAL EXPERIENCE

The terms "spiritual experience" and "spiritual awakening" are used many times in this book which, upon careful reading, shows that the personality change sufficient to bring about recovery from alcoholism has manifested itself among us in many different forms.

Yet it is true that our first printing gave many readers the impression that these personality changes, or religious experiences, must be in the nature of sudden and spectacular upheavals. Happily for everyone, this conclusion is erroneous.

In the first few chapters a number of sudden revolutionary changes are described. Though it was not our intention to create such an impression, many alcoholics have nevertheless concluded that in order to recover they must acquire an immediate and overwhelming "God consciousness" followed at once by a vast change in feeling and outlook.

Among our rapidly growing membership of thousands of alcoholics such transformations, though frequent, are by no means the rule. Most of our experiences are what the psychologist William James calls the "educational variety" because they develop slowly over a period of time. Quite often friends of the newcomer are aware of the difference long before he is himself. He finally realizes that he has undergone a profound alteration in his reaction to life; that such a change could hardly have been brought about by himself alone. What often takes place in a few months could seldom have been accomplished by years of self discipline. With few exceptions our members find that they have tapped an unsuspected inner resource which they presently identify with their own conception of a Power greater than themselves.

Most of us think this awareness of a Power greater than ourselves is the essence of spiritual experience. Our more religious members call it "God-consciousness."

Most emphatically we wish to say that any alcoholic capable of honestly facing his problems in the light of our experience can recover, provided he does not close his mind to all spiritual concepts. He can only be defeated by an attitude of intolerance or belligerent denial.

We find that no one need have difficulty with the spirituality of the program. *Willingness, honesty and open mindedness are the essentials of recovery. But these are indispensable.*

> "There is a principle which is a bar against all information, which is proof against all arguments and which can not fail to keep a man in everlasting ignorance—that principle is contempt prior to investigation."
>
> -HERBERT SPENCER

III
THE MEDICAL VIEW ON A.A.

Since Dr. Silkworth's first endorsement of Alcoholics Anonymous, medical societies and physicians throughout the world have set their approval upon us. Following are excerpts from the comments of doctors present at the annual meeting* of the Medical Society of the State of New York where a paper on A.A. was read:

Dr. Foster Kennedy, neurologist: "This organization of Alcoholics Anonymous calls on two of the greatest reservoirs of power known to man, religion and that instinct for association with one's fellows ... the 'herd instinct.' I think our profession must take appreciative cognizance of this great therapeutic weapon. If we do not do so, we shall stand convicted of emotional sterility and of having lost the faith that moves mountains, without which medicine can do little."

Dr. G. Kirby Collier, psychiatrist: "I have felt that A.A. is a group unto themselves and their best results can be had under their own guidance, as a result of their philosophy. Any therapeutic or philosophic procedure which can prove a recovery rate of 50% to 60% must merit our consideration."

Dr. Harry M. Tiebout, psychiatrist: "As a psychiatrist, I have thought a great deal about the relationship of my specialty to A.A. and I have come to the conclusion that our particular function can very often lie in preparing the way for the patient to accept any sort of treatment or outside help. I now conceive the psychiatrist's job to be the task of breaking down the patient's inner resistance so that which is inside him will flower, as under the activity of the A.A. program."

* 1944

Dr. W.W. Bauer, broadcasting under the auspices of The American Medical Association in 1946, over the NBC network, said, in part: "Alcoholics Anonymous are no crusaders; not a temperance society. They know that they must never drink. They help others with similar problems . . . In this atmosphere the alcoholic often overcomes his excessive concentration upon himself. Learning to depend upon a higher power and absorb himself in his work with other alcoholics, he remains sober day by day. The days add up into weeks, the weeks into months and years."

Dr. John F. Stouffer, Chief Psychiatrist, Philadelphia General Hospital, citing his experience with A.A., said: "The alcoholics we get here at Philadelphia General are mostly those who cannot afford private treatment, and A.A. is by far the greatest thing we have been able to offer them. Even among those who occasionally land back in here again, we observe a profound change in personality. You would hardly recognize them."

The American Psychiatric Association requested, in 1949, that a paper be prepared by one of the older members of Alcoholics Anonymous to be read at the Association's annual meeting of that year. This was done, and the paper was printed in the American Journal of Psychiatry for November, 1949.

(This address is now available in pamphlet form at nominal cost through most A.A. groups or from Box 459, Grand Central Station, New York, under the title "Alcoholism the Illness.")

IV
THE LASKER AWARD

In 1951 the Lasker Award was given to Alcoholics Anonymous. The citation reads in part as follows:

"The American Public Health Association presents a Lasker Group Award for 1951 to Alcoholics Anonymous in recognition of its unique and highly successful approach to that age-old public health and social problem, alcoholism ... In emphasizing alcoholism as an illness, the social stigma associated with this condition is being blotted out ... Historians may one day recognize Alcoholics Anonymous to have been a great venture in social pioneering which forged a new instrument for social action; a new therapy based on the kinship of common suffering; one having vast a potential for the myriad other ills of mankind."

V
THE RELIGIOUS VIEW ON A.A.

Clergymen of practically every denomination have given A.A. their blessing.

Edward Dowling, S.J.,* of the Queen's Work staff says, "Alcoholics Anonymous is natural; it is natural at the point where nature comes closest to the supernatural, namely in humiliations and in consequent humility. There is something spiritual about an art museum or a symphony, and the Catholic Church approves of our use of them. There is something spiritual about A.A. too, and Catholic participation in it almost invariably results in poor Catholics becoming better Catholics."

The Episcopal magazine, *The Living Church*, observes editorially: "The basis of the technique of Alcoholics Anonymous is the truly Christian principle that a man cannot help himself except by helping others. The A.A. plan is described by the members themselves as 'self-insurance.' This self-insurance has resulted in the restoration of physical, mental and spiritual health and self-respect to hundreds of men and women who would be hopelessly down and out without its unique but effective therapy."

Speaking at a dinner given by Mr. John D. Rockefeller to introduce Alcoholics Anonymous to some of his friends, Dr. Harry Emerson Fosdick remarked:

"I think that psychologically speaking there is a point of advantage in the approach that is being made in this movement that cannot be duplicated. I suspect that if it is wisely handled—and it seems to be in wise and prudent hands—there are doors of opportunity ahead of this project that may surpass our capacities to imagine."

*Father Ed, an early and wonderful friend of A.A., died in the spring of 1960.

VI
HOW TO GET IN TOUCH WITH A.A.

In the United States and Canada, most towns and cities have A.A. groups. In such places, A.A. can be located through the local telephone directory, newspaper office, or police station, or by contacting local priests or ministers. In large cities, groups often maintain local offices where alcoholics or their families may arrange for interviews or hospitalization. These so-called Intergroup Associations are found under the listing "A.A." or "Alcoholics Anonymous" in telephone directories.

At New York, U.S.A., Alcoholics Anonymous maintains its international service center. This consists of The General Service Board of A.A. whose Trustees administer A.A.'s General Service Office, A.A. World Services, Inc., and our monthly magazine, "The A.A. Grapevine."

If you cannot find A.A. in your locality, a letter addressed to Alcoholics Anonymous, Box 459, Grand Central Station, New York 17, U.S.A., will receive a prompt reply from this world center, referring you to the nearest A.A. group. If there is none nearby, you will be invited to carry on a correspondence which will do much to insure your sobriety no matter how isolated you are.

Should you be the relative or friend of an alcoholic who shows no immediate interest in A.A., it is suggested that you write the Al-Anon Family Groups, Inc., P.O. Box 182, Madison Square Station, New York 10, U.S.A.

This is a world clearing house for the Al-Anon Family Groups, composed largely of the wives, husbands and friends of A.A. members. This headquarters will give the location of the nearest Family Group and will, if you wish, correspond with you about your special problems.

NOTES: